Forged in a Country Crucible, 2nd Edition

by
Joseph C. White

Bloomington, IN  Milton Keynes, UK

authorHOUSE®

AuthorHouse™
1663 Liberty Drive,
Suite 200
Bloomington, IN 47403
www.authorhouse.com
Phone: 1-800-839-8640

AuthorHouse™ UK Ltd.
500 Avebury Boulevard
Central Milton Keynes, MK9 2BE
www.authorhouse.co.uk
Phone: 08001974150

First published by AuthorHouse 9/18/2006
ISBN: 1-4259-4694-1 (e)
ISBN: 1-4259-4697-6 (sc)

Printed in the United States of America
Bloomington, Indiana

This book is printed on acid-free paper.

Joseph C. White
3018 Patrick Place Circle
Clover, SC 29710 USA
josephcwhite@comporium.net
www.josephcwhite.com

A Memoir
FOREWORD

"No man but a blockhead ever wrote except for money," so said Dr. Samuel Johnson more than 200 years ago.

Call me then a blockhead, for I wrote this for my children, grandchildren, and any relatives and friends who might have the desire and patience to read it. My wife, Linda, has urged me for years to record the stories I told her about life on the farm during the Great Depression. Once I started writing, it was like eating one salted peanut—it was hard to stop.

My title for this book comes from the ancient recipe for a battle instrument that you could trust with your life. Sword makers heat their steel blades red hot and plunge them into a crucible of cooling liquid to harden and temper them. That makes them stronger so they won't break or bend during a battle. I believe the hard work on the farm made me tougher mentally and physically; so I have neither regretted my humble beginnings nor been ashamed of the dirty, back-breaking work I did there. It was good for me.

I did this because it had to be done and my family depended on me to do it. There was no one else available who could. That forced me to develop the habit of disregarding my personal feelings and doing what had to be done, and it helped me succeed later in life.

I entered the U.S. Immigration Service Border Patrol in 1953 as a GS-6 trainee, and I retired 21 years later as a GS-15. It was an old-line agency that was not known for rapid promotions. The Border Patrol gave me challenging work, including flying a four-engine airplane on trans-oceanic flights to take deportees to their home countries and return with political refugees. I qualified as a pilot because I had been trained in the Army Air Corps.

My career in the immigration service led to my selection, after I retired, as the executive assistant to Harlon Carter, the executive vice president of the 3-million-member National Rifle Association. After 18 months in that first position, I then served two years as Deputy Executive Vice President. I remarried then, and resigned to get away from the long hours and other demands of the job. Later, I was elected to serve three years on the NRA Board of Directors.

I had some natural ability and an interest in shooting begun in my early days hunting game for the family table. That shooting ability helped me get into the Border Patrol, where I became a part of the competition teams. Successes included five National Team Championships won as a firing member of the Border Patrol Team, plus six individual National Senior Pistol Championships after I retired. The first was at age 64, and the last at age 70.

I've heard that success is five percent inspiration and ninety-five percent perspiration. In all these endeavors, I owe most of my success to the work habits that were forged in a country crucible on a hardscrabble farm during the Great Depression.

CHAPTER ONE

I woke to the sound of the coffee grinder. It was below freezing outside, and Dad had banked the fire the night before by covering the burning backlog with ashes. The only warmth during the night had been the heat remaining in the fireplace bricks and that generated by the bodies of two adults and seven children living in the house. I knew dad had already started fires in the fireplace and the kitchen stove, because he always did that before he ground the coffee beans.

It was New Year's Day, 1936, and I was 15 ½ years old. I was big for my age, and had been working in the fields since I was eight or nine and doing hard work since age 12. I had one sister and five brothers, all born after I was.

I slept in a room behind the kitchen in a weather-beaten farmhouse in Tennessee. We had no gas, no electricity, no running water, and no plumbing. The toilet was either out the front door, across the road, and into the woods; or out the kitchen door, behind the house, and into the privy in the edge of the field. The Works Projects Administration (WPA) had built the privy for us in 1933. Before that we went either into the woods or behind the barn.

I dreaded going to bed when the weather was cold. I had no way to warm the sheets except to lie still until my body heat warmed a spot, and if I moved I had to warm another spot. Pioneer families put hot coals into a metal box and slid it over the cold sheets to warm them, but we had nothing like that.

I wore long underwear and a long-sleeved work shirt in bed. Mama had sewed the shirt, the pillowcase, and the sheets from cloth salvaged from empty fertilizer sacks. It was coarse, but I didn't mind because I had worn such clothing for years. The material was oyster white and had a tighter weave than brown burlap. Sometimes we bought flour in cloth sacks with red or blue patterns, but Mama used that cloth to make dresses and underwear for herself and my sister.

The fertilizer company printed the chemical analysis in big black numbers on the fertilizer sacks, and we were never able to remove them. The cheapest fertilizer available was 2-10-2, commonly referred to as 10-2-2, and for years we used only that. A slightly more expensive formula was 4-10-4, or 10-4-4. Recently Dad and Mama were sitting on the front porch while the kids were playing in the yard. Dad said times must be getting better, because last year all the shirts had 10-2-2 on them, and now two of them have 10-4-4.

The old iron bedstead was spotted with rust. The homemade mattress was four inches thick and stuffed with cotton. It lay on a section of woven wire mesh, attached to the bed frame by pull springs spaced six inches apart along each side of the metal bed frame and across each end. The patchwork quilts were stuffed with cotton.

I knew that either Mama or Eunice, my sister, would be up soon and making biscuits and thick, white gravy—the standard morning meal for the family. Soon I would have to get up and wash my face and hands for breakfast. My bladder was full, but I didn't want to use the slop jar (chamber pot) under the bed because I would have to empty and wash it later. So I lay in my warm spot and thought about the year ahead.

We expected to plant twenty acres of corn, ten acres of cotton, five acres of hay, and five acres of miscellaneous crops such as watermelons, potatoes, sorghum cane, and peanuts. We had a half-acre plot reserved for a garden and ten acres under fence for pasture. We did all the planting, cultivating, and harvesting with manual labor, using two mules and a few basic farm tools. Dad used to say he farmed the way an Irishman played the fiddle, by main strength and awkwardness. He was Scots-Irish, so he was poking fun only at himself.

I knew I would be busy in January and February going to high school, cutting firewood and cook wood, repairing fences, cleaning stables, and spreading manure for fertilizer. In March I would be following the two-mule turning plow after school and on Saturdays, preparing the land for planting. High school ran from early September to late May.

In April we would plant corn and Irish potatoes, and in May we would plant cotton and several other crops. During most of the year, some crop would need planting, some would need cultivating, or some would need harvesting. There might be a week or two of slack time in August, after the last cultivation ended and before the harvest of the sorghum cane began.

I wondered if there would be enough rain to produce a good crop—some recent years had been so dry the land produced very little. I wondered if there would be enough money to pay for the seed, feed, and fertilizer we would need. These were Dad's worries, but I shared his anxiety. He always hoped to have enough money left at the end of the year so he wouldn't have to borrow to put in a crop the following year. So far, it had never happened.

My parents thought it was important to own the farm rather than to sharecrop. But mortgages were risky, because the entire balance came due each year. Most borrowers paid only the interest and renewed the mortgage for another year. If the mortgage holder insisted on all the money, the borrower was in trouble and might have to move.

Since Dad and Grandpa had owed their mortgages to the man who sold them the land, they worried he might not let them renew at the end of the year. So they had gone to a bank and refinanced their mortgages to pay off the original mortgagee, Cullen Bass. Later I heard my dad say they had dodged lightning, because Mr. Bass had decided to call in some of his other loans and would not renew them.

Compared to some we were poor, but I was happy. Since my parents were buying the farm, we didn't have to move frequently as some sharecroppers did. Dad said we were better off than people who lived in town and had to live out of a paper sack. We always had food from the produce we grew. It was rarely elegant, but it was wholesome.

We were quietly proud of our independence, and our parents taught us the satisfaction of earning a living by hard, honest labor. Dad said we could look anyone in the eye because we kept our word and paid our debts. We had been through some hard years, but we were thankful for what we had.

The Nashville Tennessean newspaper had recently run stories about a German named Hitler and about the possibility of war in Europe. That was disturbing news, but I had farming and high-school algebra to worry about, and that helped take my mind off what was happening thousands of miles away.

Finally, I got out of bed, retrieved my overalls and my denim jumper from a nearby chair, and dressed quickly. It would have been too dark to see inside the privy, so I hurried out the front door, crossed the road, and relieved my bladder beside a little path in the woods. That was closer and more convenient. When somebody said he had to go out, nobody thought he was looking for fresh air or sunshine.

Someone I knew told me a story about a farmer who went to visit his cousin in the city. They showed him how their indoor plumbing worked, and that afternoon they cooked and ate barbecue in the back yard. "I wouldn't have believed it if I hadn't seen it with my own eyes," he said later. "They eat in the yard and pee in the house."

CHAPTER TWO

I came through the living room and into the kitchen. "Shore is cold, " I said to no one in particular. "Yep, shore is, " Dad replied. "But that was good kindlin' wood you brought in last night. Fire caught up real easy this mornin.'" Each night I brought in enough firewood, cook wood, and kindling wood for the following morning and stacked it on the front porch near the door. If I did this, Dad got up first the next morning and made the fires in the fireplace and in the kitchen stove. But if the wood was not on the porch, he woke me and sent me out to bring the wood from the woodpile and make the fires myself. That had happened one cold night the previous winter, and after that I never forgot.

I took a dipperful of water from the bucket and poured it into the metal wash pan on a table by the back door. Then I went to the kitchen stove and dipped some warm water from the reservoir. I poured it into the wash pan with the cold water, washed my face and hands, and dried them on the community towel that hung on a nail in the corner. Then I opened the back door and threw the used water into the back yard.

The biscuits were in the oven, and Mama was stirring the gravy as it simmered in an iron skillet on the stove. We called it Hoover gravy because Herbert Hoover had been the president during the early days of the depression, and most people blamed the hard times on him.

To make the gravy she had put ¼ cupful of lard into the skillet and heated it until it melted. Then she added flour and salt and cooked the mixture, stirring constantly, until the flour turned brown. Next she added milk until the skillet was almost full, and stirred it until it boiled and became thick and smooth.

All the kids except the twins were now in the kitchen with both parents. The babies were only nine months old and were still asleep. Mama poured the gravy into a big bowl and put it in the middle of the table. When the biscuits were brown, she took them out of the oven, put them on a platter, and placed them near the gravy.

Dad had built the table of pine boards, and had attached two wooden benches that ran the length of the table, one on each side. Our parents usually sat in cane-bottomed, ladder-backed chairs, one at each end of the table; and the kids sat on the benches. Sometimes on Sundays or on special occasions we covered the table with a clean sheet, but most of the time the table was bare wood.

Mama made big biscuits. She had started with a bowl of flour and added salt, baking soda, an egg, and melted lard. She made a depression in the middle of the flour mixture and poured in milk slowly as she stirred it into the flour. She kept on pouring, stirring, and mixing until the dough had the consistency she wanted. If the dough was too loose she added more flour, and if it was too stiff she added more milk.

Then she picked up dough a handful at a time and rolled it between the palms of her hands to form a biscuit. Finally, she flattened it and placed it into a greased pan. When the pan was full, she put it into the oven. Her biscuits were usually at least three inches in diameter.

I put a helping of gravy on my plate, sprinkled it with black pepper, and took one of the biscuits. I broke a chunk from the biscuit and wiped it across my plate through the gravy. Then I put the piece of biscuit in my mouth, making sure not to drop gravy on the table or into my lap. After I chewed and swallowed that bite, I took another piece of biscuit and repeated the process. We all ate biscuits and gravy that way, and so did our neighbors. I usually ate five or six biscuits and at least a cupful of gravy.

Someone wrote a country song about this kind of food, and it became a favorite on the Grand Ole Opry. The chorus was: "Pass the biscuits, Mirandy, I'm jest as hongry as sin. Pass the gravy, Mirandy, I need some sop to sop 'em in."

Sometimes in summer we had cantaloupe to go with biscuits and gravy. That may sound like a weird combination, but to me, a ripe sweet cantaloupe with hot biscuits and gravy was a treat. But the melon season lasted only a month or two, and we had no way to keep them in that ideal condition. Sometimes we ate biscuits with butter and sorghum molasses, and sometimes on special occasions we had biscuits with chocolate gravy.

Mama made that gravy with butter instead of lard, and she added chocolate flavoring and sugar. That, too, was a delicacy to be savored.

We all liked home-made grape jelly and watermelon-rind preserves with our biscuits for breakfast, but one of the best was pear preserves. We didn't grow pears in our orchard, but sometimes we got a bushel or two from Uncle George Roberts, who lived three miles away and was married to my mother's aunt. They had several trees, and occasionally had more fruit than they could use. They were Bosc pears, but we called them sand pears. My sister told me that when Uncle George sold that farm the new buyer cut down all the pear trees. I heard about it fifty years after the fact, but it still made me sad. Of course by the time he sold, the trees may have been so old they were no longer productive.

Mama cut the pears into bite-sized pieces and cooked them in water and sugar to make preserves. She liked to get them when they were barely ripe, and undercooked them so they would be slightly crisp. The sugar water she cooked them in was thick and syrupy when they were done. When they were still hot she put them into fruit jars and sealed them immediately so they would keep for months.

Having any one of these sweets was a treat, because most of the time we had only biscuits and thick, white gravy for breakfast. But I liked that too, and I never felt underprivileged for having only that for breakfast. In the summer we also had eggs on occasion, but our hens didn't lay many in cold weather. We traded most of our eggs and our chickens to a peddler for sugar, salt, coffee, flour, and other things we didn't grow ourselves. We sold most of our hams, pork shoulders, and side-meat bacon for cash.

We kept and ate the cured sowbelly bacon and the sausage, which we preserved in Mason jars. Any farm family who ate the more expensive hams or shoulders was said to be eatin' high on the hog.

I enjoyed the smell of coffee, but never drank it. We had an old coffee pot made of gray enamelware, and my parents boiled the coffee grounds in it. Little holes on one side near the top let the coffee into the spout but kept out most of the coffee grounds. Dad often put freshly ground coffee into the pot with the old grounds and boiled them together. He said coffee couldn't be too strong for him, so long as the spoon didn't bend when he tried to stir it. Sometimes when country people were out of coffee beans, they browned corn meal in a skillet and boiled it, just to have something hot to drink and to pretend they had coffee. I suppose that is like giving a pacifier to a baby. Our parents never offered coffee to any of the kids when we were young.

After breakfast I did the chores around the barn and let the cows and mules out into the pasture so they could go to the pond and drink their fill of water. They could come back to the barn when they were ready. I knew there would be ice around the edges of the pond, but not enough to prevent them from drinking. The sub-freezing weather would have to last several days before the pond would freeze all the way across. A story in the Nashville Tennessean said ice had paralyzed the Atlantic area, but luckily for us, it hadn't hit Middle Tennessee that hard.

We didn't let the mules graze in the pasture when they were doing heavy work in the summer, because eating the green grass made them short-winded. We fed them dry corn, together with hay, cured corn tops, or fodder when they were working hard, and we took them to the watering trough for fresh water from the well at least four times a day. After doing the chores I came back into the house and sat around the fire all morning. It was the last day of the school break for the holidays.

* * * * *

My brother Quinton had gone into the woods the week before and gathered a bucketful of hickory nuts. When he couldn't find enough on the ground, he climbed a hickory tree and shook the branches to make the nuts fall off. Everybody in the country called them hicker nuts. We older kids sat on the floor and used flat irons to crack the nuts on the cement hearth. We dug out the meat with horseshoe nails because they are flat. A round nail slid around the nut meat and left part of it in the shell.

Eating them took time. People made jokes about staying up all night trying to fill up on hicker nuts, or about somebody who ate hicker nuts 24 hours a day until he starved to death. Eating nuts from Scaly Bark hickory trees went faster, because they were easier to crack open and the nutmeat was thicker. The trees got that name because they had pieces of bark hanging loose on the tree, as if about to fall to the ground.

The fireplace was four feet wide and we burned three-foot logs, but it couldn't heat the room when a cold wind blew. The outside walls were unpainted weatherboarding, with each board overlapping the board below. But they didn't fit snugly together, and there was no insulation behind them. Once after a snowstorm I found snow on my bed near the wall. The wind had blown the snow through the cracks.

My parents had finished the overhead of each room with narrow beaded ceiling and had planned to finish the inside of the walls the same way. They ran out of ceiling material and money, however, and the ceiling on the walls went only about half way from the floor to the top. Above that, we could see the two-by-four framing. Like most country houses, ours had a galvanized metal roof, and so did the barn, the corn crib, the potato house, the smoke house, and the outhouse. I liked the metal roof, because I enjoyed listening to the drumming of raindrops when it rained.

The floor was four-inch pine boards, fairly smooth but not sanded and finished. Mama cleaned them by scrubbing with a mop made from corn shucks. She used either home-made lye soap or wood ashes. The floor in front of the fireplace had several blackened spots, burned by embers that popped off the burning logs in the fireplace. Most farm homes had similar burned spots.

Dry wood threw more embers than green wood, and dry chestnut wood threw the most of all. A blight had killed the chestnut trees a few years previously, and many still stood in the woods, their dead bare limbs like giant skeletons against the sky. Dead chestnut made great firewood except for the flying embers, and we burned it often in our fireplace

There was something hypnotic about staring into the flames, listening to the crackle, and enjoying the distinctive aroma of the burning wood. But sometimes the crackle got loud. Pockets of moisture in the dry wood caused little explosions. As the wood burned, the moisture turned to steam, and pressure from the steam caused popping sounds. Sometimes a loud pop blasted a chunk of burning wood off the log, and a flaming ember went skittering across the floor. If left alone it might set the house on fire, so nobody dared go to sleep with a fire blazing in the fireplace.

There were no fire trucks or fire hydrants in the country. Once a house was on fire it usually burned to the ground, leaving nothing but a blackened brick chimney standing alone by the side of the road. Banking the fire with ashes at bedtime kept the embers in the fireplace during the night and preserved live coals for starting a fire the next morning.

The floor was about two feet above ground, and the sills rested on columns of concrete blocks spaced some ten feet apart around the house. The only solid foundation was for the fireplace. They built it up from a big block of concrete poured into the ground. The boards of the floor did not fit tightly together, and there were no carpets; so a cold wind came under the house and up through the floor. In addition, wind came in between the boards of the walls. But when it was only moderately cold and there was no wind, the fireplace could warm one room reasonably well.

I could not be comfortable in our house on a cold windy day unless I wore several layers of clothing. If I sat facing the fire, the front part of my body was hot and the back part was cold. Then when I turned around with my back to the fire, my backside was hot and my front was cold.

At eleven o'clock in the morning, Mama mixed up batter to make enough cornbread for the rest of the day. She greased the fireplace oven with lard and put the cornbread dough in it. The cast-iron oven was a foot in diameter. It was three or four inches deep and had a matching iron lid with a handle.

She raked out a level bed of live coals and covered them with ashes. Then she placed the oven on the ashes and covered it with more ashes. Finally she covered those ashes with live coals and let the batter cook that way for more than an hour. When the cornbread was done, we ate some of it with canned vegetable soup for dinner and put the rest of it in the warming closet to save for supper.

I brushed my teeth with a mixture of baking soda and salt. I don't recall when I got my first toothbrush, but I remember rubbing the salt and soda on my teeth and gums with my forefinger. Mama had told me to add the salt, perhaps for its healing properties. We all gargled with salty water when we had a sore throat, and it helped.

I don't remember ever going to a dentist until I was in the army, but I remember grandpa saying once that he had gone to a "tooth dentist" and had his teeth cleaned. I have no idea how often he went, but it must have been an unusual occurrence for me to remember it some seventy years later. My father had a full set of false teeth before he was 50. But in those days if neither castor oil nor sulfur and molasses would cure whatever was wrong with you, the next thing they thought of was pulling your teeth.

* * * * *

In the afternoon I put on extra clothes and went into the fields to hunt rabbits. I had been hunting with the family shotgun since I was twelve. The gun was old, the inside of the barrel was pitted from rust, and the action would not lock tightly. The firing pin hit the bottom half of the primer, but it never failed to fire. It held a single shell, and the barrel was 30 inches long with a full choke. A little hole on top of the barrel and about a half inch from the end had once held the front bead sight, but it had been missing for years. I saw only one rabbit all afternoon, and it got into the woods and out of sight before I could shoot.

The only wild game we could get with any frequency was rabbits. They were especially good in the fall and early winter, after they had grown fat on soybeans and other crops. They were more plentiful in some years than in others.

Rabbit meat was as good as chicken if cleaned carefully, soaked overnight in salty water, then rinsed and smother fried. Mama always made thick gravy in the same skillet, using the cooking grease from the rabbit. That gave the flavor of the rabbit meat to the gravy. We didn't have meat often, so a meal of rabbit, biscuits, and gravy was a treat for all of us. She made gravy the same way when she fried chicken or sausage. We had fried chicken or chicken and dumplings only on special occasions or when we had company.

In the fall and winter, rabbits didn't move much during the day. They scratched out a bed under a bush or a clump of grass and stayed there. A person walking in the fields or woods could often see old forms where rabbits had spent a night. They were bare spots about six inches wide and a foot long, usually with dead grass or weeds hanging over them. Rabbits made new forms each night, probably to avoid predators. When a hunter came close enough, he jumped out and ran. We called that jumping a rabbit.

We never had a rabbit dog. Dogs could help find a rabbit, flush it out of its bed, and follow it by scent. When chased by a dog, a rabbit tended to circle around and come back to the starting place. The dog rarely caught it, and the hunter waited for the rabbit to return, hoping for a clear shot. I always had to hunt with no dog and with a single-shot gun, so if I missed with the first shot the rabbit was home free.

I hunted often in open fields and looked for big clumps of dead grass or weeds where rabbits could hide. Bushes and trees made it hard to get an open shot in the woods. When it snowed I followed rabbit tracks in the snow, and sometimes found one that way. From the tracks I could tell which direction he went, and could usually tell if the tracks were new.

A rabbit is easier to see in the snow, because of the brown fur against the white snow. In winter, the dead weeds and grass are about the same color as a rabbit's fur, and often the first thing a hunter can see is the eye. It is big and shiny, and looks nothing like the grass cover. When I hunted, I stopped for a few seconds every ten or fifteen feet and looked carefully at potential hiding places nearby. If I kept walking, a rabbit would let me step almost on him without running, because he thought I didn't see him. But if I stopped walking and stood still when I was close to him, it made him think I saw him even when I didn't, and often caused him to jump and run.

When I found a rabbit sitting in his bed nearby, I always wished for a .22 caliber pistol that I could carry in a holster. Then the ammunition would cost me only 1/3 of one cent, instead of three cents for a shotgun shell. As much as I hunted rabbits and as much as I liked to eat them, I still felt sorry for them.

I have since read that the average life span of a wild rabbit is one year. They either fall prey to predators or die from exposure to severe weather in the winter. That's why they need to produce so many young. A mother rabbit may have two litters during the summer, and a baby doe rabbit born in the spring will have young of her own before winter comes.

I never saw squirrels, turkeys, or deer around our woods. Bob White quail usually flew before I saw them, and I didn't shoot at them in the air. My chances of hitting a running rabbit were much better, and it would provide five times as much meat as a quail. I had only two shotgun shells at that time and no money to buy more, so I didn't want to waste one. I had heard bird hunters from town say they would never shoot a bird on the ground because it wasn't the sporting thing to do, but I was hunting for food and not for sport.

Most of the farm families had dogs. Some were hounds or bird dogs, but all we had was a Feist. In one of Faulkner's stories, he referred to a dog like that as what local people called a Fice. The American Kennel Club did not recognize the Feist as a breed, but they look something like Jack Russell Terriers. The J R people have their own organization, and in the past they did not choose to be included with AKC breeds. But I have heard the AKC now recognizes the Jack Russell breed. Those dogs are naturally aggressive and will climb over or tunnel under almost any fence.

Some of the Feists were good squirrel dogs or 'possum dogs, but ours was useless as a hunter. We had tried to take him 'possum hunting one night, but he wanted to stay home. We finally persuaded him to go by feeding him a piece of biscuit every twenty or thirty feet. We got him about two hundred yards into the woods by doing this, until a covey of quail flushed under our feet. The drumming of their wings made a loud noise when they flushed, and the dog took off like a streak for the house. After that we gave up on him.

* * * * *

Just before sundown I came home, pulled the shucks off several ears of corn, and fed the livestock and chickens. The mules got six or eight ears each in the feeding trough, and they bit the corn off the cobs to eat it. Any grains that fell off the cobs stayed in the trough, and the mules picked them up with their lips and ate them separately. They didn't eat the corn cobs because they had no food value and apparently no taste that the mules liked. We took the old cobs out of the troughs each day before we put in more corn.

Most country people used old dry corn cobs instead of toilet paper. There were always plenty of them around the barn, and they were better than anything else that was readily at hand. Country people never had to wonder where the expression rough as a cob originated. After the WPA finally built us a privy, we kept old newspapers or old Sears Roebuck catalogs in it.

In the stables, we had a manger next to each trough, and I put hay in the mangers for the mules. We always fed the mules corn, but sometimes we fed them fodder—dried corn leaves—or corn tops instead of hay. We also fed the cows either hay, fodder, or corn tops; but we gave them either cottonseed or cottonseed meal instead of corn. I shelled some corn from the ears and threw it on the ground for the chickens to eat. I gave the hogs ears of corn plus shorts mixed with water. That was a by-product from flour milling.

We had a wooden trough for feeding the hogs, and we always poured the water and shorts mixture into the trough. We also used the trough to feed them slop, which was water mixed with any leftover table scraps that we didn't want to save for ourselves. The trough was not quite level, so the liquid feed ran toward the lower end and the pigs fought with each other to position themselves there.

Little pigs fought when they nursed the mother. She had two rows of nipples from front to back, and the pigs soon learned they got more milk from the front nipples than from the back ones. The unfortunate pig that had to take the rearmost nipple didn't get as much milk. He's sucking hind tit was a crude country expression to describe someone down on his luck.

Dad had already milked the old red cow, because she was so cantankerous nobody else could deal with her. I brought in enough wood for the evening and the following morning and went in to sit by the fire.

Our supper was the usual cornbread and milk. When our meal supply got low, we shelled a bushel of corn, put it in a bag, spread a blanket or quilt over the shoulders of one of the mules, and put the bag of shelled corn on top of the blanket. We didn't fill the bag to the top, so more of the corn could be in the ends of the bag and less of it in the middle. That allowed the bag of corn to adjust to the contour of the mule's back and made it less likely to slide off during the trip. Then one of the kids got on the mule behind the bag of corn and rode to the gristmill.

The miller ground the corn into meal and kept one eighth for the grinding. The kid then rode the mule home with the meal, and we had plenty of cornbread for a while. We ran the meal through a sifter to get out the worst of the husks. Then we put baking soda, salt, and milk in it—and sometimes an egg—and baked it. It may have been crude and coarse, but we liked it with milk for supper, or with soup, peas, boiled greens, or vegetables for dinner.

Water power drove the gristmill. A dam across a creek formed a mill pond, and a trough made of boards delivered a stream of water to the top of the water wheel. The trough had slots where a board could be inserted to turn off the flow to the wheel. Several wooden "buckets" were constructed all around the wheel, and the water poured into the buckets on the far side of the wheel.

The weight of the water in the buckets made that side of the wheel heavier, so it pulled downward, causing the wheel to turn. As the filled buckets reached the bottom of the rotating wheel and then started back up on the other side, the buckets were then upside down and the water poured out into the stream. When the wheel was turning the buckets on one side were always full and heavy, and the buckets on the other side were always empty and light. That kept the wheel turning as long as the water kept pouring down on one side of the wheel. The grinding mechanism consisted of two huge millstones with grooves cut into them. They were geared so they turned slowly and in opposite directions, and the meal came out in a small stream.

We made sure we saved enough corn, peas, cottonseed, and other grains to plant a new crop the next year. When they say don't eat your seed corn, a farmer knows exactly what they mean.

We had only one cow giving milk, so we had a limited supply. Our other cow was expecting a new calf and would not give milk again until it was born. Sometimes we had plenty of milk and a limited amount of cornbread, and sometimes we had plenty of both. I usually broke up the bread and put it into a bowl with the milk. I then ate it with a spoon, taking a bite of the moistened bread along with some milk at the same time. If there was plenty of milk and a limited amount of bread, I didn't mix it together in a bowl. Instead, I took a small bite of cornbread and a big sip of milk and let it mix in my mouth as I chewed.

In this case there was plenty of bread and not much milk, so I prepared the bowl as usual but ate it with a fork instead of a spoon, allowing the excess milk to drain through the tines of the fork and back into the bowl. I still had a bowl half full of milk when I finished, and then I put in more bread. This may sound silly today, but it was serious then.

After supper it was getting dark, so we lit the coal oil lamp in the room where the fire was burning. We had no radio and had never heard of television. I sat there a while and then went through the kitchen to the back room and got into bed early, as I usually did in cold weather. Once I got my space warmed, I could be more comfortable in bed than around the fireplace.

CHAPTER THREE

A double fireplace stood in the middle of the wall between the two front rooms. One fireplace faced the room on the North side, which we used as a living room. Directly behind it, and using the same chimney, the other one faced the other front room. An old organ sat in a far corner of that room. Pumping the two pedals near the floor provided the compressed air to make the sounds. When we had company for singing sessions we sometimes used both fireplaces at the same time, but usually we had only one going at a time. Each of the front rooms had two double beds, and the storage room back of the kitchen had another.

In the same room with the organ, a wooden telephone box hung on the front wall by the door. The mouthpiece stuck out in front and a receiver hung on a hook on the left side. The front could swing open to reveal two large batteries standing inside. They were shaped like cylinders and were about six inches tall. A magneto rang the phone when we turned a crank on the right side of the phone box.

We grounded the phone batteries by wrapping the ground wire around an iron rod and driving the rod into the ground. People also grounded their battery-powered radios that way. When the ground was very dry in the summer we poured water on the ground around the rod, because dirt conducts electricity better when it is wet.

There were a dozen telephones on our party line, but never more than one to a household. Anyone who picked up a receiver of one phone could hear anything said on any of the others. When one rang they all rang, and each had its own signal. The central operator answered to one long ring, another phone was a short and a long ring, another was two shorts and a long, another was two long rings: We had the last phone on the end of

17

the line, and our signal was nine long rings. We could call anyone on our line by ringing the appropriate signal, but if we wanted to call someone who was not on our line we had to call the central operator and ask her to place the call.

Nobody else within a mile had a telephone, and we probably had ours only because Dad was a peace officer. A neighbor sometimes came to our house to make a call, usually to a doctor when someone was sick. I remember one night a neighbor was calling Doc. Harris. I wondered what he meant when he said, "Hurry Doc., her water's done broke."

Doctors routinely saw patients in their homes, and a visit to a hospital was rare. Old Doc Harris charged two dollars for a house call. If that sounds low, consider that an average adult worker would have to pick cotton for three days to earn two dollars. Doc Harris had a new car just about every year, and he always drove fast.

Our house was built in the shape of an upside down T. The two front rooms formed the bottom of the T, and an open porch ran across the front. The stem of the T was a combination kitchen and dining room plus a catch-all back room behind the kitchen. That room served as a storage room, as a bedroom, and as a place to bathe. Before I was old enough to do the plowing we had a hired man in the summer, and he slept in that room and took all his meals with the family. Mama washed his clothes on Saturday afternoon. He worked five and a half days a week and Dad paid him twelve dollars a month. He had a good job: It cost him nothing to live, and in three months he could save thirty-six dollars, enough to buy a good used car and gasoline to run it several months.

In the kitchen we had a cook stove, a safe, and a table. The safe was a freestanding wooden cabinet that we used as a pantry. We had no refrigerator because we had no electricity, we had no icebox because we lived too far from the ice plant, and we had no sink because we had no running water. A big metal pan served for washing dishes and a smaller one for hands and faces.

Our wood-burning cook stove was made of iron except for the warming closet, and that was of thinner metal. The stove was three and a half feet wide, three feet high, and two feet deep. As you faced the stove, the reservoir was on the left, and it held two or three gallons of water. As the fire cooked the food it also heated the water. Next to the reservoir was a firebox that took sticks of wood up to sixteen inches long. To the right of the firebox was the oven, which extended to the other side of the stove.

The heat passed from the firebox through a metal passageway behind the oven to a metal stovepipe that went up through the ceiling and the roof. A damper controlled the flow of hot air. It was inside the stovepipe between the stove and the ceiling, and we opened or closed it by turning a lever on the outside of the pipe.

In the vertical position the damper was open and allowed a maximum flow of air through the pipe. This made the flue draw better and the fire burn faster. After the fire was established we closed the damper part way to reduce the air flow through the pipe. That slowed the rate of burning and made the wood last longer.

The top of the firebox and the top of the reservoir had eyes that we removed to start or replenish the fire or to put in or take out water. The eyes were round iron plates about ten inches in diameter and 3 / 8 inch thick. Each had a receptacle milled into it to accommodate an eye lifter, which we used to take the eyes off the stove or put them on again. The receptacle was a little square hole that went down into the eye near the outside edge and then toward the center about half an inch, leaving a strip of metal over the inside half of the hole. The metal eye lifter was curved on the end and we hooked it into the hole to lift the eye off the stove.

The warming closet was above the stove and surrounding the stovepipe and was supported by a thin sheet of metal from the back of the stove. This metal cabinet was as wide as the stove, and in it we stored leftover food. It had metal doors, one on each side, and when we were hungry, we looked there first. A baked sweet potato or a crust of cornbread coated with molasses was a treat for a hungry kid. Sometimes we found leftover biscuits, and maybe even a fruit tart. But that was rare, because leftovers didn't last long at our house. Baking was uncertain because it was hard to control the oven temperature. We made coffee and did most of the cooking on top of the stove, on one or more of the eyes.

We bathed only on Saturday except for special occasions, as did most of our neighbors. Each person bathed in a metal washtub, usually in the back room for a modicum of privacy. Hot water from the reservoir of the cook stove took the chill off the cold water in the tub. None of the farms had running water or bathtubs. We were only 107 years behind the times, because the presidents bathed that way in the White House until the first bathroom was installed in 1829.

When I came in from plowing I took off my shoes on the porch and beat the heels and soles against the porch floor to dislodge the dirt that had collected in them during the day. Then I turned the shoes upside down and poured the dirt on the ground. I didn't wear socks with plow shoes. We had a small galvanized container —-we called it the foot tub—-that held about four gallons of water. In hot weather the sweat on my legs combined with the dirt and dust from the plowing, and my feet and legs were always dirty at the end of the day. Instead of taking a full bath, I put one foot at a time into the little tub and washed my feet and legs.

The main living room had an entrance door from the front porch and an exit door into the kitchen. An interior door connected the two front rooms, and the other room also had a door leading to the front porch. An exit door led from the kitchen to a tiny back porch on the right side, toward the barn. The barn and the corn crib were about fifty yards from the house.

* * * * *

Sometimes we had overnight company and not enough beds, so we had to sleep on pallets. A pallet was a quilt on the wooden floor, and I slept on it fully dressed. If I had only one quilt, I slept on one side of it and folded the other side over me for cover. If I had two quilts, I folded one of them so I had two layers under me, and then used the second quilt for cover. If I didn't get a pillow for my head, I folded a jacket, a sweater, or a towel and used that.

Sleeping at the foot of the bed was another emergency measure, especially for young children. Adults required more room for their shoulders and upper bodies than for their legs, so sometimes two adults slept in a double bed with one or two youngsters. The kids had their heads at the foot of the bed with the legs going up the middle of the bed. The legs of the two adults were on the sides of the legs of the kids.

Two country songs enjoyed temporary popularity. One was *Pallet on the Floor,* and the other was *Sleepin' at the Foot of the Bed.* The song writer thought sleeping at the foot of the bed injured his psyche and caused all the troubles he suffered later in life. He recalled how hard it was to "rassle for cover on a cold winter's night with a big foot a-settin' in your face."

* * * * *

The barn had no floor, and it had a passageway running lengthwise through it, wide enough for a loaded wagon. The second floor loft provided storage for hay and fodder, and built-in wooden ladders afforded access.

The floor of the loft was in the shape of a U with the front part open, so we could pull a wagon into the passageway and unload it into the loft. On each side of the passageway were stalls for the cows and mules. The two stalls for the mules each had a trough for feeding corn and a manger for feeding hay or fodder. A fenced area surrounded the barn, so that the animals could walk around without getting into the main pasture, which could be entered only through a gate behind the barn.

As you looked at the barn from the house, the corncrib was in the left front corner of the corral. The barn was on the left side of the corral, and the left side of the barn was a part of the corral fence on that side. The barn was totally inside the corral, with one side of the barn serving as part of the fence. The corncrib was not within the corral, but the front of the crib served as part of the fence.

The corncrib was approximately 20 feet wide, 20 feet deep, and eight feet high; with a wooden floor suspended two feet off the ground. The door was in the middle of the front, and just to the right of the door an area was partitioned for storing cottonseed. The wall around the cottonseed bin was four feet high on two sides. The other two sides were the front and sidewalls of the crib. When filled with cottonseed it was a comfortable place to sleep, and it came in handy when there were too many overnight visitors for the available beds. I preferred sleeping in the cottonseed bin to sleeping on a pallet on the floor or sleeping at the foot of the bed.

CHAPTER FOUR

When we moved from Winston County to Tennessee In 1925, Dad and Grandpa bought an 80-acre farm from a man named Cullen Bass. Grandpa took the north 30 acres, which had a house, a barn, and a well; and Dad took the South 50 acres, which had none of the above and was mostly woods. Most of grandpa's 30 acres was already under cultivation, and part of it was fenced. Dad was 35 years old and grandpa was 65. We had rented a house for a year while he cleared land for cultivation and had a house and barn built on our fifty acres.

My first memory of Tennessee is riding in a buggy with my mother. We were on the way to Fairview Elementary School, where she was a teacher. I think she dropped Eunice and Quinton off at grandma's house and picked them up on the way home. She took me with her just to watch me, because I wasn't old enough for first grade and we had never heard of kindergarten then. The buggy had two wheels and was pulled by one mule. The cloth top was open on both sides and in the front, and two large springs on either side of the seat softened the ride.

All the farm homes had wells, because there was no electricity for a pump and none had a spring good enough to supply the needed water. I was six when my father was deciding where to dig our well. He cut a forked branch off a nearby tree and walked around the general area holding one of the forks in each hand. When he passed over the place where water would be found, the branch was supposed to dip toward the ground. People called it witching for water. They thought there were streams of water underground and you would find water only if you hit one of those underground streams. Since then I have read that if you dig anywhere in that area you will find water ninety-five percent of the time. It is not necessary to hit a stream of water—just dig the well down below the water table and let it fill.

Dad dug the well himself. It was about four feet in diameter and thirty-five feet deep. As he dug he made notches into the sides of the well, one row on each side of the shaft, to provide footholds and handholds for climbing into and out of the well. The water at the bottom was three or four feet deep, depending on the time of the year. Our well never went dry in the summer as some did. When that happened to a well, it was necessary to dig deeper to get water. Our water came from a limestone aquifer, and the taste was excellent.

We had no ice or refrigeration, so we tied a bucket on a rope and lowered it into the well near the water. The air was cooler near the water, and that kept our milk and butter from spoiling. Once in a great while the bucket tipped over and the milk spilled into the well water. We then had to draw all the water out of the well, go down there and clean it out, and wait for it to fill up again. There was still a faint taste of milk in the drinking water, but it went away eventually.

* * * * *

Dad knew how to use dynamite from his years as a coal miner, and he blasted the tree stumps out of the corral after our barn was built. Pieces of some of those stumps flew high into the air and landed on the tin roof of the barn. The dents they made were still there the last time I saw it, although there wasn't much left of the barn by then. He didn't blast the stumps out of the fields, because there were too many of them. We plowed around them until they decayed enough so we could hook the turning plow to them and let the mules pull them out of the ground. Each year we had a few more stumps to pile up and burn.

It took four or five years for a stump to decay enough to be removed, and the middle of the stump usually started to decay first, leaving a hole in the top of the stump. That was a favorite nesting place for bluebirds, and we always left those stumps alone until after the little birds had left the nest.

Our ten acres of pasture was enclosed by three strands of barbed wire fastened to white oak posts, the most durable and decay-resistant wood we had. The fence began at a corner of the corncrib and went straight back for several hundred yards. It then turned right to the boundary of the farm and then right again. From there it followed the property line along the road until it came to a point even with the back of the barn. Finally, it connected to the corner of the corral that was diagonally across from the corncrib. The pasture was half cleared and planted in grass, and the other half was in woods. Bitterweed and wild onions (ramps) kept trying to grow in our pasture, but we dug them out by the roots and burned them in the fireplace or in the cook stove. If a cow ate either of them it gave her milk a disagreeable flavor.

Down a gully across the back part of the farm, water flowed toward the pasture when it rained. A few springs in the grassy area of the pasture supplied enough water to make it an active stream except in the driest months of the summer. Farther into the woods, this stream ran into a pond fifteen feet long, ten feet wide, and deep enough to make a swimming pool for the kids. It was big enough to retain water for the livestock to drink during the dry season, when the springs above the pond dried up.

Below the pond the stream was bigger, meaning other springs fed the pond from the bottom. About thirty yards farther downstream the water flowed under our barbed wire fence, across a dirt road (under a small wooden bridge), under another wire fence, and into the woods on Harvey Keener's farm. That was part of his pasture, and his mules and cows had access to drinking water from the stream..

In and around the stream and pond we had tadpoles, minnows, bullfrogs, turtles, mosquitoes, and big flying creatures that walked on the water. We rarely saw a snake, and then it was only a non-poisonous black racer. Copperheads and rattlesnakes were in the area, but we never saw them near the pond. Sometimes the Keener boys joined us in the pond on Sunday afternoons, because it was a way to cool off in hot weather.

One other large ditch ran across the farm, and it also was dry except when it rained. It was near the house, about fifty yards away. The slope ran downhill from the house to that ditch, and then uphill for about a hundred yards; where we had an orchard of 10 or 12 trees, mostly peaches and apples. The land then went downhill for another hundred yards or so to another ditch. The second ditch was the one that continued into the stream in the pasture. We also had ditches between our farm and grandpa's farm. They ran straight downhill to the other two ditches. Water from rains followed the terraces and emptied into these ditches and then ran downhill and emptied into the two main ditches.

From the second ditch, the land went gradually uphill as far back as we cultivated the farm. Sometimes we had trouble hauling crops out of the field, because the ditches were too deep for the wagon to cross. So we made a road across the ditches by digging a slope down each side, so the wagon went gently down one side and up the other. That was the only place we could cross the ditches with a wagon.

Where the nearest ditch crossed under the fence and into the pasture, we filed with rocks and timbers to keep the cattle from crawling up the ditch and under the fence to get to the growing crops. Rainwater formed a temporary pond behind this dam and caused a deposit of silt to build up next to the fence. A volunteer peach tree grew out of this silt, and we called it an Indian peach because the fruit inside was deep red. It was the heaviest- bearing tree we had, probably because of the rich silt soil it grew in. Mama peeled the ripe peaches and pickled them whole in mason jars with various spices. We never knew where the seed came from that started the tree, because we had no others like it. Someone probably ate a peach and threw the seed away, and it washed down our ditch in the rain until it stopped at the barrier under the fence. Whoever it was did us a favor.

* * * * *

Farmers in the neighborhood bought and sold cattle among themselves. A young bull calf sold for a dollar, but a young heifer about to have her first calf might bring fifteen dollars. The buyer could then look forward to a year or more of milk production before she went dry and had to have another calf to start producing milk again. We usually let a new calf have all the milk for the first few days, then cut him back to not more than half of it. The cow's udder was caked and hard at first, and we didn't want to drink any of it for about nine days. As soon as possible we weaned the calf and fed it other food. The purchaser of a pregnant young heifer could hope for several calves and many years of milk production during the cow's lifetime.

We always had a flock of chickens, and they roamed free around the yard and in the woods. We prepared nests lined with straw for the hens, and had a porcelain egg in each nest to give the hens the idea. Normally a hen would not try to set on the eggs until she had twelve or more in the nest, and it took three weeks of incubation for the eggs to hatch. The incubation process did not start until the hen stayed on the nest and kept the eggs warm constantly, so eggs laid two weeks earlier hatched at the same time as the others. Once the baby chicks started pecking out of the shells, they were all out within a day.

We didn't have a brooder house, but we tried to have at least three or four hens hatching eggs during the summer. We raised the chicks to frying size within six weeks to two months, and then sold them to the peddler or to the Columbia Produce Company in Lawrenceburg. By then they weighed about 1.5 to 2.00 pounds each.

I learned more about chickens 60 years later when I visited Gerald Bailey, my cousin, in Cullman, Alabama. He was field operations manager for Gold Kist, Inc. the parent company for Gold Kist Farms, and they sold more than a million chickens a week. He took my brother Bruce and me through one of their hatcheries and explained the process to us.

His company buys purebred hens from a specialty company and buys purebred roosters of a different breed. This crossbreeding produces hybrid baby chickens that are stronger and more vigorous than either parent. The ratio is usually one rooster to twelve hens. Any fewer roosters might not keep all the hens fertilized, and any more might cause too much competition and fighting among the roosters in the flock. One mating is sufficient for three to five eggs, and that is a week's production for an average hen. This arrangement keeps the roosters busy, but none of them show signs of being overworked.

The company controls egg production by controlling light. They get the hens when they are one day old, and for several weeks they keep the chicken house dark more hours a day than they have it lit. Than when the hens are old enough to start laying, they put the roosters with them and turn the lights on bright for several more hours than they have them off. That makes the hens think it is springtime, and they start laying eggs. The company gets maximum egg production from hens for about forty weeks. By then they have new hens ready to start laying eggs, and they send the old ones to market.

They keep the eggs at a temperature below 70 degrees until they put them into the incubators, so they will all hatch at the same time. The incubating racks that hold the eggs rotate 90 degrees automatically every hour, and that prevents the baby chickens from sticking to the insides of the shells. The temperature varies no more than one degree plus or minus for the first eighteen days of incubation.

After eighteen days they put the incubating racks on a machine that injects a vaccine into the big ends of the eggs and then moves them to hatching flats, where they stay three more days until they hatch. The inoculation protects the baby chickens against certain diseases that might otherwise occur within a few weeks. The hatching flats remain stationary and don't rotate. Each one holds more than a hundred eggs, and usually they all hatch within 24 hours.

Male and female chickens grow equally fast up to four or five pounds, but then the males grow faster. After that, it costs 1.5 cents more to add a pound to the weight of a hen bird, because hens are smaller by nature.

The company has different markets for different-sized birds. Some fast-food chicken places want 3.5 to 4.00 pound birds for bone-in chicken. Others that sell de-boned meat want big birds; eight or nine pounds each, for strips, patties, and nuggets. Specialty markets want very small birds that they sell as Rock Cornish Hens. Supermarkets want four or five pound birds to sell as fryers, and full-sized hens to sell for baking. Separating the baby chickens by sex makes it easier and more economical to produce birds of uniform size.

Eight or ten sexing specialists sit around the outside of a conveyor belt that runs continuously, forming a U at each end. As the flats full of baby chicks come from the hatchery, they dump them on the conveyer, and by the time the belt makes a full turn they have all been sorted. In front of each person are two receptacles, one for males and one for females. These receptacles connect to chutes that take the chickens to two other conveyors, one for males and one for females. In the interest of speed, they toss the baby chicks into the receptacles as if they were socks or mittens, but obviously it doesn't harm them.

Other workers load the chicks into shipping crates and put them into climate-controlled trailers, one for roosters and one for hens. The hen chicks go to local chicken farmers who keep them in their buildings for six weeks, by which time they are ready for market. The rooster chicks go to a sister operation in Russelville, Alabama, where they specialize in marketing to fast food places and other locations that want larger birds. When the hatchery at Cullman sends a trailer load of rooster chicks to Russelville they send back a trailer load of hen chicks from the hatchery there. The humidity in the trailers is strictly controlled, and the temperature varies no more than one degree either way.

By having all male birds, the operation at Russelville can save six or seven cents on the cost of producing each bird that they grow to eight or nine pounds. They market a half million such birds a week, so that translates into savings of at least $30,000 a week, or $1,500,000 a year. With an operation of that magnitude, the pennies add up to real money.

Determining sex is fast and simple. The operator picks up the chick and spreads the feathers on the tiny wing. The feathers of a rooster are all the same length, and the feathers of a hen are alternately longer and shorter. It is just that easy.

The chicken farmers provide the buildings, built to company specifications, and they watch over the chickens during the growing period. The company delivers the baby chicks and provides all feed and medication. Computers control the feeding and add medication to the feed as necessary to prevent disease. In six weeks, when they are ready for market, the company comes and picks up the chickens and takes them away. The farmer spends one day thoroughly cleaning and sanitizing the building and then the company delivers another load of one-day-old chicks for another growing cycle. The Russelville operation takes a few weeks more to get their birds to the heavier weights.

* * * * *

But in 1936 we had no such facilities, and our chickens ran free around the house and into the woods. We had no lighted and heated henhouse to encourage the hens to lay eggs, so most of our baby chicks were hatched in the spring when the days got longer and before the hot weather set in.

A hen cackled when she laid an egg, and it sounded like, "Cut-Cut CutAAWWWK, Cut-Cut-CutAAWWWK, Cut-Cut-CutAAWWWK." She repeated it several times, with not more than a few seconds between outbursts. Occasionally a hen did that when she had not laid an egg, but she always cackled when she did. That's how we found some of the nests they tried to hide in the woods.

> "The codfish lays a thousand eggs; the hen lays only one
> Yet the codfish never cackles to tell what she has done
> So while we praise the cackling hen, the codfish we despise
> And all this only goes to show it pays to advertise."
>
> Anonymous

A mother hen kept her chicks around her with a gentle clucking sound. They spent a lot of time under her outspread wings when they were first hatched. They slept there at night, and during the day she called them to her and got them back under her wings if a hawk or a crow got too close. Eunice says there is a reference to this in the Bible. Chicken hawks could not carry away full-grown hens, but they were always looking for young chickens.

She scratched in the dirt to uncover seeds or other bits of food suitable for little chicks. After they got too big to hide under the mother's wings, they roosted in the chicken house with the others. Chickens, like other birds, bend their legs backward when they sit on a perch. That forces the claws to close naturally and grasp the perch. The weight of the chicken keeps the legs bent backward and the claws closed tightly on the perch. That's how chickens and other birds can sleep without falling off the perch.

Each flock needed a rooster to fertilize the eggs so they would hatch. Some farmers got a new rooster every two or three years to guard against inbreeding, and this leads to a story about an old rooster that was being replaced by a new purebred rooster:

When the farmer put the new rooster in the barnyard the old rooster approached him. "I know you are here to replace me," he said, "but I would feel better about it if I could be sure you are a better rooster than I am. I will race you five times around the barn, and if you beat me, I will go quietly and never give you any trouble." The new rooster was sure he could win, so he agreed.

He let the old rooster have the five-foot head start he asked for and they started the race. After the third time around the barn there was a loud "Ka-boom" from the direction of the farmhouse, and the new rooster rolled over dead in a cloud of feathers. The old farmer blew the smoke out of his shotgun barrel. "I'll never buy another purebred rooster," he muttered. "That's the third one this month, and every one of them has been gay."

Animals require a separate mating for each birth, although there may be multiple births each time. Cows rarely have more than one calf at a time. One mating by a boar with a sow hog will produce six to ten pigs in one litter, just as one mating by a rooster with a hen will fertilize several eggs. Commercial egg producers who sell eggs for food do not keep roosters with their flocks. They don't need roosters to make the hens lay eggs, but just to fertilize them so they will hatch.

The sun does not sit at the end of the day—it sets, and a hen does not sit on her eggs—she sets on them. A setting of eggs was fifteen eggs. A hen might set on fewer, but fifteen was about all she could manage at one time. If we wanted a hen to stop laying and produce a brood of chicks, we left the eggs until the nest was full. That encouraged her to stay on the eggs day and night until they hatched. She left the nest only for brief periods, so the eggs were always warm.

If we wanted to eat or to sell the eggs, we took the eggs out of the nest as they were laid, leaving only the nest egg and sometimes one more in the nest. If we left no eggs in the nest, the hen would go somewhere else to lay her eggs, perhaps to a nest in the woods. Sometimes a hen started her secret nest and we didn't know it until she came out of the woods leading a dozen or more baby chicks.

The chickens foraged for food in the yard and in the woods. They ate grasshoppers, bugs, and all kinds of seeds. We threw grains of corn on the ground for them once a day, and they ate bits of gravel and tiny pieces of glass that helped grind up the corn in the craw.

Hens liked dust baths, and all around the farmyard they scratched up little patches of dust and flopped around in them as if they were birdbaths. The mules liked to roll in dust also. Every evening after work we took the harness off and turned them loose in the corral. They immediately looked for a place to "lay down and waller." Usually a mule wallowed on one side and then got up and lay down again to wallow on the other side. One of our mules could roll completely over on his back to the other side, so he didn't have to get up in order to roll on both sides. Before harnessing them the next morning, we used a curry comb to clean off the dirt and debris that stuck to them.

A chicken house sat between our house and the corncrib, but farther back toward the fields. Chickens like to roost off the ground, so we had roosting poles across the chicken house. The pole nearest the door was one foot off the ground, and the next was a foot higher and a foot farther back. They continued in this progression all the way to the back of the chicken house. Each row was above and behind the row in front, so each chicken had an unobstructed view forward. The door was on the right front corner of the house as you approached it, and if you walked into the door and kept going in a straight line, you went parallel with the roosting poles on your left. We had three or four nests built on low platforms on the right side wall, and wide boards that served as ramps for the hens to walk up to get to the nests and the roosting poles.

Chickens cannot see well in dim light. They started for the chicken house in the late afternoon, and by sunset they were all on the roost. If someone went to bed unusually early we said he went to bed with the chickens. Dad told us there had been an eclipse of the sun when he was young. It got so dark the chickens thought night was coming and went to the hen house.

* * * * *

We had a pen for hogs just outside the corral, on the side away from the barn. Our hogs grew to about 250 pounds by slaughtering time. We tried for at least one litter of pigs each year, but we had to use a neighbor's boar because we didn't have one.

The County Agent had recently announced that the County bought two Jacks, four White-Faced Hereford bulls, one Jersey bull, and one Duroc boar. All were brought into the county for breeding purposes. He also announced that Mr. C. C. Gunn set out five acres of Locust trees through the forestry Department of the Tennessee Valley Authority. Our school bus passed that grove on the way to high school. I understand that Locust wood makes good fence posts.

When the testicles of the male pigs became prominent, Dad sharpened his pocket knife and castrated them. He always poured coal oil on the open wounds to help them heal, and I never saw one develop an infection. Some farm families fried and ate these mountain oysters, but I never got that hungry.

* * * * *

Dad was a law enforcement officer ever since I can remember. He was elected to be constable several times, and he had some income from fees he collected for various duties. Sometimes he served warrants of arrest, and sometimes had to arrest a drunk who was causing a public disturbance. Usually he farmed during the week and performed these duties on weekends and holidays.

Many Sunday mornings a man rode a mule past our house on his way to the Lum Crews place, about a mile away on Big Oak Road. A few hours later he always came by in the other direction, riding the same mule. He was usually so drunk he swayed to one side or the other, and the mule seemed to be weaving from side to side to keep him balanced on his back. We watched him each time as he went by and never saw him fall off. We heard that Lum Crews made some kind of wine called raisin jack, and this was one of his relatives who came over on Sundays and drank it with him. Dad never arrested him for public drunkenness, because he didn't bother anybody and caused no disturbance.

Dad's duties also included looking for wildcat distilleries (stills), but the operators usually ran away and escaped arrest. Since he could not identify the owners or operators, all he could do was destroy the equipment. Such stills were illegal in Lawrence County for two reasons: The county had voted dry and made whisky illegal, and they were unlicensed and didn't pay federal and state taxes on the production of whisky. The officers who hunt down these stills are called revenuers, because the operators are depriving the government of revenue. The penalty for operating a moonshine still was a year and a day in jail. I suppose the law made the penalty one day more than a year to make sure the offense was counted a felony.

Officers looked for smoke from the wood-fired boilers to help them find stills, so some of them made whisky on dark nights in the woods. One man had his still in his house and directed the smoke from his boiler through his fireplace chimney. But his luck ran out when officers investigated smoke coming from his chimney one hot day in August.

Later dad was elected to be Justice of the Peace, and now and then he earned fees for the duties of the position. A cartoonist with the Nashville paper published a series of cartoons showing a very fat man with a three-day growth of beard smoking a big cigar and clutching wads of money in each fist. He always labeled the cartoons "Fee-grabbing J. P." They may have made big money in the cities, but certainly not where we lived.

I recall Dad's holding a civil trial one Saturday afternoon on the front porch of our house. He had to settle a dispute between a well digger and the farmer who employed him to dig a well. The well digger said he was obligated only to get water, and he got water. The farmer said the amount of water was not sufficient, and the well digger had to dig the well deeper to get a sufficient supply. I don't recall how it was settled, but it was a temporary diversion from hoeing cotton and picking bugs off of potato plants.

We raised a crop of spuds each year, and the potato bugs ravaged the plants if we didn't do something about them. Dad sometimes put arsenic on cotton plants to kill the boll weevils, but we were afraid to put it on our potato plants and then eat the potatoes. Therefore, one of the chores for the younger kids was to follow the row of potato plants and pick off the potato bugs. We killed them by dropping them into a jar of kerosene or of soapy water. The bugs multiplied so fast we did this once every two days.

Someone told a story about a farmer who saw an ad for something that was guaranteed to kill every potato bug in the field, and it cost only three dollars. He sent the three dollars and got back a little package with two wooden blocks in it. On one block was printed, "Put bugs on this," and on the other block, "Mash bugs with this."

* * * * *

Mules provided most of the power for farming during the depression. A mule sold for a higher price in the spring than in the fall, when he would have to be fed all winter and might not be needed for several months. Active buying and selling took place at the annual Mule Day at Columbia, about 30 miles north of Lawrenceburg. Traders prided themselves on the shrewd deals they made at Mule Day, and some made several trades during the day. Lynchburg also had a Mule Day, and there may have been others around the state.

A buyer always looked in the mouth of a horse or a mule before buying. The teeth gradually wear away with age, and their condition gives the most reliable indication of an animal's age.

A mule is a cross between a male donkey (Jack) and a female horse (mare.) Mules are tougher and more durable than horses but not quite as big. The size of the mule depends mostly on the size of the mother mare. A bigger mare produces a bigger mule.

There are mare mules and male mules, but as hybrids they are sterile and cannot reproduce. A hinny is a cross between a male horse (stallion) and a female donkey (jenny.) I never saw a hinny, but they would be smaller than mules and would have limited usefulness.

Most animals don't cross breed. Horses don't breed with cows and dogs don't breed with sheep. Horses can cross breed with donkeys because they are so much alike except for size. Dogs can cross with other breeds of dogs, and the puppies are usually stronger and healthier dogs than the parents. Unlike mules, mongrel dogs can reproduce.

Jacks like to bray, and they pass on their vocal abilities to their mule offspring, especially to the male mules. The words HEE HAW are often used to describe the braying of a jackass or a mule, but it actually sounds more like AAAGGGHHHH EE AGH EE AGHH EE AGHH. The first sound is long-drawn-out, deep throated, and coarse. It has an argumentative tone, something like the cawing of a crow, except it is lower in pitch and considerably louder. The EE's that come between the loud parts sound like whistles, and may be caused by a sharp intake of breath taken for the next part of the braying.

Our two mules, Jack and Jim, were mismatched. Jack was slow and plodding, while Jim was quick and jumpy. After they got going they kept about the same pace, but when they first started Jim jumped ahead and then fell back about the time Jack got started.

Near the end of the day the mules plodded along slowly when going away from the barn. But when I turned at the end of the row and started back toward the barn, they walked much faster. They were motivated to get to their drink of water, their wallow, and their corn and hay.

But sometimes it takes more than food to motivate a human: A rich old man, together with all of his children and their spouses, was preparing to eat Thanksgiving dinner. "Before we eat," he said, "I want to announce that I changed my will yesterday. As I have told you often, the fondest wish of my life is to have a grandchild before I die. You all are married, yet none of you has provided me with that pleasure. So now my entire estate will go to the couple who gives me my first grandchild. Now let's bow our heads while I say the blessing." After he said the blessing, he looked up and there was nobody at the table but him.

Somebody said once that Wesley Hayes went to Mule Day with nothing but a Barlow pocket knife, and after trading all day returned with a pair of mules. That was an obvious exaggeration, but he certainly was a shrewd trader. He was a farm kid who never went to high school. Yet he was trading horses and mules by the time he was fourteen years old and trading cars when he was sixteen.

A few years later, after he married, he hired a couple of out-of-work carpenters to build a house for him on Fall River Road, two or three miles from Lawrenceburg. Soon someone offered him so much money for it he sold it and had another one built. After this happened two or three times, he went full time into the house-building business.

He expanded eventually and built nursing homes and large apartment complexes. The last time I saw him, he was still living in the little brick house across from Lawrenceburg High School where he had lived for thirty or forty years. I had no personal knowledge of his net worth, but I'm sure it was into the millions. Wesley may have been short on formal education, but many college graduates would have traded their degrees for what he had in his head.

Wesley wanted to go into business with me after World War II. I had learned to fly in the Army Air Corps, and he offered to buy an airplane if I would use it to sell short rides on weekends. I didn't accept, because I was afraid we would never sell enough rides to pay for the plane. Also it sounded like a commitment for a longer time than I wanted.

It's easy to have 20 / 20 hindsight, but if only I had accepted his offer to go into business with him it might have led to something much bigger. I had known him for years and had always been on good terms with him, and a partnership in the flying business might have led to a partnership in his building business. At that time he didn't know any more about building than I did, and we could have learned the business together and perhaps could both have become millionaires. But you can't cash an if-only at the bank. If only a frog had wings, he wouldn't have to bump his behind on the ground all the time when he wanted to go somewhere.

CHAPTER FIVE

After the school vacation for the holidays was over, I walked north a mile and a half to the little country store at Gum Springs, where I always caught the bus for the high school in Lawrenceburg. The dirt road was usually muddy in the winter and dusty in the summer, but now it was frozen and solid underfoot. The freeze had pushed little short columns of ice—something like horizontal icicles—out of the sides of the ditches along the road. After a lot of rain in the spring or winter the ground got so saturated little rivulets of water flowed out of the sides of the ditches

In dry summers a car stirred up a cloud of dust, and it deposited a whitish-gray coat on all the trees, bushes, and weeds along the road. A hard rain always washed it off, but we hadn't been having many hard rains in the summers lately. Wildflowers grew along the road except in winter. Some blooms were red and blue in the spring, and others were yellow and brown in the fall.

The land around our farm was rolling but not hilly. The road in front of our house was level for the length of a football field, about half the distance to Grandpa White's house, then it was uphill the rest of the way. From there it leveled out for about a hundred yards before going uphill another three hundred yards to the Joe Voss house. Our house, Grandpa's house, and the Voss house were all on the eastern side of the road, the right side going north toward Gum Springs. Every thing on that side was open farmland from our house to just beyond the Voss house.

Otis (pronounced Ah'tis) Roberts, a son of Mama's aunt, owned the store at Gum Springs. The kids called him Smiley because of his glum expression. "Man who have not smiling face should not open shop," is a

Chinese proverb, and it fit Otis Roberts. Maybe he was grumpy because the school kids came in to get warm and rarely bought anything.

Alton Jordan, pronounced Jerden, drove the school bus. The kids said he was "Blind in one eye and couldn't see out uv the other'n." Tennessee didn't have a driver's license law until a year or two later.

A half-mile before reaching the school, Fall River road went down a long hill, curved sharply to the left, crossed Shoal Creek on a narrow two lane concrete bridge, and continued up a steep hill. Mr. Jordan always gunned the engine as he approached the bridge, so he could reach the top of the hill without shifting into lower gear. The bridge had four-feet-high concrete walls on each side, and I feared he would crash the left side of the bus into the wall of the bridge. He always raced around that curve and onto the bridge with his head cocked to the left so his good right eye could look straight ahead. He never put a scratch on that bus, but I looked for a seat on the right side when I boarded at Gum Springs in the mornings. In case he ever hit that concrete wall, I didn't want to be sitting on the bloody side.

On his morning run he picked up the first passengers at Fall River, and then collected others along the Fall River Road until he reached Crossroads. There he turned left and went toward Leoma until he passed the Jim Moses farm, and where the road divided he took the left fork down the Steadman Ridge Road as far as Dave Webb's store at Revilo. Then he backtracked to the Fall River Road, turned left, and continued up that Road to the school in Lawrenceburg.

When I got on the bus at Gum Springs it was more than half full. Noah and Paul Hillhouse, Ivorine and Bertie Jackson, Albert Ward, A. C. Springer, and Sally Howell lived in or near Fall River. They were the first ones picked up. A couple of miles farther up the road two brothers got on. I don't remember their names, but the older one was thin and had yellow fingertips and stained teeth from smoking Country Gentleman tobacco rolled in brown paper. The younger brother's first name was Dorcus, and they pronounced it Dawkus. At Revilo the driver picked up the Webb kids, Annis, Arras, and Zirkle (an older brother, Zenas, was away in the Navy, and the younger kids were still in Elementary school.)

Then he backtracked toward Crossroads and stopped at the Cantrell farm for Jim and Bernie (Bernice). They had an older brother, Bill, but he had graduated already. All the Cantrells had teeth so perfectly shaped and so dazzling white it was hard to believe they were real. Jim tried hard to be a comedian, but never had much success. Bernie sang and played the organ in church. She was charming and lovely, and Ezra Voss thought she was the sweetest peach on the tree. She was friendly with him, as she was with everybody, but beyond that she gave him no encouragement.

The next stop was for Alfred Prosser, who had to walk more than two miles from near Fairview Elementary School, which was on the road to Leoma. He often wore woolen dress pants to school, and had them dry cleaned when they got dirty. He had a minor impediment in his speech, but he did well in school. Alfred was the marble champion of the community, and he had a bucketful of marbles he had won playing keeps. Now and then someone challenged him, but he always won all the marbles and added them to his collection.

The two Moses brothers, Barney and Charlie, boarded next. Then Glayden and Trula Fox got on at Crossroads. They lived two miles down the Old-Florence-to-Pulaski Road, near the pond in Rossboro creek where the Gum Springs Baptist Church held their total-immersion baptizing ceremonies twice a year. At Gum Springs the bus stopped for Ezra Voss, Lacy Williams, and me. Farther up the road we picked up Elizabeth Guthrey, and that completed the load.

Many kids went only to elementary school, because the law didn't require any more. My cousin Noah Robinson went to high school a month or two and then dropped out. He said when he asked his teachers what benefit he would get from some subject he was taking, they always said he would need it when he got to college. But he didn't intend to go to college, so he thought he was wasting his time.

LAWCO HIGH was short for Lawrence County High School. Our principal's name was E. O. Coffman, but everybody called him Teeb behind his back. I never knew why. He was the only teacher who had a Master's degree. I learned that one day at a meeting of students in the gymnasium when he read the names of all the teachers and the kind of degree each one had. Everybody else had only a Bachelor's degree, and I think he wanted everyone to know it that he was the only one with an MA.

The school was in an old, three-story, and red-brick building with no elevator. A coal-fired furnace in the basement provided heat; and Bob Bailey, the janitor, kept the fire going. He had one wooden peg leg from the knee down, but it didn't seem to bother him. He made good brooms in the basement and sold them for thirty-five cents each. He used one machine to flail the seeds from the broomcorn and another machine to bind the brooms to the handle. The school probably considered his income from the broom-making business when deciding what to pay him to be the janitor. Hughes Cheatwood, one of my classmates, told me much later that Mr. Bailey made brooms for all the schools in the county system.

We had a fine new gymnasium next to the school building. They built it the year before to replace the old one, which was down in a valley one block away. The new one was named the E. O. Coffman Gymnasium, and the school held many functions and meetings there.

We usually had a respectable basketball team, but never a state champion. Their glory days were before my time, when Clay and Clyde Whitehead, brothers, were on the team. Basketball legends in Lawrenceburg, they also played baseball in the Industrial League for Salant & Salant, the local shirt factory, now out of business for many years. One of the boys, I never knew which, eventually developed an enlarged heart and had to give up sports.

The starting forward on the 1936 basketball team was Zollie Webb. Charlie Kirk was the substitute player for that position, but he played more minutes and scored more points than Webb, the starter. After one game the *Democrat Union* displayed the headline: *"Substitute" Kirk scores 34 points in basketball game.*

I tried out for the basketball team one winter but didn't make it. We practiced after school, and I walked home six miles in the dark because the bus always left two hours earlier. The coach drove one of the players home after practice, but he was a star player and would not have been available to play otherwise. We couldn't share the ride because he lived in the opposite direction. Coach Walter Hooker gave me every opportunity, and even let me use a pair of his basketball shoes, because I couldn't afford a pair of my own. But I soon learned I didn't have the talent or the experience to make the team, so I stopped going to practice.

Most of the good high-school players came from the elementary school programs. Lawrence County held a tournament each year for the basketball teams from the elementary schools, but Gum Springs never advanced very far. The coach was Drudie Greene, the principal, and I don't think he had ever played the game. We had a center, two forwards, a running guard, and a standing guard. The standing guard was supposed to stay back in the middle of the court when his team had the ball and was trying to score, and be there to head off anybody who stole the ball and headed for the other team's goal. Naturally, the standing guard was not expected to score any points. The few times I played they always made me the standing guard, and that said something about my inability to score.

T. D. Rayfield was the coach of the Dunn Elementary School, probably the best team year after year of all the elementary schools. Rayfield must have been a good player in college, because he was light years ahead of Drudie Greene as a coach.

I wanted to try out for the high school football team, because I was big for my age. But I couldn't do that, because the football season conflicted with harvest time on the farm and I had to work every day after school.

We had a cafeteria, but I don't recall anything about it. I took my lunches, usually wrapped in pages of newspapers. Many times they consisted of biscuits filled with butter and sugar or with butter and molasses. Sometimes I took boiled eggs or fried eggs inserted into split biscuits, and other times I took baked sweet potatoes.

* * * * *

I was a mediocre student in high school. We had six periods during the day, with four classes and two study halls. The grading was numerical, and 75 was a passing grade. My grades were usually in the high seventies, and rarely in the eighties. I had made good grades in elementary school by listening in class and never studying, but that was not enough in high school.

I had just failed the first semester of Algebra and would have to take it again. Teeb had taught the class, and I found him arrogant and sarcastic. If a student asked a question when he should have known the answer, Teeb ridiculed him and make him feel like an idiot. Since my name started with W, I was in the back row, and I seldom raised my hand for fear of being humiliated. My sister, Eunice, later had a part-time job in Mr. Coffman's office and took some of his classes, and she thought he was a great teacher. She made good grades, which may account for her different opinion.

Boyd Phagan Davidson was a star in my algebra class, and so was Barney Lumpkin. Teeb often had one of them go to the blackboard and solve long complicated problems to show us dummies how to do it, but I didn't understand it any better afterwards. I heard years later that Boyd had become a doctor, and a good one.

I was glad to learn that Mr. Emerson Hendrix, the coach of the football team, would teach my beginning Algebra class when I took it again. He had taught my Manual Arts class the previous semester and I liked him. He was easy to relate to, and I was sure I would pass the course. Taking it for the second time would also make it easier.

* * * * *

A wooden building 150 yards east of the school provided three of the school's classrooms. The Manual Arts, General Science, and Agriculture classrooms were in that building. It was on the other side of the football field, but I didn't mind the walk unless it was raining or unusually cold.

I was a no-thumbs student in Manual Arts. While others were making cedar chests, I was trying to build a three-legged stool thirty-six inches high. I managed to finish the octagonal top, but the stool wouldn't stand solidly on the floor. When one leg was a trifle too long and I cut it off, another leg was then too long. The legs were almost even after I did this a few times, and I decided to take my chances and leave things as they were.

But by then I had a stool that didn't measure three feet tall. I passed the course with a mediocre grade, perhaps because Mr. Hendrix took pity on me. I was like the man who said he had cut off his pants legs three times, but they were still too short.

Mrs. Whittaker taught the General Science class. She was very thin and had white hair. I remember three things about her class. She heated one end of an iron rod with a small torch, and the other end got hot quickly, demonstrating that iron conducts heat well. Another thing I remember was her thick southern accent. I can still hear her saying, "Aiahh is a pooahh conductahh of heat, but aiahh is a gooooud carriahh of heat." She went on to explain that hot air is a good way to move heat from one room to another, but dead air between walls makes good insulation. The last thing was the way she demonstrated static electricity. She tore up bits of paper and put them on the desk. Then she took another iron rod, wrapped a piece of sheepskin around it, and rubbed it to generate static electricity. She got a tense look on her face as she gripped the sheepskin tightly and pumped it up and down very fast on the iron rod. Then she passed the rod over the pieces of paper and they attached themselves to the rod because of the static electricity she had generated in the rod.

Mr. Melvin South taught my classes in Agriculture and in Ancient History. The Agriculture class was interesting, because it concerned something I was doing. But the history course was dry, and Mr. South never managed to get me interested in the Medes and the Persians. The course in Agriculture reminds me of a County Agent whose job was to go to the various communities and hold meetings to teach the local farmers better farming methods. One old man would never come to the meetings, and the agent asked him why:

"Waste of time," he explained, "cause I ain't farmin' now as good as I know how."

The school offered a business class that included typing, but I never took it because it cost a dollar and fifty cents for each six weeks, including the rental of a typewriter. Walter Hooker, the basketball coach, taught it. One kid named Martin Harris could type sixty words a minute on a manual typewriter. I had never seen anyone type that fast.

In my first semester Miss Ruby Ussery taught my English class. I had a crush on her, but couldn't possibly let her know it. I was fourteen years old and still three years away from having anything resembling a date. She was perhaps twenty three, and I was jealous because I thought she liked Mr. Hendrix, the football coach. It took me a year to get over it.

Two things from that English class still linger in my mind. One was a line from The Rime of the Ancient Mariner: "A fair breeze blew, the white foam flew, the furrow followed free." The combination of meter and alliteration fascinated me. The other thing was an example of a misplaced modifier: "Lost: A fountain pen by a woman full of green ink."

Laura Lou White—no relation to me—was in that class. She was probably 14 or 15 and already a beauty. Two years later I saw her come into the conference hall when we were having a meeting of all the students. By then she had a figure that would have made any woman proud, and when she sauntered down the aisle most of the boys started clapping their hands. I never considered asking her out, because I had no money, no transportation, no dressy clothes, and no nerve. She was the daughter of the owner of White's Hardware, and after she graduated she married F. L. Coffey, the son of the owner of Coffey Motors, a car dealership in Lawrenceburg. Many years later I saw her brother, Jimmy White, when I was in Lawrenceburg. He was manager of the restaurant in the Greyhound bus station there.

In high school I excelled only in plane geometry. Miss Particia Springer, the teacher, was tall and thin and about fifty. For some reason the course was easy for me; and I never missed a question, never failed to solve a problem, and never failed to make a perfect score on any quiz or test for the semester. I especially liked statement problems that presented a set of facts and asked us to answer one or more questions using geometry. One day I happened to overhear Hassell "Speck" Brewer talking to another of our classmates. He said, in amazement, that I had worked one of the problems a different way from how the teacher had, and the teacher said my way was just as good.

I had a study hall just before the class, and spent the entire hour studying geometry. When they gave out report cards at midterm, I picked up my card in the morning and took it to all my classes. Each teacher then entered the grade for that class on my card. Since my Geometry class was at the end of the day, Miss Springer saw my 76's, 77's, and 78's from the other classes. She couldn't understand why my grades were so low in the other classes and so high in hers. I told her it was because I had a better teacher in her class.

She taught a music class in a room next to one of my other classes, and the singing voices came faintly but clearly through the wall.

I didn't take the music class, but I studied poetry in an English class. They taught us about feet and meter, but I have since forgotten many of the details. I remember Iambic Pentameter best because of Gray's Elegy Written in a Country Churchyard, one of my favorite poems. Webster's dictionary says an Iamb is a metrical foot of two syllables, the first unaccented and the second accented; and Pentameter is a line of verse having five metrical feet or measures. Iambic Pentameter, therefore, sounds like duh DUH, duh DUH, duh DUH,duh DUH, duh DUH. In Gray's Elegy, the first line is "The CHURCH bell TOLLS the KNELL of PART ing DAY."

* * * * *

The Librarian was Miss Mildred Looney, and I recall her trying to teach us the Dewey decimal system. The school assessed a library fee of fifty cents a semester for each student. Most of the 400 kids in the school resented the fee. One afternoon as the principal was leaving, he backed his car into a fence post next to the parking lot. "Tear it up-" Snotty Norton yelled. "Buy a new one with the library fee." Mr. Coffman gave no indication that he heard it.

Mrs. McCrory taught my Biology class. Her husband, Raymond, taught there also, but I don't recall ever having a class with him. She was a proper lady with dark eyes, black hair, and olive skin, and it embarrassed me to listen to her talk to us about bodily functions and reproduction. She didn't make us dissect frogs, for which I will be forever grateful, but I had a problem when she told us to bring to class a complete menu of what we ate for a week and read it aloud to the class.

My parents had always stressed the importance of telling the truth, but I didn't want to tell the whole class that I ate biscuits and Hoover gravy seven days a week for breakfast, cornbread and milk seven days a week for supper, and cornbread and peas or beans or turnips or vegetable soup most of the time for lunch. That seven-day menu I turned in, with my fingers crossed, was a combination of the best meals I had for the previous year. I rationalized my fudging by thinking it was nobody's business but mine and it didn't hurt anybody else.

* * * * *

On the way home from school the bus always stopped for a few minutes at a store run by a Mr. Franks. That gave the kids a chance to buy pencils, paper, or other things they needed for school; or to get a soft drink, a piece of candy, or some cheese and crackers. I usually stayed on the bus because I had nothing to spend and we had been riding for only ten minutes. I always refused any offer from a friend of a soft drink or a piece of candy. It was better to pretend I didn't want it than to feel obligated when I knew I wouldn't be able to return the favor.

The students in the school ranged from financially comfortable to poor as dirt. William Kidd's father owned a service station and garage on the edge of town, and his wallet usually held several bills. Many others rarely had two nickels to rub together. One kid had the nickname of Loan-me-a-nickel because he said it so many times to so many other students. I asked him once why he wanted to borrow a nickel, and he said to buy an R.C.Cola. I didn't have a nickel, but I wouldn't have lent it to him anyway. That nickel would have been gone forever, and for a nickel I could buy one shotgun shell and six 22 cartridges. With that much ammunition I could hope to put some meat on the table.

The Whitten family owned a trucking company and had an impressive home a few blocks from the school. One of their sons, Rolla, had very little use of his legs and had to use crutches to get around. He rode a pony to school and tied it up in the schoolyard when he was in class. I don't recall how he got on and off the pony.

CHAPTER SIX

Dad had not been healthy since World War I, and that was the primary reason he had to stop digging coal. He had Spinal Meningitis and Influenza at the same time during the war. He didn't trust doctors, and he threw the pills they gave him out the window. Late one night a doctor was making his rounds and said to the nurse, "There's one who won't be here in the morning," thinking Dad was asleep. He thought to himself "You SOB, I'll be here when you're gone."

When they had processed him for demobilization, he insisted there was nothing wrong with him. He thought his problems were temporary, he wanted to go home, and he was afraid they would keep him in an Army hospital instead of letting him leave. After he got home and tried to do a hard day's work, he discovered he had made a mistake. In later years he could not prove his disability was service connected, because his medical record showed nothing wrong when he left the Army.

Sometimes he had chills and fever and took a patent medicine called Grove's Tasteless Chill Tonic. The directions on the bottle said shake before using, and the shaking stirred up something that looked like metal filings in the bottom of the bottle. I tried it once, and the taste was horrible. They should have named it Grove's Taste Bad Chill Tonic.

* * * * *

My only sister, Eunice, was born in January 1922, a year and a half after I was, and my brother Quinton Merrit a year and a half later. Next came Edgar Reeve, Oland Bruce, and finally the twin boys, Billie Gene and Bobbie Dean—-born when I was not quite fifteen. They were premature and weighed a little more than four pounds each. Both were injured at birth and had cerebral palsy. We kept them in a wash tub lined with cotton and heated by warm water in mason jars. We had to boil their milk, mix it half-and-half with water, and feed them every thirty minutes. The whole milk caused them to develop jaundice, so we switched them to buttermilk.

It was a full-time job around the clock to keep them warm and fed. Dad later built a wooden box with legs—-a country incubator—-to replace the washtub. Old Doc Harris came to the house and delivered the twin babies. He had his office in his home near Lawrenceburg, about six miles away.

Besides his physical handicaps, and probably because of them, Billie developed serious psychological problems in his late teens. When Dad died in 1957, Billie was already in a state hospital in Nashville. Bobbie was never able to walk and died at age five.

My sister is a gentle, loving person; and more than anyone else she has helped to keep the family together. Circumstances put a heavier load on her than on any of the rest of us, and for many years she was the only source of comfort for Billie

He needed crutches from the beginning, and was in either a hospital or a nursing home the last forty years of his life. Medicare and Medicaid took care of most of the expenses. Through the persistent efforts of his sister he ended up in a good nursing home near her, but he suffered a stroke and was totally helpless for the last three or four years. She went to see him every day, and did everything possible to make things easier for him. He never led a normal life, and died at age sixty-one. In his later years he frequently tried to talk, but his words were so garbled we could rarely understand him.

Edgar developed Epilepsy when he was eighteen years old, and we thought it was because he suffered an injury playing football in high school. When they drafted him he told them about the epilepsy, but they thought he was making excuses to avoid serving. After he had been there a few months they discovered their mistake and discharged him.

But he had served in the army long enough to be eligible for free medical treatment, and he spent more than half of his life in the Alvin C. York Veterans Administration hospital at Murfreesboro, Tennessee, about thirty miles from Nashville. During the first few years they let him come out for a weekend, or sometimes longer, but he got worse until he had to wear a football helmet at all times to guard against injury from sudden falls.

They couldn't control his Gran Mal epilepsy with drugs, so he could never drive a car. He always talked about getting his driver's license, but never did. I went to see him every chance I got, and was usually able to take him somewhere nearby to eat.

He told me once that the food was good in the hospital, except they kept giving him green peas on his plate. Edgar talked with a slow drawl. "I tole them I cain't eat them ole English peas " he said, "but they kept on givin' 'em to me. One day the doctor said if I didn't eat them peas I wouldn't never get another bite to eat in that hospital as long as I lived. So I eat 'em, and I thrrrowwed up. They didn't give 'em to me no more."

He got progressively worse and finally died in the V. A. Hospital at age forty-five. Edgar and Billie are resting next to each other in a memorial garden just north of Lawrenceburg.

For many years Billie and Edgar were in hospitals 25 miles apart, and Eunice was the only sibling that lived in the same state. Quinton eventually retired and moved to the area, but his wife, Beverly, was bedridden for years and needed his constant attention. He also became seriously ill and died a few months before Billie did. I always lived several hundred miles away, and Bruce lived even farther away, so we didn't go there often. Eunice deserves sainthood for the way she looked after her helpless brothers.

During our early years we kids all had turns with measles, whooping cough, and colds. We had occasional boils—we called them risins—stubbed toes, and cuts or puncture wounds in our feet from stepping on nails or other sharp objects while we were barefoot. We soaked any open wound or puncture in coal oil, and usually there was no infection. I had scarlet fever when I was three, but I don't remember it. Quinton had pneumonia at an early age, and it stunted his growth for a while. I had a tougher time than most with my case of measles, because I started to break out after I came home one evening from hunting rabbits all day—- slogging through six inches of snow in a cold wind.

* * * * *

The first year in Tennessee we had rented a house from the Bishop family on Fall River Road. It was almost a mile down the road from the Gum Springs Baptist Church and the Gum Springs Elementary School.

One of the Bishop children was Carrie, a girl whose club feet were so bad she spent all her time in a wheel chair. Another was a boy whose name was spelled Emit but pronounced Emmitt. Carrie had a sister who worked years later at Old Hickory, Tennessee, until she saved enough money for surgery to correct Carrie's handicap; but Carrie did not survive the surgery.

In July, the Tennessean reported that Infantile Paralysis had hit 81 Alabamians, with 70 diagnosed since June 1. No fatalities had been reported as yet, but they speculated that many might be crippled. The disease usually affects children between ages four and ten, and I had four brothers in that age group. On July 11, Montgomery, Alabama, reported: "Eight dead as epidemic strikes 126—— Infantile Paralysis spreading into Tennessee." We were lucky, because the disease didn't get to anyone we knew.

CHAPTER SEVEN

The Tennessee River flows through Tennessee from north to south, then through Northern Alabama from east to west, then through Tennessee again from south to north on its way to join the Ohio River at Paducah, Kentucky. Thus it creates three natural divisions of the state: East, Middle, and West Tennessee. That's why the state flag has three stars.

Lawrence County is in the southern part of Middle Tennessee, and Lawrenceburg is the County Seat. It is located at the intersection of Highways 64, and 43, about half way between Chattanooga and Memphis and ninety miles south of Nashville. Lawrence County extends about thirty miles farther south to the Alabama State line.

Lawrenceburg had a population of three thousand when I started high school in 1934. The courthouse sat in the public square in the middle of town. Around the square were two banks, a Piggley Wiggley grocery store, a restaurant, two hardware stores, a dry-goods store, a five-and-ten-cent store, a small hotel, a movie theater, a Chrysler-Plymouth dealership, one drug store, and a pool hall. A family named Beckham owned the drug store, and one of their sons went to high school when I did. He worked in the store when he had free time from school activities.

Jack Seymour's restaurant was just off the square. I went there one afternoon looking for my friend Lacy Williams, and saw Paul Campbell, another friend from Gum Springs. He was sitting at the counter eating from a plateful of meat in a thick brown sauce.

"Whatcha eatin' Paul?"

"That's an order of steak."

"What comes with it?"

"Nuthin."

"What did it cost?"

"Fifteen cents."

Paul was a picky eater and left two or three bite-sized chunks of meat on his plate. I never understood how anyone could do that. I wanted to order a serving for myself, but I didn't have fifteen cents. Besides, for that price I could buy five shotgun shells or a box of rifle cartridges.

North Military Street ran north from the courthouse, and there were several stores and other business buildings on that street. It went out to the general area of the National Guard Armory, which probably accounted for the name of the street.

The local funeral home had a burial society, and Dad joined it. When someone in the group died they assessed each member twenty-five cents to pay for the funeral of the deceased person. The funeral home provided free cardboard fans with flat wooden handles to churches in the area. On one side of each fan they printed advertising for the funeral home. The church members used them to fan themselves on hot days. We had never heard of air conditioning, and the country churches didn't have electricity to run electric fans.

* * * * *

The wagon yard, commonly called the hitch yard, in Lawrenceburg was an open space a city block in size near the Louisville & Nashville railroad tracks; and the farmers parked their wagons there when they came to town. They usually unhitched their mules from the wagons and tied the reins to a wagon wheel. The mules were then unable to pull the wagon and run away, so they stayed hitched to the wagon wheel until the farmer returned from whatever he was doing.

Trains frightened the mules because the steam engines were big and scary. They made loud hissing noises as they blew off clouds of steam and smoke, and made a KER-CHUNK, KER-CHUNK sound when they started off after being stopped. In addition, the engineer always blew the steam whistle and rang the bell as he got the train going, in order to warn the traffic at crossings down the line.

The hitch yard not only was alongside the railroad, it was near the depot where the trains stopped. That kept the engines next to the hitch yard longer than if the trains just passed by. The farmers knew when a train was scheduled to come, and they tried to be there to hold the bridles of the mules and calm them until the train was gone.

Tennessee had a local option law that allowed the voters in each county to decide whether whisky would be legal. Davidson County (Nashville) allowed whisky, but Lawrence County was dry. But many confessed they voted dry and drank wet, and it was easy to find a bootlegger. The half-pint bottle was the most popular size, because it was small and easy to conceal.

Sometimes a drinker hid a bottle in his wagon and came back from time to time to get a nip. That was safer than carrying the forbidden stuff around in a pocket of his overalls. People went to jail for possession of illegal whisky. Someone wrote a song about a man who got drunk in town and had all kinds of trouble. The song title was "I wish I'd a-bought me a half-a-pint and stayed in the wagon yard." That was also the last line of each verse.

Most of the trains were freights, but the L & N had one passenger train that ran five days a week. The engine was a diesel, and it pulled only two passenger cars, probably because they never had enough passengers to need a third car. We called it the Hucketybuck, and its warning horn sounded like "GAROOOONK, GAROOOONK." The steam engine whistles sounded more like "WHOOOOOO, WHOOOOO, WHOOOoooooooooooo" It sounded louder as the train approached; and the sound faded sharply when it passed and started going away, especially when the train was going at full speed. I learned later that was the Doppler effect.

Once we rode the Hucketybuck to Alabama to see our grandparents. There were a few stops on the way where the train did not stop unless someone signaled. One such stop was Dunn, between Lawrenceburg and Leoma, and another was Bear Creek. The station at Dunn looked like a telephone booth there beside the railroad tracks.

Farther down the road I remember the conductor calling out "BEAR CREEK, BEAR CREEK," but then the train did not stop. I asked Mama why, and she said nobody was getting off there and nobody was waiting to get on. A passenger had to pull an overhead cord to signal that he wanted to get off. If nobody was standing out by the station building, they assumed nobody wanted to board, so they didn't stop unless a passenger signaled.

The rest room had a round metal pipe with a toilet seat at the top. The pipe was about a foot in diameter and it was open straight down to the end, just above the railroad bed. When you looked down through the toilet seat you could see the crossties flying past.

The Hucketybuck went south toward Alabama in the afternoon, and we could usually hear it when we were working in our fields. We could tell time by watching for the mail carrier who came about 11:00 AM and by listening for the horn of the Hucketybuck that went south about 4:00 PM. If we were working behind a hill when the mail carrier came we could still see the cloud of dust that always followed him, unless it had been raining.

At other times we estimated the time by the position of the sun in the sky. I'll come by this evenin' about an hour by sun, meant an hour before sundown. Our neighbor Harvey Keener was the exception. He had a railroad watch made by the Illinois Company, and he carried it with him everywhere he went. He kept it in a little pocket in the bib of his overalls, and he looked at it and wound it frequently. If you asked him for the time, he told you the hour, the minutes, and the seconds. We considered a railroad watch to be the ultimate timekeeper.

* * * * *

Highway 64 was two blocks north of the courthouse and ran east and west through Lawrenceburg. East Gaines Street went due east from the courthouse, parallel with, and just south of Highway 64. Lawrence County High School was a half mile out East Gaines Street. A turn to the right at the high school and a left turn three blocks later led to the beginning of Fall River Road. This road was paved to the city limits and unpaved after that. It ran southeast from Lawrenceburg to Fall River, about a dozen miles away.

The Gum Springs School and Church were on Fall River road, five miles from Lawrenceburg. Wesley's Chapel road began there and ran North past Wesley's Chapel Methodist Church to intersect Highway 64 at the community of New Prospect.

Aldridge Road began ½ mile beyond Gum Springs and ran south about a mile to the Harvey Keener place. The road got its name from the family living in the first house on the right side of the road. They called it White-Voss Road for years, but started calling it Aldridge road after the White and the Voss families moved away.

Dill Peppers and his family lived in the Aldridge house previously, but they moved to a house on Fall River road near Crossroads. I always wanted to ask Mr. Dill Peppers if he had a cousin named Dill Pickles.

The road ran south past the Aldridge farm and then past an old house on the left that had been occupied by a succession of sharecroppers. Next came the Abercrumbie farm, which sat on the right just beyond a small stream spanned by a little wooden bridge. The little stream originated on the Aldridge farm and they had fenced the area surrounding the stream as pasture for their livestock.

The Joe Voss farm was on the left three hundred yards farther up a slope, and Grandpa White's farm was also on the left and five hundred yards down the other side of the hill. We lived just beyond Grandpa's place, and Harvey Keener lived two hundred yards beyond us and on the right side of the road. From the Abercrumbie farm to the Keener farm, the west side of the road was all in woods.

The road was straight from the Fall River Road to Harvey Keener's place, then it turned left and followed our property line, crossed a small stream, turned right, and went past the Lavato (Vader) Williams farm. Farther on the road passed the Crum farm, meandered through the woods and across a creek, passed Blackburn Frazier's little house on the right and the Big Frazier house on the left, and joined the Big Oak road near the Lum Crews farm.

Blackburn Frazier had been married before and had a daughter, IvaNell, who turned out to be a real beauty. Blackburn was living with another woman, while IvaNell lived with her grandparents in their house on the hill about 300 yards away. Blackburn finally married the other woman, and she had a baby the next day, according to reports.

Beyond the Keener place the road was rough, bumpy, and sometimes rocky. It twisted and turned and went up and down hills, and at one place it crossed a fairly wide creek with no bridge. It didn't cause a problem unless the water was high from rain, because the creek was shallow there and the bottom was mostly flat rocks.

The Crossroads community was two or three miles farther down Fall River road from Gum Springs. Crossroads Baptist Church was the first building on the left, and fifty yards beyond the church was the Crossroads country store. A dirt road (The Old Florence-Pulaski Road) from Giles County came from the left. It began at Highway 64 near the little community of Bodenham, near Pulaski. It passed between the church and the store and continued past the Oak Hill church and on to Big Oak, near the little town of Leoma.

The nearest drinking water to the Crossroads Church was a well at a farm house two hundred yards up Fall River Road. No country store was ever open on Sunday, so soft drinks were not available. The well was 70 feet deep, and it made me dizzy to look down into it. The pool of water at the bottom looked the size of a dime. I wondered who had been brave enough to go that deep into the ground to dig that well.

Oak Hill church was half way between Crossroads and Leoma, and it also had no well on the property. Everybody who needed water came back down one hill and then up another to the well on the farm of Frank James, and it was only half as deep as the well at Crossroads. Each well had a community dipper, used by everyone for drinking. It was either a metal dipper, a metal cup, or a hollowed-out gourd with a handle on it more than a foot long.

The road curved slightly to the right between Crossroads and Oak Hill, and it curved some more to the right between Oak Hill and the dead-end intersection with the Rabbit Trail Road. A huge oak tree grew at this intersection, and everybody called the location Big Oak. Even 50 years later after the tree died and was cut down, they still called that road intersection Big Oak. Turning left, the Rabbit Trail Road led to the community of Five Points, and to the right led to the town of Leoma, about a half mile from Big Oak. Leoma was on Highway 43, and five miles south of Lawrenceburg.

Dick Massey, the diminutive son of the Chrysler-Plymouth dealer in Lawrenceburg, described Leoma as, "Two stores, two whores, and a cotton gin." It had five or six houses, a couple of stores, a post office, a sawmill, a cotton gin, a blacksmith shop and a service station—only everybody called it a filling station then. I didn't know anything about any girls. Our address was Route Three, Leoma, Tennessee. We didn't have a box number, because the rural mail carrier knew everybody on the route and names were painted on the mail boxes.

Until the early 30s Fall River Road had a dirt surface, kept in passable condition by work crews made up of volunteers from the community. Mules pulled the grading machine, and an operator maneuvered the blade by turning big wheels to change the angle of the blade and the depth of the cut. The operator sat on a high seat near the back, so he could watch the blade and easily reach the operating controls. In the early thirties men in the neighborhood applied a chert surface to the road. That was a clay-like substance that packed down harder than dirt, and was less likely to develop potholes in the winter.

They did this with mules and wagons and picks and shovels. The wagons had boards about two feet high on each side and at the front. The board in the back slipped into a retaining slot and could be lifted out when it was time to unload. The floors of the wagon beds were two-by-fours standing on edge. They were long enough so they stuck out a foot or two behind the wagon. The extended part was trimmed and the sharp edges rounded off, so a man could grasp one of the two-by-fours and pull it up through the load of chert. Pulling up first one 2-by-4 and then another allowed the chert to fall to the road. They parked the wagons where they wanted to dump the chert.

At the chert pit they loaded the wagons with picks and shovels, but unloading was faster and easier. When they had enough chert on the road, they smoothed and shaped it with the grading machine and then let the subsequent traffic pack it down.

Several years later they put a chert surface on our road. It ended at Harvey Keener's place, about two hundred yards beyond our house. They did this soon after Dad was elected to be a Justice of the Peace, making him a member of the County Court.

* * * * *

Our rural mail carrier came six days a week. He never had a car more than two years old, and I liked to go to the mail box to meet him so I could lean over and sniff that new car smell through the open window of his car.

Uncle Roy Reeve said the mail carrier job for the route where he lived in Alabama had been vacant during World war I, and they asked him to take it. They told him he would have to pass a written test, but he could easily make a hundred on it. He had no competition, and the job was his for the asking. He turned it down because he was working in a plant in Birmingham at the time, and was making more money than the Mail Carrier job paid. He said he thought the good jobs and the good money would never end.

"Now the man they persuaded to take the job is driving a new car every two years," he said later. "He gets off work at three PM, a perfect time to go bird hunting. He makes more money in two months than I make farming in a year, and he will have a guaranteed pension for life when he retires."

* * * * *

We kids liked to go barefoot in the summer, but our parents always made us wait until the Dogwood trees bloomed. That was usually in April, and the soles of our feet were tough by the end of the summer.

Sometimes we bought our clothes at stores in Lawrenceburg, but most of the time we ordered them from Sears Roebuck or Montgomery Ward. I remember seeing shoes on one page of the Sears catalog for $1.98 and another pair on the next page that looked the same but cost $2.00. I wondered if the difference was worth two cents or if the shoes were identical and Sears was playing pricing games with the customers.

Work shoes had uppers above the ankles. Dress shoes were low cut, and we called them slippers. When a shoe sole wore through, we put cardboard inside temporarily to keep dirt from coming in through the hole, and sometimes we used a commercial product called Sav-A-Sole. It came in a tube and looked something like thin peanut butter. We applied it with the blade of a knife, as we would apply plastic wood to fill a hole in a board, or spackling compound to repair drywall. When it had dried completely it was better than nothing, but was never as good as advertised.

A pair of good overalls cost two dollars, and those of lesser quality as little as a dollar and a quarter. One of the better brands was Oskosh B'Gosh, but we usually bought the Sears Roebuck intermediate quality. We didn't throw them away until they got so threadbare they wouldn't hold a patch. The blue denim faded to gray before we discarded them.

On Easter Sunday and on Decoration Day we dressed in our best. Last Easter I had worn a white, sleeveless, V-necked sweater and a pair of cotton pants. The sweater had cost $1.98 from Sears. When I was in elementary school, I had one pair of overalls that still looked blue and had no patches on the knees. I saved these to wear to church on Sunday or to wear if we went into town on Saturday afternoon.

* * * * *

People said if you stood on a street corner on the Public Square on Saturday afternoon you saw everybody you knew. That was an exaggeration, but it was a favorite place to go and hang out.

For the men and older boys, the pool hall was a big attraction. Identical twins owned it, Fred and Flo Gilbreath. They were chiropractors by profession, but they spent more time in the pool hall than they did in their offices. The manager was a skinny, balding, nondescript character called Tip, who collected the five cents a game from the players and racked the balls between games. Flo Gilbreath said he paid Tip $10.00 a week and all he could steal. The house charged 2 ½ cents a cue, or a nickel a game for two players and a dime a game for four. The loser or losers paid for the game.

Six full-sized pool tables were lined up down the middle of the room. On the right side looking from the front, racks of pool cue-sticks lined the wall, and on each side was a row of benches for the convenience of the spectators and the players.

Each pool table had a wire stretching along the length of the table and reaching from one side wall of the poolroom to the other. The wire was higher than the players' heads and had a divider in the middle. A hundred wooden buttons on each side of the divider were threaded on the wire, and all were pushed to the middle.

When two players played straight pool, each took one section of the buttons to record his score. They could shoot at any ball on the table but had to call each shot—-designate which ball would fall into which pocket. The first player kept shooting until he missed, and then used his cue-stick to move the appropriate number of buttons to the other end of the string to record how many balls he had made. Then the other player shot until he missed, and he in turn recorded his count on the other end of the string. The first one to reach 50 won the game. For games like this, the pool hall charged in segments of time.

A rest room in the back of the pool hall had one stool and a long metal trough on the wall for a urinal. It slanted downward toward the back of the room, and had a drain at the lowest point. A sign said "Don't throw cigarette butts in the urinal." Many years later I saw a similar sign over a urinal at Camp Perry, Ohio, where they were holding the national pistol matches. Underneath it some wag had scribbled, "They get soggy and hard to light."

Several brass spittoons along the row of benches were provided for tobacco chewers, but the juice didn't always hit them. Day's Work, Spark Plug, and Mail Pouch were favorite brands of chewing tobacco, and Bruton's and Copenhagen were popular brands of snuff. They painted ads for Mail Pouch chewing tobacco on the roofs and walls of barns along the highways in Tennessee.

Gambling was illegal, but pool players gambled. The best test of skill was straight pool, but it was a slow game; and two of the more popular games for two people were nine ball and eight ball. In the first they used only nine balls. The players played rotation pool until one of them made the nine-ball, and then the game was over, making it a fast game.

In eight ball, all fifteen balls were used. One player started with the number fifteen ball and worked down to the eight, and the other player started with the number one ball and worked up to the eight. The first one to make a ball could choose high or low. A player could shoot at the eight ball only after all his assigned balls were made. Whoever did this first and then sank the eight ball in a designated pocket won the game.

If either player accidentally knocked the eight ball into a hole before he made all his assigned balls he lost the game. He also was not allowed to hit the eight ball first on any shot unless all his assigned balls had been made. A player had a problem if the cue ball came to rest directly behind the eight ball and it was not possible to hit his next object ball first. He was literally behind the eight ball.

Dad liked to play pool, and he had a favorite pool room story: A stranger came into the pool room one day and sat and watched the action for a while. He was drinking a Coca Cola and he offered to buy one for the man sitting next to him.

"No thanks—-I tried it wunst and I didn't like it."

"Then can I buy you a Baby Ruth?"

"No thanks—I tried it wunst and I didn't like it."

"Would you like to play me a game of pool?"

"No thanks—I tried it wunst and I didn't like it; but that is my son over there, and he'll play a game with you."

"He must be your only child."

* * * * *

Once each year the community held a box supper at Gum Springs School to raise money for some project. Each of the women who participated prepared a box of food and wrapped it in colorful paper. Someone served as auctioneer and sold the boxes to the highest bidders. Each successful bidder then sat and ate the box meal with the woman who prepared it.

The boxes had no labels, but the bidders could usually find out who prepared the boxes. When some man was sweet on a certain woman, the other men bid against him and made him pay more for the privilege of eating with her. Occasionally this backfired when the victim stopped bidding and someone else was stuck with the high-priced box.

They raised money also with a prettiest-woman contest and an ugliest-man contest. They charged a nickel for each vote, and the ugliest man prize always went to Slats Jordan, a brother of the man who drove the school bus.

His name was Clayton, but he was almost as thin as a bed slat, so everybody called him Slats. He had a big nose and a sharp face like a ferret, and his receding chin almost disappeared into the skin that ran from his lower lip down to his Adam's apple. But everybody liked him, and his friends made sure he always won the ugly-man contest. His appearance was surprising, because all the other Jordan children were better looking than average. Slats was happily married to a woman named Florene, who was as much overweight as Slats was thin. When I saw them together it reminded me of a nursery rhyme and the picture that went with it.

"Jack Spratt could eat no fat; his wife could eat no lean. So 'twixt them both they cleared the cloth and licked the platter clean."

* * * * *

I had graduated from Gum Springs Elementary School in 1934, after going there eight years. I don't recall any special graduation ceremonies, and there certainly were no robes or mortarboards. We had no Junior high school then, just eight years of elementary and four years of high school. By the time I got my diploma, the senior class was down to almost nothing. I remember only three other kids who graduated with me, and I believe I was the only one who went on to high school from that class.

The wooden building had only three rooms. The first room housed the first and second grades, taught by Mrs. Bertie Greene, the wife of the Principal; the middle room housed the third, fourth, and fifth grades, taught by Miss Mae Beard; and the third room housed the sixth, seventh, and eighth grades, taught by Mr. Drudie Greene, the Principal.

Some of the more rowdy boys speculated about a romance between Mr. Greene and Miss Beard, but I never thought that was possible. She was big boned and strong and vigorous, and compared to her he was small and sort of mouse like. I wondered how much longer he could live if he started an affair with her.

Two long benches sat in the front of Mr. Greene's room, facing him. The class he was teaching at the time sat there. The other students kept their seats in the back of the room and studied for their next classes. After dismissing one class, Mr. Greene would look at his watch and say, "Let's have the seventh grade arithmetic," or "Let's have the eighth grade English," or whatever was next on his schedule. Then the members of the next class would come up front and take their places on the front benches.

A wood-burning stove in the middle of each room provided heat, and water simmering in a tin can put some humidity into the air. Once I saw Mr. Greene pour some of the water on the hot stove, presumably to create steam and raise the humidity. Once on a Monday morning there was a strange smell in the schoolroom. Mr. Greene walked over to the stove, pointed to the water can and told me to pour it out. I thought he meant pour it on the stove, so I did.

I didn't know that someone had come into the unlocked schoolroom over the weekend and filled the can with urine. Mr. Greene meant for me to take it outside and get rid of it. I was humiliated, and I can still remember the smell of the clouds of steam that rose from the stove.

Mr. Greene was not more than five feet and five inches tall and weighed about 130 pounds. He had a sharp little nose, wore round eye glasses, and squinted his eyes when he talked. On his desk he had a brass bell, which he used to signal the start of classes in the morning, the end of classes in the afternoon, and the beginning and end of the recess and lunch periods. In the meantime, the teachers in the other two rooms called and dismissed their own classes.

Mr. Greene's bell had a round wooden handle, and the open end of the bell was some four inches in diameter. It was eight inches long including the handle. Mr. Greene seemed to enjoy ringing the bell, perhaps because it showed he was in charge. He bought it when he became the principal, and when the school house finally burned, the bell was the first thing he saved. They replaced the building with a bigger one made of brick. When they finally closed the school, someone converted the building to a residence, but that was after I left.

At the beginning of each school year Mr. Greene crowded everybody into one room and read aloud the thirteenth chapter of First Corinthians, verses one through thirteen—-the discussion about Faith, Hope, and Charity. In later years I heard it called Faith, Hope, and Love. I don't know when it was changed or who changed it, but in Mr. Greene's bible it was Charity. After he finished the reading, he closed his bible and we didn't see it again until the beginning of the following school year. At least once during each school term he mentioned that General Nathaniel Greene was one of his ancestors.

I remember a little girl named Hazel Shannon in the sixth grade at Gum Springs. She was beautiful, mature for her age, and very friendly. Most of the boys were salivating over her. They wrote notes to her and when she replied, they proudly showed her responses to the other boys, who were naturally jealous. I would never have dared to write her a note or even to approach her, and on the few occasions when she smiled at me I thought I would faint.

* * * * *

We used the baseball diamond in front of the school to play shove-up during recess and the noon break. It was a variation of baseball, played with nine players in the field and three batters. When one of the batters made an out, he went to the left field position. The left fielder moved over to center field, and the center fielder went to right field. The right fielder replaced the third baseman, who replaced the shortstop, who replaced the second baseman, who replaced the first baseman, who replaced the pitcher, who replaced the catcher, who became the third batter. They all shoved up to the next position, working toward one of the three batters.

We didn't have enough time to play regular baseball, and we rarely had enough players for two teams. When school let out for recess, someone yelled shove-up, one bat. The next two who yelled were the other two batters. Others called out pitcher, catcher, or whatever position each wanted to play. We didn't have gloves or mitts, and we seldom had real baseballs. We got by with home-made balls that we made by winding string together tightly into a ball.

When we found a discarded rubber inner-tube, we cut it into thin strips and wound them tightly into a ball, using a little glue to hold it together. Sometimes we completed the ball by wrapping it tightly with string on the outside and tying the end of the string securely. This made a ball that was more lively than one made of string only.

Sometimes older players had a pick-up baseball game on Saturday, using real baseballs. Home plate was near the well, which was about fifty yards in front of the school building and on the right side of the school grounds looking out from the school. The people from Gum Springs church also used this well, one of the few that had a concrete curb. There were three big sweet gum trees and two little springs about a hundred yards from the school, to the right as you faced the school building. That is how the community got its name. Sap from the trees formed clumps of gum on the bark, and the kids scraped it off and chewed it.

The school had two privy buildings, one for boys and one for girls. They had six seats each, with holes cut in a long plank. The one for boys was on the left side of the school grounds and the one for girls was on the right side. They both were about fifty feet behind the school building and a hundred feet apart. The people from the Gum Springs Church also used them om Sunday, because there were no other facilities.

Nobody had electricity, and when they had church at night, they used lamps hanging on the walls. Each lamp had a round, shiny, reflector between the lamp and the wall. They were Coleman type lamps with a mantle, and that made a brighter light than the simple flame of a wick. They used white gas, and built-in pumps provided air pressure to change the gas into vapor.

The mantle was a cloth bag made of a fine grade of cotton with draw strings at the open end. It fit over the small tube where the flame would be, and the drawstrings held it in place. The air pressure in the fuel compartment filled the mantle like a balloon, and the flame from a match started it burning. After it had burned a while it turned into a white powder that disintegrated if touched.

Blowing the light out would destroy the fragile mantle, so they extinguished the light by turning the adjustment so low the flame went out. To light the lamp again, they turned the adjustment up and held a match or some other flame close to the mantle. They could turn the light off and then on again many times so long as nothing touched the mantel or jarred the lamp. The mantles lasted a long time, but they had to be replaced when they broke.

At home we had oil lamps, but they were not bright enough for easy reading. Each had a glass chimney to intensify the light and protect the open flame from air currents. The bottom part was a glass tank to hold the coal oil, and a wick extended from the oil to the flame. The wick went through a mechanism controlled by a knob that protruded from the side of the lamp. Turning this knob caused the wick to go higher or lower, depending on which way the knob was turned. Moving the wick higher caused the flame to burn brighter because there was more of the wick on fire. Turning the wick lower caused the flame to diminish, since there was less wick exposed to the flame. As the wick passed up or down, the mechanism compressed it tight enough that the flame never got into the oil compartment. The wick was made of fire-resistant fiber, and it drew the oil up to the flame by capillary action.

We lit an oil lamp by grasping the chimney at the bottom and lifting it off the lamp and then touching a lighted match to the wick. We extinguished the light by blowing down the chimney. It was extremely hot immediately above the lamp chimney, so we held one open hand next to the top of the lamp chimney and blew our breath hard against the hand. The hand directed the air down into the chimney to put out the flame and saved the face from being seared by the heat. The globe was too hot to touch after the lamp had been burning. The glass lamp chimney got smaller near the top, and then flared slightly, a design that intensified the heat near the top and made it hot enough to light a cigarette just above the top of the lamp chimney.

If the lamp was ever knocked over or dropped on the floor, the glass oil tank might break, exposing the oil to the open flame. That kind of accident caused houses to burn in some cases. They say the great Chicago fire started when a cow kicked over Mrs. O'Leary's lamp while she was doing her milking. It set fire to the straw on the barn floor and the fire got out of control.

Besides the coal-oil lamps, we had a lantern for use outside or in the barn at night. A handle made it easy to carry, and a glass enclosure protected the flame of the wick from the wind. It did not give off much light, but it was better than nothing when we had to milk a cow or feed the livestock after dark or before daylight. People also used lanterns when they went hunting at night for 'possums or raccoons.

Most people hunted 'possums and 'coons for the hides, as a way to make extra money. Some of them ate the 'possums, but I never heard of anybody eating raccoons. I don't know why, because raccoons are cleaner and neater than 'possums and more fastidious about what they eat. Grandpa White liked 'possum and 'taters. He said sweet potatoes went well with 'possum because the meat was rich and greasy. I didn't like to look at them, and we never ate them.

* * * * *

Gum Springs was a Missionary Baptist Church, and our parents were Baptists. A Methodist church, Wesley's Chapel, was about a mile farther away, and we went there sometimes, but most of the time we went to Gum Springs. On Sunday mornings we had Sunday School first and then church, when people would talk about what God had done for them. During these testimonials I watched members fidget in their seats because they knew others expected them to get up and witness for Jesus. Yet some were nervous and timid and kept waiting for somebody else to get up first.

Finally one would slide out to the front of the bench and stand up, after waiting as long as he dared. The first words were usually, "I'm proud to stand up for Jesus," or "I'm not ashamed to stand up for Jesus." Most of the testimonials lasted about a minute, but occasionally someone talked a long time.

The Pastor was Brother Speakman, who earned his living as a farmer and lived two miles from the church. He usually preached on Sunday at one church or another, and for two weeks in the summer preached every night at a revival meeting. He never accepted money for preaching; and once when some of the members took up a collection and tried to force him to take it, he told them if they insisted on paying him he would resign and never preach there again. He said he was preaching to serve God, and not to make money.

He never studied at a seminary. He preached the Ten Commandments, love thy neighbor, and help the needy; and he never wrote a prepared sermon. He read from his bible and referred to it often, but never looked at notes. He didn't mention politics and he didn't criticize any other church or faith.

He shouted and pounded on the pulpit, and when he described Hell I could almost smell the nauseous smoke of the smoldering brimstone and the singed hair and scorched flesh of the sinners. I never saw any other human being who seemed to believe so fervently in what he was doing. In Summer he was wet with sweat when he finished speaking. He ended every sermon by having the choir sing _Almost Persuaded_ or _Why Not Tonight._

During those songs he stood in front of the pulpit and begged sinners to come to Jesus. He collapsed in front of the pulpit and died of a heart attack on one of those occasions. I wasn't there and didn't witness it, but I would guess his last words were, "Won't you come?—Won't you come?" I'm sure he wouldn't have wanted to die any other way. When I see some of the modern day evangelists on television, I think how much times have changed.

I went down front one summer night when I was twelve. Some other kids were already at the Altar and the choir was singing:

Whyyyyy not tonighttttttt, Oh whhhyyyyyy not toniggght,

Wilt thouuuuuuu beee savvvvved, then whyyyy not tonigghtttt?

Maybe there really was a Hell as the preacher described, and maybe I would go there if I didn't "get right with God." Suddenly I found myself walking down the aisle to the Altar and soon Brother Speakman was slapping us all on the back and shaking our hands and saying over and over, "Praise God, Hallelujah; Praise God, Hallelujah".

At the appointed time we all went to the pond in Rossboro creek and stood in line to be baptized. Brother Speakman stood in waist-deep water and took us one at a time. He stood with me, raised his right hand toward the heavens, and chanted:

"By the loving grace of him, our Father,

and on a profession of faith by him our brother,

I baptize thee in the name of the Father, the Son, and the Holy Ghost."

(He always said Holy Ghost, not Holy Spirit.)

Then he put his hand over my face with his thumb and forefinger holding my nose closed and his palm over my mouth, put his left hand between my shoulder blades, and pushed me backward and dipped me into the water. In about three seconds I was back upright, and with a "God bless you brother," he sent me back to dry land and motioned for the next one in line.

There was one more formality. The recently baptized ones stood in a line and all the church members came by and extended the right hand of fellowship to us. We were then members of the Gum Springs Missionary Baptist Church.

I was a passive member. I never "Stood up for Jesus" in the Sunday meetings, and I never was an every-word-literally-true Bible believer as Grandpa White was. I always suspected that many of the members considered their membership in the church as insurance, just in case there really was a Heaven and a Hell. But nobody dared to question the existence of a living, personal God in the image of a human. I knew of only one person in the county who openly professed to be an athiest—-or infidel, as everybody called him. Almost everyone mocked that person and sneered at him; and if there were other atheists around, they were careful not to announce it publicly.

A preacher named Yeager told a story about asking everybody in the church who wanted to go to heaven to raise their right hands. Everybody raised hands except one man:

"Brother Jones, you didn't raise your hand. Don't you want to go to heaven when you die?"

"Sure I do, preacher, but I thought you meant right now."

One member of the Gum Springs church got drunk and made a public spectacle of himself, and the church Deacons counseled with him to try to straighten him out. A week or two later he did it again, and they brought him in to have a public hearing with the other members to consider withdrawing fellowship from him. The members realized they didn't have the power to expel someone from the church, so they simply withdrew fellowship. I don't remember the outcome, but I do remember his only defense: "The Bible says take a little wine for the stummick."

I listened recently to some cassette tapes, recorded by university professors, about the old-time philosophers. I learned that a man named Spinoza was excommunicated twice, first by the Jews and later by the Christians. Apparently they found his opinions on religion to be outrageous, especially since he was so open about expressing them. He claimed to be religious in his own way, but he believed man invented God for his own purposes, instead of God creating man.

In those days drinking and gambling were sins, and so was dancing. Grandma White saw Quinton and me playing with a deck of Rook cards one day and really laid us out. We never gambled, and Rook was a harmless game, but she insisted, "Playin' cyards is a SIN."

One house on Big Oak road, not far from the Hester place, provided grist for the gossip mill. Whispers went around that the couple who lived there as man and wife were not really married. According to the rumor, the woman was getting a survivor's benefit of some kind from a dead husband, killed in the war, and if she married again before a certain age she would lose the benefit.

Sunday evenings we had BYPU, Baptist Young Peoples Union. The meetings rarely lasted more than two hours, and this gave the younger people somewhere to go. They also had Wednesday night prayer meetings, but a smaller and older group attended.

The year before, some man had gone around to many of the churches and talked about the coming end of the world. He quoted scriptures, gave examples, and made arguments that the world would end sometime in the spring of 1936. Most of us thought he was a screwball, but others believed him. Some people entertained such thoughts as the year 2,000 approached.

* * * * *

I don't remember much about going to funerals. My mother died while I was in California, and all of my grandparents died while I was away. In 1930 they brought my uncle Buren home from Arizona for burial, but I can't remember anything about the funeral. I know that when there was a funeral at Gum Springs, Brother Speakman "preached" the funeral. He always reminded everybody of the certainty of death and of the importance of being ready to meet your maker when the time comes.

Grandpa White was devoted to his church and his faith. He never missed a Sunday at church if he was physically able to get out of bed and go. He never missed a Wednesday-night prayer meeting or a Saturday business meeting of the church. In his younger days he ran a country store. Dad said grandpa finally went out of business because he was too generous. He often gave thirteen eggs for a dozen, and he continued to give credit to poor people when he had no realistic hope of ever being paid.

Someone once wanted to buy two hundred pounds of sugar for cash; and he refused to sell it to him, because the customer couldn't possibly use that much sugar unless he was making whiskey. A friend remarked that he would just buy it somewhere else. "Maybe so," Grandpa replied, "but I won't be a party to it."

An old gray mare pulled his one-horse plow, and when he got really angry with her he said, "AAHHHH, YOU OLD HEIFER!" That is the most profane thing I ever heard him say. But I did hear him comment once about a neer-do-well in the neighborhood, "If he was starving and you offered to give him a bushel of corn, he would ask you to shuck it and shell it first."

Next after gospel hymns, Grandpa's favorite song was Grandfather's Clock. He particularly liked the part that said it stopped short, never to go again, when the old man died. He was extremely regular in his habits. He wanted his meals at the same hour each day, and he got up and retired at the same hour each day also. I ate lunch with them one day, and just as we sat down the clock in the living room struck the chimes. "Eleven thirty," he commented, "a mighty good time to eat dinner."

Many years later I went to a church in Florida and listened to a minister spend an hour talking about how wrong other churches and other denominations were in their beliefs and practices and saying his church had the truth and none of the others did. Later one of the members of that church insisted on arguing religion with me He said anybody who did not belong to that particular church was surely bound for hell. He said if I would just read my Bible I would see that he was right.

I finally shut him up by telling him in detail how Grandpa White lived his life as a member of the Missionary Baptist Church. "If that man goes to Hell because he didn't belong to your church," I told him, "I would be ashamed to show my face in Heaven."

* * * * *

Once a year they had Decoration Day at the local churches, and Gum Springs had theirs the first Sunday in May. They always had Children's Day in the morning, and the young kids recited verses, sang songs, put on skits, or otherwise provided entertainment for the audience. They rehearsed for a month beforehand.

The star of these programs was little Jewell Hatch, the Shirley Temple of the Gum Springs community. She died soon after she started to school, and is buried in the first grave at the cemetery nearest the church.

At noon they moved some church benches outside and used them as tables for a feast that all the women had brought from home. After lunch everybody put flowers on the graves of the relatives and loved ones who were buried in the nearby cemetery. In the afternoon they sang gospel songs in the church.

This program, or something similar, was conducted each Sunday during May. The churches in the area took turns, so there would be no conflict. When five Sundays occurred in a month, the Fifth Sunday Singing Convention met. They rotated this event between the churches, and they met in the afternoons to sing gospel songs.

Sometimes during the summers the church sponsored a free singing school, put on by the graduates of the James D. Vaughan music program. I didn't learn much, and most of it I have since forgotten. One thing I remember, however, is the result of mnemonics. The instructor, a youngish man named Theo Powell, gave us a memory device to help us remember the musical notes F, B, E, A, D, G. Someone told me later these letters represent the musical keys that have flats. He said to think Foolish Boys Eat Apple Dumplings Greedily.

"If you can't remember that," he said, "think Five Boys Eat a Dead Goat."

* * * * *

My Uncle Stacy Abner was a gospel singer and song writer, and I once went with his son William Ray Abner to the James D. Vaughan Museum in Lawrenceburg to find out more information about his career in the music business. In 2001, we had attended an annual meeting in Lawrenceburg of the descendants of Noah and Lucy Reeve, our maternal grandparents. The museum was closed at the time, and I tried unsuccessfully to reach them by telephone. More recently I called the Chamber of Commerce in Lawrenceburg. They sent me some information about Lawrence County, and the following quotations are from that material:

"The glorious history of Southern Gospel Music comes alive in the James D. Vaughan Museum in historic Lawrenceburg, Tennessee.

"The museum honors the Father of Southern Gospel Music, James D. Vaughan, who sponsored the first professional southern gospel quartets, established the first southern gospel magazine, recorded the first southern gospel quartets, established the first southern gospel music radio station, and taught the South how to sing with the renowned Vaughan school of music.

"The United States Congress has declared and recognized Lawrenceburg as the Birthplace of Southern Gospel music.

"Beginning in 1911, Vaughan began holding a regular music 'normal' school in Lawrenceburg to train shape note singing school instructors. These instructors then fanned out across the country teaching the Vaughan method to the nation.

"During the 1920's James D. Vaughan had sixteen southern gospel music quartets traveling the country and into Canada. Vaughan kept America singing during the first half of the 20th century.

"James D. Vaughan published millions of shape note songbooks. . . .. The Vaughan music enterprise included music publishing, songwriting, radio, and the famed Vaughan School of Music, all headquartered on the public square in historic Lawrenceburg, Tennessee.

"Always the pioneer, James D. Vaughan put radio station WOAN on the air in 1922. Two tall towers dominated the Lawrenceburg skyline for nearly a decade. WOAN was the first radio experience for many of the early southern gospel music legends."

* * * * *

"The bronze, life-sized statue of Colonel David Crockett, proudly standing on the south side of the public square in Lawrenceburg, Tennessee, is the only statue erected to honor the memory of Tennessee's famous hunter, frontiersman, soldier, legislator, statesman, patriot and Hero of the Alamo, Colonel David Crockett.... A state park of 950 acres was started in 1856 and dedicated to the memory of David Crockett in 1959. . . . "

"A replica of the Crockett cabin was built by Mr. R. A. Carvell on the original site of the Crockett cabin. The cabin on South Military Avenue is now a museum and contains many artifacts of the Crockett period."

"The Amish community in Ethridge numbers more than 200 families of highly productive farmers and craftspersons. Lawrence County residents since 1944, the Amish drive horse-drawn vehicles and avoid modern evils such as electricity and cameras."

* * * * *

Once or twice a year they had a fa-so-la singing meeting at the church, usually on a Sunday afternoon. The songbooks were huge, and instead of having seven shaped notes in their songs, they had only three or four. I think there was one more note they used besides fa, so, and la. I don't remember which one it was, but I would guess it was mi since that is the one just below fa; and that would allow everyone to sing comfortably in the middle range of the scale.

They were called sacred heart song books, and a limited number of hard-core fa-so-la singers used them. They always started by singing the notes before starting on the first verse, and then they sang every verse of every song. That is unlike the often-used practice in gospel music of singing the first two verses and then the last one. Also the song leader did not follow the usual practice of standing in front and holding the songbook in one hand while he marked time with the other. The songbooks were so big the leader had to sit with the songbook spread out in his lap. I have never encountered that kind of singing anywhere else.

My parents enjoyed singing gospel songs. They both played the organ or piano and frequently played in church. When we were early teenagers, my sister and I sang as a quartet with our uncle Mack White and Cousin Grace Canada. We practiced at home and sang several times in church, but when puberty came along and my voice started changing my singing career ended.

Dad could read music, and he could sit at the piano with the music to a gospel song and play it, even if he had never seen it before. Yet when he was in the army during world war I, they wouldn't use him in the band because he had learned by the Vaughan method and couldn't read round notes. In most music, the position of a note on the staff determines the sound of the note, and all the notes are round. In the Vaughan gospel song books, the positions of the notes are the same as with round notes, but the notes also have a different shape for each tone. Dad could sing and play the shaped notes by their shapes but not by their positions on the staff.

He was more mechanical in his organ playing and rarely improvised, but Mama enjoyed playing the lively songs, such as Over There, which was still popular from the war period. She also played the guitar and sang, and Dad harmonized with her. One of their favorites was When You Wore a Tulip and I Wore a Big Red Rose. She knew only a few basic chords on the guitar, and she taught them to me. I never played well, but my brother Quinton was good enough to play in a string band, years later when he lived in Detroit.

* * * * *

Lawrence County had two newspapers, The Lawrence News and The Lawrence Democrat Union. The Democrat Union had a correspondent in each community who wrote news items about what was going on there, and Mama was the correspondent for Gum Springs. Most of these items would be something like: "Mr. and Mrs. Alford Keener visited Mrs. Keener's mother, Mrs. Horton, in Haleyville, Alabama last week. Mr. and Mrs. Joe White visited the Roberts family in New Prospect last Saturday and brought back two bushels of beautiful pears, which they plan to make into preserves. Mrs. Joe Voss is expecting another baby in the fall. This will be number twelve for her. She says she doesn't care if it's a boy or a girl, so long as it's healthy."

Every time she wrote something about Mr. and Mrs. Monroe White, it always came out in the newspaper as Mouse White. We never knew if they couldn't read Mama's handwriting or if they were trying to be funny. Grandpa didn't think it was funny. If he had been six feet tall and had weighed two hundred pounds perhaps he might have been able to accept it more gracefully. He suspected the editor of the paper did it deliberately, because grandpa was small and mousey in physical appearance. Mama finally started referring to him as Mr. M. White in her correspondence. When she wrote her column, she prefaced it with, "I know not what the truth may be. I tell the tale as 'twas told to me."

Mama also wrote poems and had several of them printed in the local newspaper. She always wrote them under the pen name Betty Joe. Sometimes she composed the poetry from the happenings in the community. When the World War I veterans finally got their long-awaited bonus payments, she wrote:

Daddy got his bonus pay
Ain't that wonderful news
Now we can pay our doctor bills
And buy the kids some shoes.

Mama had dark eyes and dark hair, and my brother Edgar got his coloring from her. She was overweight, but most considered her a beautiful woman nevertheless. She could bend over and put the palms of both hands flat on the floor without bending her knees. Perhaps that was because her legs were short, compared to the rest of her body. Both of Eunice's daughters are beautiful, but Judy looks more like mama did when she was young. One of our neighbors, Stella Hunter, told me that Miss Ider, as she called her, was the finest woman she had ever known.

* * * * *

A Mrs. Baxter conducted an adult-education class several nights a week at Revilo School, next to Dave Webb's store on the Steadman Ridge road. Her pay depended on the average attendance each week, so she had entertainment on Friday nights to swell the attendance and increase the average. She invited anyone who could play an instrument or who could sing or whistle to come on Friday nights and perform. Revilo got its name from Oliver spelled backwards. The Oliver Company made farm implements.

Anybody could participate in the program. A tall skinny guy who lived across the road from Mr. Webb's store played the French harp. He liked to play Eighth of January and Hop Light Lady, Cause the Cake's All Dough.

Two of the Huntley brothers had good voices and sang duets. Two of their favorites were St. Louis Blues and There's a Hole in the Bottom of the Sea. This last song was patterned after Partridge in a pear tree, but with a different tune. It started with a hole in the bottom of the sea, and followed with a rock in the hole, a frog on the rock, a wart on the frog, and a hair on the wart.

Their younger brother, Hillard, played the mandolin. He rocked side to side as he played and sang, shifting his weight from one foot to the other and keeping time by rocking his head to the right and to the left. He expected someday to become a star on the Grand Ole Opry. If someone hinted it might not be easy to do, he said, "Why not? Look at Eddy Arnold: He was just an old Tennessee plowboy." There were no televisions then and few radios, so people would listen to almost any kind of music. Occasionally I walked across the woods to the Hunter house to listen to The Grand Ole Opry on Saturday night. Then when the singers and pickers had done their last number near midnight, I was disappointed when Mrs. Hunter turned the radio off before the commercials were finished.

Charley Price played the guitar and sang in a trio with Fount Webb and Ray Baxter. One of their best was Back to Old Smoky Mountains. Charley had served with the Army in Hawaii at one time, and sometimes he tuned his guitar differently and played it Hawaiian style with a steel slide.

I played harmony on the French harp as a duet with Lacy Williams, and Wildwood Flower was one of our favorites. Sometimes I played Lost John or Freight Train Blues as a solo. I had a Marine Band model by M. Hohner in the key of A. It cost 55 cents, and it was my most prized possession until I got my new rifle when I was sixteen. Hohner made a less expensive version called the Attaboy, which cost 35 cents, but the Marine Band was heavier and sturdier.

Shorty Shultz was one of the regular performers. He was a member of the Shultz Quartet, who sang at churches and singing conventions around the area. They also sang sometimes at WSM radio in Nashville. I don't recall the Shultz Quartet ever singing at Revilo on Friday nights. Mrs. Baxter was always nervous when Shorty was performing, because he liked to sing risqué songs, such as Red-hot mama, turn yore damper down.

"Red hot mama, red hot mama, you're the one I need
Red hot mama, red hot mama, yes, indeed.
You're just like the girls in folly, hot tamale,
Remind me of a great big baby dolly
I confess that you possess the sweetest love in town
And unless I miss my guess, the boys are following you around

You make a music master lay down his fiddle
Make a bald-headed man part his hair in the middle,
Red hot mama, red hot mama, turn yore damper down."

The original Shultz Brothers Quartet was Link, Mutt, Shorty, and Boss Shultz. I never heard them called by their real names. Link sang the lead, Mutt sang alto, Shorty sang tenor, and Boss sang bass. Boss died before I knew them, and they recruited Claude Roberts to take his place. After that they shortened the name to the Shultz Quartet. I think they were as good as any of the popular quartets that came along later. They say the things we remember improve with passing years, so perhaps I remember them as being better than they were.

Howard Shultz, Shorty's younger brother, did not sing with the quartet, but he sang love songs and played a guitar. Two of his favorites were that's the Story of Love and Darkness on the Delta. All the members of the Shultz family pronounced darkness as dorkness.

After the end of the program in the schoolhouse, Howard sometimes sat on the grass outside and played the guitar and sang. He usually had several listeners. Howard was dating Annis Webb and later married her. They had one child, Phyllis.

Revilo was some four miles from our house, and I walked there and back on Friday nights. There was no good way to get there. Going the long way by Fall River Road and Crossroads would have doubled the distance, and going the shortest way meant following a narrow path through the woods and across a little stream. Coming back in the dark was the problem. I turned from the road at the James place near Oak Hill Church and walked along the fence at the edge of their field. At the end of that farm I entered a wooded area that was part of Old Man Crum's place. For two hundred yards I was in the dark, following a trail with weeds growing so close they often touched me on both sides.

The path was wider where it crossed the stream, but I still got my feet wet many times. If it had been raining the stream was often too wide to step across, and sometimes it was so dark it was hard to see the water. Eventually I came out onto the road that led from the Crum house to our house, and from there it was the better part of another mile.

CHAPTER EIGHT

Grandpa was 75 years old but still active. On Saturdays during the winter, weather permitting, I helped him saw logs to make firewood and stove (cooking) wood. We looked for trees that were either dead or dying. First we determined which way the tree wanted to fall and made sure it would not fall into another tree. Next we used an ax to cut a notch on the side in the direction we wanted it to fall. Sometimes we started the notch by cutting into the tree a few inches with the saw, about a foot above the ground. Then we chopped out the wood above this saw cut, starting a foot above the cut and chopping down on an angle to the bottom of the cut.

When done, the notch was about a foot from top to bottom and extended across the tree on the side toward which we wanted it to fall. We then sawed with the crosscut saw from the side opposite from the notch, and planned the cut to come out in the notch on the other side. This helped insure that the tree would break off cleanly and not split.

We carried an iron wedge with us, as well as either a pole ax or a sledge hammer. A pole ax has a blade on one side and a flat surface on the other that can be used as a heavy hammer. A double-bit ax has two blades with a hole in the middle for the ax handle, and Grandpa had a new one. "From now on," he said one day, "I ain't gonna neither lend ner borry double-bit axes." Then he smiled a sly little smile and we knew he had just bought one.

Sometimes we miscalculated the way the tree wanted to fall, and as we sawed it started to bind on the saw blade when the cut was almost through the trunk. When the tree started to lean backward, the opening of the saw cut closed and squeezed the saw blade. Then we put the thin edge of the iron wedge in the saw cut and drove it in with the sledge hammer or with the blunt side of the pole ax. As the wedge went deeper into the cut, it forced the gap to open wider and forced the tree to lean in the direction we wanted it to fall. We could then easily pull the saw to finish the cut, and the tree fell in the direction we wanted.

We always looked for an old log that the tree could fall on, so the log we were working on would not be lying flat on the ground. We didn't want the saw blade to dig into the ground when it went all the way through the log. Once the tree was down, we cut off all the branches with the ax and got them out of the way. We cut the larger branches into usable lengths and added them to our pile, and left the smaller ones in the woods. If we were cutting for the cook stove, we cut the log into lengths less than sixteen inches to make sure they were short enough to fit into the firebox.

Dad taught me how to use the crosscut saw, and I could saw wood with him for hours at a time. It took two people to use it, because it was too long and too limber for one person to push through a log. The saw had a wooden handle bolted to each end. The handles were round, about a foot long, and stuck straight up from the saw. They were a little bigger than a broom handle. He taught me to let the saw do the work, because the weight of the saw was enough downward pressure. I pulled my saw handle toward me all the way and then he pulled his handle toward himself all the way. When one of us was pulling the handle, the other's hands were merely following the other handle to the log, so they would be there to pull it back again. This required little effort, and the sawdust flew while the saw went through the log.

But Grandpa believed bearing down on the saw made it cut faster, so he pressed down on his end of the saw when I was pulling it toward me. I was pulling him as well as the saw, and he wondered why I got tired. He had a deep voice that belied his diminutive size, but he was only a few inches more than five feet tall and weighed probably 130 pounds. Nevertheless, he felt heavy on the other end of the saw. Dad was almost six feet tall, and so were two of his brothers, but they got their height from my grandmother's side of the family.

The crosscut saw blade was an eighth of an inch thick, five inches deep, and five-and-a-half feet long. The bottom of the blade was milled to form saw teeth, a half inch apart. Each tooth was divided into two smaller teeth, an eighth of an inch apart. Starting from the middle, the saw blade curved gently upward toward the two handles. That allowed a natural rocking motion as the saw went through a log.

Dad had to sharpen the saw now and then. He held it in a vise with the teeth pointing up, and went along the blade with a file and sharpened each tooth. He changed the position of the saw several times in the vise, so the section he was working on was held securely. After they were all sharpened, he set the teeth by bending one tooth slightly to the right, the next one to the left, and so on. This made the saw cut a groove slightly wider than the saw blade so it would go through the log easier.

To set the teeth he laid the saw down on its side, putting a block of iron under the saw tooth. He let about one third of the tooth stick out slightly beyond the iron, and then tapped the end of the saw tooth with a hammer to bend it slightly downward. He did this to every second tooth in the saw. Then he turned the saw over and bent the alternate teeth in the opposite direction.

Once a log had been cut to the appropriate lengths we hauled the blocks to the house, so we could split the blocks up into smaller sticks at our leisure. Oak or hickory was the best for cooking or for the fireplace. It was best after it had dried for a few weeks, but we needed to split the blocks into smaller sticks as soon as possible, because it was harder to split after it dried. We always tried to have some wood from a poplar tree to use for starting the fires, because it would ignite easier and burn faster than either oak or hickory.

We started a fire by whittling some shavings from a dry poplar stick and lighting them, either with a match or with some leftover coals. Then we put some slightly larger poplar sticks on the fire, crossing them back and forth so the air and flames could go through them. Next we put some small dry oak or hickory sticks on that, and let them get to burning briskly. Finally we put on bigger oak or hickory sticks for a longer-lasting fire.

A year or two before, Dad and I had taken a wagon load of stove wood into Lawrenceburg to sell. The wood was split and seasoned and stacked in rows in the wagon bed. We were lucky that day, because someone flagged us down at the top of the hill on the outskirts of town and bought the load. We took it to a small building on the back of his lot and threw it through a little window-sized opening into the building. The man paid Dad with a brand new two-dollar bill in the new small size, and it was the first one we had ever seen. I must have been about fourteen at the time, because prior to 1934, paper currency came in much larger sizes. The old bills were about fifty percent longer and fifty percent wider than the new bills of the 1934 issue.

Wood sellers often waited all day in the hitch yard without success. Then late in the afternoon buyers came around and offered less than the asking price, hoping to get a bargain because the farmer was anxious to start home.

When we split the cook wood into smaller sticks we stood one block on top of another, so the ax would not go through the first block and into the ground. We wanted the ax to stay sharp, and driving it into the rocky dirt would make it dull. We split the blocks into halves, then quarters, and then eighths. When the smaller sections would not stand up on the block by themselves, we held the stick with the left hand and wielded the ax with the right. The right hand moved up near the ax blade for more control, and the left hand pulled away a split second before the blade got to the wood.

We cut our fireplace logs three feet long, although four-foot logs would fit. We put in a backlog first and built the fire in front of it. It was bigger than the other sticks, and usually was of green wood, preferably gum. Gum logs burned slowly, providing staying power for the fire. We banked (covered) the fire with ashes at bedtime, and the backlog provided the live coals that lasted through the night.

We tried to pile up enough firewood to last all winter, and to split and pile up enough cook wood to last a year. A big woodpile gave us a great feeling of satisfaction. It was like having a corncrib full of corn and a barn full of hay.

When the log is on the ground it doesn't matter which side of the saw you stand on, because each sawyer can saw either right or left handed. When felling a tree, however, the saw blade must be horizontal. The hands need to be at the bottom of the handle near the saw blade for better control, so one worker needs to saw right handed and the other left handed. I cut, hauled, and split firewood and cook wood for many years and had only one accident. Quinton and I were sawing down a tree one day and I was sawing left handed at the time. The saw was almost through the tree trunk when I let the blade get too close to my right knee. As he pulled the saw toward him the blade cut through my overalls and sliced a gash in the inside of my leg at the knee. It was a nasty looking cut, but I doused it with coal oil and it healed. I still have a small scar there after all these years.

When I was fourteen and feeling spry I liked to jump over the barbed wire fence on my way to the barn. One morning the grass was wet with dew, and my foot slipped as I took off for my jump. I didn't make it all the way over, and my left leg went between the top strand and the second strand of barbed wire. The barbs ripped my overalls and made several gashes in my left leg. Generous applications of coal oil healed the wounds, but some of the scars never disappeared.

* * * * *

After we finished our woodpile and Grandpa finished his, I started on the most unpleasant job on the farm, cleaning out stables. Large animals like mules are constructed so their leg joints lock when they relax. This allows them to sleep standing. Sometimes they lie down, but not for long. Their heavy weight presses their rib cages against the ground and makes it harder for them to breathe.

We didn't muck out the stables daily during the winter, and by springtime the manure was at least a foot deep and packed hard. As the oldest boy in the family I was elected to dig it up and shovel it out of the stables into a wagon. We then took it to the fields and spread it as fertilizer. We had to use it selectively, because there was never enough to go around. It was the best fertilizer we could use, but it was no fun to apply.

I could stand the normal smell of the stables, but digging the manure and moving it around made it worse. The odor was so bad I had to go outside every few minutes and take a few breaths of fresh air. Dad had an old gas mask that he brought home from the war. I tried using it, but it didn't help much.

Rufus Hunter told me about a strawberry grower who was hauling a load of manure in a wagon. He passed by the grounds of an insane asylum, and one of the inmates hailed him from inside the fence.

"Hey! Whatcha gonna do with that manure?"

"I'm a-gonna put it on my strawberries."

"I put sugar and milk on mine, and they think I'M crazy! "

Several years later Harry Truman was president, and he often used salty language. At a press conference he mentioned he was planning to put manure on the White House lawn. One lady reporter asked Mrs. Truman if she couldn't persuade the President to call it fertilizer instead. "I don't think so," Bess replied. "It took me twenty years to get him to call it manure."

CHAPTER NINE

We didn't get much mail except the newspapers. We got the local weekly papers and we subscribed to the Nashville Tennesseean, the morning daily paper out of Nashville. A truck came from the presses early each morning and delivered papers to the post offices. The rural carriers then picked them up early for delivery on that day's run. Nashville also had an evening paper, The Nashville Banner, but by the time they could have delivered it by mail it would have been yesterday's newspaper.

One of my classmates sometimes brought clippings from the Washington Post and let me read them. Many years later, I went to the archives of the Post and copied some of the headlines and some of the more interesting stories from 1936. I also went to Lawrenceburg and looked for records of the stories in the Lawrence News and the Lawrence Democrat Union, but no records could be found in either paper for that year. Nobody seemed to know why.

The following headlines and stories are quoted from the <u>Washington Post</u>, so I will not use quotation marks unless they are used in the text:

Headline December 29, 1935:
NEW DEAL COMMUNITY FAILS AFTER 220 YEARS
Amana Colony In Iowa, A Perfect Communist Experiment, Reverts to Individualism For Lack Of Spiritual Zeal. By Hilding Siverson.

The assumption that the New Deal of 1933 is something liberal, progressive, and the result of advanced social thinking is an assumption that will not stand scrutiny. As a matter of fact, the outstanding principles of the Roosevelt New Deal were discarded by the Amana Colony of Iowa in the very year that the American people, under the goad of depression, unknowingly adopted a fabric and tissue of collectivism under the impression that they were voting the Democratic ticket.

It is a paradoxical coincidence that a member of the New Deal Cabinet who is a foremost exponent of so-called "new order" should have come from the very state of Amana Colony, which had just abandoned the collectivist system which began with the teachings of Eberhard Ludwig Gruber in the year 1714.

The Community of True Inspiration was established first in Germany, but because of long persecution it sought a new haven, and after many tribulations a settlement was made early in the last century on a tract of 5,000 acres near Buffalo, New York. Then in 1885, the Inspirationalists followed the westward course of empire and settled on the Iowa River, at the present site of Amana. Their entire social structure was founded on an ideal of communism, which worked beautifully as long as a singularly pure religious motivation was provided by the individual members.

Here, at Amana, Iowa, for nearly 80 years, existed a working experiment in collectivism. The Colony owned 28,000 acres in common. There were community factories, community bakeries, community butcher shops, community kitchens, comfortable community housing, common ownership of land. In fact, one would think that Prof. Tugwell with his resettlement enterprise and his voluminous theories concerning the abolition of the profit motive, would have Amana a most idyllic object lesson in his project of "making America over."

There is not a single objective in the so-called New Deal that has not been already tried out in principle in the Amana Colony. It provided social security in abundance. There were subsistence homesteads in effect. The farmer and the business agent shared alike in the produce of the land, the factory, and the shop. Sales effort, advertising and promotion, which are anathema to the Brain Trust, were practically unknown. There was no competition, and the NRA, (National Recovery Act) as far as virtual principle was concerned, was fully effective. Under Christian Metz, its leader, planned economy was found in perfection. At least, so it seemed up to about the World War era.

The members of the colony were earnest, intelligent people. Their experiment actually worked. Ostensibly communism, in its best possible sense, had come to beautiful, idyllic fruition.

However, every student and advocate of communism should study carefully the entire history of the Amana Colony. He will find that the collectivist philosophy worked only as long as the personal units of the community were actuated by an exceptionally strong religious spirit. Long ago a historian wrote of this colony: "Communism is only incidental to the life and thought of this community. Its chief concern is spiritual. . . . It has ever remained primarily a church.. . . . That their ideal of a simple religious life might prevail, they substituted a system of brotherly cooperation for one of selfish competition.

* * * * *

Gradually a change came, shortly after the turn of the century. Many of the members began to shirk their duties as laborers for the common good. Worldly thoughts entered. The telephone, automobile, radio, and other modern inventions brought increasing contacts with the outer sphere and the inhabitants tasted of the seductive apple of knowledge. Discontent came to the younger people who became acquainted with the ways of the world. The inspiration of religion lost some of the dynamic pull on the hearts of the people. At one time it was found necessary to import 200 hired laborers to do the necessary work on the farms and in the shops because there were so many shirkers. The colony went into debt and the deficit approached half a million dollars. (Thus, it seems, another phase of the New Deal technique was anticipated long before 1933). One of the elders of the church gave this reason for the change: "You can't have socialism without its spirit, the spirit of sharing." At this critical time that saying ought to be blazoned in neon letters a mile high in every city and town of the United States.

Parasitism became rampant. The individual found it was possible to exist without work, and the lack of incentive caused him to remain idle, for no longer did he have the spur of a poignant religious motivation.

Finally came the inevitable liquidation of the great dream. In June, 1932, almost at the very moment that the two major political parties in the United States were holding their gatherings which were to decide a momentous issue, the old Amana quietly disappeared, and in its place came the new Amana of individualism, substituting a co-operative corporation employing the individualistic profit system for the old methods of communism. "It meant that everyone who would eat must work," wrote a historian hitherto friendly to the experiment. "Amana itself has never regarded its communism as the working out of a social theory," says this same historian, Bertha M. H. Shambaugh. This statement is profoundly significant and needs to be studied in the light of Amana history and the annals that go clear back to Pastor Gruber in 1714. "Without its spiritual significance the communism of Amana was as empty as a chrysalis from which the butterfly has flown."

* * * * *

And now, what of the results of the change back to sturdy individualism? Perhaps another quotation from this historian will serve to tell, in a few words, what happened.

"Women who formerly dropped out of the kitchen and garden routine on the slightest pretext (but sent their baskets to the kitchen-house with great regularity) learned for the first time what it means to prepare three meals a day for a family and to cultivate a family garden if the family were to eat. Deduction in wages for time out resulted in a marked improvement in the general health of men who had formed the habit of being ' too sick' to report for work in the fields or factory when the apple trees in their own yards needed spraying or the currants were ready to pick—and perhaps to sell. . . .Men who had been 'too sick' to do an honest day's work in 20 years were loud in their demands for something to do. . . .Here and there an overweight brother regained his youthful figure in the new experience."

The cancer of idleness and degeneracy had been working a long time, even though it had come to the surface rather suddenly. The new, stiff dose of individualism brought Amana back again to earth and its people are now happy and prosperous again.

The enervating effects of collectivist philosophy on a large scale are now being witnessed in the Nation. The country should have been forewarned by the experience of Amana, for what is true of Amana is true of human nature everywhere. A flabby spirit of helpless dependence which is foreign to American genius has been introduced into social system.

Good government cannot be blueprinted or made the object of predictions of social psychologists. It is rather the result of a complex wave of personal relations and ethical attitudes. Amana has conclusively proved this, for as long as the Amana people were motivated and implemented by an intense and almost fanatical religious fervor, their plan worked beautifully, but as soon as that attitude failed, that very same plan failed dismally, and that is all there is to it. The mechanics were incidental.

Amana has tried the collectivist philosophy and finds that in a world of average, moderate selfishness and indolence, it doesn't work. Social security guaranteed by the government not only won't work—-it is positively and malignantly harmful, and if the American Nation does not awaken to this fact a tragic mess will result. An intelligent society profits by its own errors. Why repeat an impossible folly on a grand scale? (Reprinted by permission of the *Washington Post.)*

1935—-A Year of Violent Struggle: Historic Decision on Gold Clause:

It began in January, on Tuesday the eighth, in the later-to-be-abandoned stuffy little Supreme Court chamber in the Capitol, when Attorney General Homer Cummins, beautifully morning-coated, made notes and chewed gum with equal vigor as a slight young man from New York, who tripped over the word "constitutionality" every time he came to it, and who had no spats, no tailcoat, and no stick, talked about thirty-eight dollars and ten cents.

This was the beginning of the Gold Clause case that had the citizenry of the financial world hanging on the hook of suspense for a month.

The young man was Emanuel Redfield, not long from law school, who represented Norman C. Norman, of New York, in the case. The issue, almost incalculable in its possible effects, was the most drastic of New Deal actions, the "repudiation" of the Gold Clause in nearly $100,000,000,000 of public and private bonds. The actual case in point was small—-whether the Baltimore and Ohio railroad owed Mr. Norman the sum of $22. 50, or the sum of $38. 10 as interest on one gold bond.

For more than a month the public interest, whipped high by the possibility that President Roosevelt's 59 cent devalued dollar might not be sound, flared in the most general public discussion of an involved and highly technical issue in many years, and in long lines of would-be spectators on Mondays—decision days—in the Capitol halls.

Then on Monday, February 18, at high noon, the little black-robed justices filed between the plum-colored plush ropes to their black-leather chairs, sat, and listened to the reading of their five-to-four decision that all gold clauses in Liberty bonds, private contracts, gold certificates, State, municipal, and other obligations could be paid in present-day devalued dollars.

But one of the dissenting four—old gloomy-eyed, gaunt Justice James Clark McReynolds, the sound-money man, said, "The Constitution is gone.

This is Nero at his worst." (Reprinted by permission of the *Washington Post.)*

January 6, 1936: The Supreme Court declared the Agricultural Adjustment Act unconstitutional, leaving a great part of the work unfinished. Said Congress cannot use taxing power to regulate agriculture. Public reaction mixed.

January 6: Dr. F. E. Townsend sponsors a plan to pay $200-a-month pension to persons over sixty.

January 17: New Jersey Governor Hoffman Gives Hauptman two weeks' reprieve. Says he is not sure the case is solved. Supreme Court refuses to hear appeal. (Note: This refers to the trial and conviction of Bruno Richard Hauptman for the kidnapping and murder of the Lindberg baby.)

January 21: Governor Hoffman ordered New Jersey State Police to reopen investigation of the Lindbergh baby kidnapping and murder. Doubts that Hauptman is guilty.

January 21: King George V died last night. Oldest son, Prince of Wales will be Edward VIII.

January 28: House and Senate override FDR veto of veterans' bonus. Will pay in June.

March 6: Hitler remilitarizes Rhine—-France to fight if League of Nations peace efforts fail.

March 12: King Edward VIII may wed Greek Princess Eugenie. Asks permission to increase expense allowance to cover possible taking of a Queen.

March 13: Hitler refuses to withdraw Rhine army. France and Belgium demand withdrawal.

March 30: 98. 74 percent of German poll backs Hitler's defiance of world powers.

April 4: Hauptman was electrocuted last night, without uttering a word, for his conviction on March 1, 1932, of kidnapping and murder of Lindbergh baby.

(Comment: The Hauptman case stirred up a lively debate among the students at Lawrence County High School. Some were absolutely certain he was guilty, and others were equally sure he was innocent.)

April 27: An AFGE survey showed that 10,000 were faced with loss of U. S. jobs because of the U. S. Supreme Court holding the AAA unconstitutional and because of proposed personnel reductions in the Works Projects Administration and the Resettlement Administration.

April 28: A political cartoon on the editorial page showed Uncle Sam holding a scroll that said, "Results, proven by facts and figures, show that we are on our way. . .very definitely on our way." FDR

In the background was a black cloud labeled BANKRUPTCY
At the bottom were four placards:
"Unemployment now 12,000,000."
"Dollar now 59 cents."
"Budget now non-existent."
"National debt now $31,000,000,000."
Legend at the bottom: "Broad is the way that leads to destruction.

April 28: The Works Projects Administration has built more than 600 public golf courses. Picture of golfing legend Bobby Jones conferring with Harry Hopkins, WPA Administrator, and his assistant. "This will make golf everybody's game," Jones commented, "even more than it is now." (Comment: The 2002 US Open Golf Championship was held at Bethpage, New York, on a course that was built by the WPA.)

April 29: The Townsend plan organization sent a delegation to Washington, D. C. in 1935 to lobby for legislation paying a $200-a-month pension to anyone over 60 years old. The organization raised $22,000 to send this delegation. Otto Moore, a Denver lawyer, told a congressional subcommittee that Robert E. Clements, when he was Secretary of that organization, once said, "We don't give a damn about the old people." That was in response to a question: "What are the old people going to do? They are expecting so much."

May 17: A Townsend plan caravan is due in Washington today. Twenty-five autos are bringing a group from the coast to urge the pension cause. They decided to come from California after a House Committee began investigating Dr. Francis C. Townsend, author of a plan to pay $200-a-month pensions to anyone 60 and over. Already it has been shown that he and Robert E. Clements, co-founder of the foundation, received fat incomes from the pennies, nickels, and dimes that came in from pension seekers.

May 22: "Townsend stamps out of hearing in rage. Refuses to return except under force."

May 3: "FHA unit aids young people to build home. Title I of the program provided credit for purchase of small home by a couple of modest means. They will now be able to pay off the loan over a long period of years at a low interest rate and without short-term refinancing borrowing."

May 4: FHA is financing 80 percent of the value of homes with 20-year amortization. Speculative home building operations increased considerably in past 15 months, and the program also caused banks to offer competing loan programs.

May 12: Agnes Meyer, in a story titled votes at any cost, quotes John Buckley Bryan, Regional Director of a WPA office in New York, as saying, "Franklin Roosevelt is the man who gave us this money, and I would be the dirtiest kind of a dog-traitor if I didn't see to it that people who are 100 percent for him receive the first consideration." "How do you vote," Meyer says, "is the first question asked of WPA job applicants."

May 14: "Absolute power seized in Austria by Schuschnigg. Nazis rejoice. He became Europe's fourth dictator: Mussolini of Italy, Hitler of Germany, and Stalin of Russia."

May 14: "Senate Finance Committee agrees to raise the individual income tax rate from four percent to five percent.

May 19 headlines: "Supreme Court rules Guffey Coal Act Unconstitutional." "R A Model Housing is voided by District Appeals Bench." This shut the door to future federal regulation of hours, wages, and working conditions in production industries. The marketing and price fixing provisions also fell.

Cartoon May 20, Washington Post:
Seven graves with tombstones labeled as follows—
Guffey coal
Rice millers
AAA
Farm Mortgage moratoriums
National Recovery Act
Railroad pensions
Hot oil
Two fat men looking on, labeled Wagner Labor Act and Social Security Act.
Legend at the bottom "The last of a long line."

After having several of his new programs declared unconstitutional by the Supreme Court, FDR proposed new legislation to add several new Justices to the Court. He hoped to appoint Justices favorable to his views so he could get these unfavorable rulings overturned. This effort failed, because many of the members of his own party thought that was going too far. "That is more power than a bad man should have," one Senator said, "and more than a good man should want."

"Tony Manero sets new mark of 282 to win U. S. Open golf crown at Baltusrol Golf club in Springfield, New Jersey. First prize paid $1,000, and the total purse was $5,000.00. Second place paid $750, third $650, fourth $550, fifth & sixth $137.50 each, and seventh $100.00."(Comment: That does not add up to $5,000.00, so there must have been many lesser prizes.)

June 12: GOP nominates Landon to run against FDR. Col. Frank Knox for V. P.

Advertisement: All wool worsted tropical men's suits $12. 95 and $14. 95.

Headline: Louis-Schmeling fight at Yankee Stadium postponed because of rain. Next day headline: Schmeling wins—-Knocks Joe Louis down in 4th and knocks him out in 12th. (Comment: Some time later Louis knocked out Schmeling.)

June 14: N. Y. Yankee rookie Joe Dimaggio hits two home runs and a pair of doubles in an 18 to 11 win over Chicago White Sox. Both home runs in same inning, equaling a major league record.

June 22: Country's largest airplane to visit local airport. Picture of DST- 21, passenger flagship of American Airlines. Nashville will be only stop between Los Angeles and New York, where plane will be put into regular service Thursday. It has two engines and carries 22 passengers.

June 26: Happy democrats pick Roosevelt to run for re-election.

July 9, 1936: 50 counties to get drought aid. Deaths mount to 112 as record heat wave ruins crops. 171 counties in seven states, including 50 in Tennessee, were today officially added by the Agriculture Committee to the list of emergency drought counties. This designates them as drought areas in the administration of the relief program for distressed farmers. Lawrence County was not included, but two adjoining counties were.

June 29: Heat sizzles at 101 Sunday to break all-time June mark. No hope for rain as drought goes into 80th day in this area.

July 4: Rains in area average two to eight inches.

July 13: Heavy damage felt from Saturday night's storm in mid-state. Barn struck by lightning and burned to the ground. Tobacco plants badly stripped, corn and other crops knocked to ground.

July 14: Tennessee heat blocks cool wave. Death toll over 1,700. No relief due in Nashville. Mercury hits 101—breezes smothered. Heat spreads damage and fatalities. 390 die in Michigan, and G. M. C. may close plant. Relief from showers only temporary.

July 15: Rain, cool wave moving eastward. 1,000 die during day to increase deaths to 2,996. Federal officials speed relief. Conditions are described as second only to the great influenza epidemic of 1918.

July 16: Drought areas greet relief. Western plains skirted by cool waves as deaths from heat reach 3,848.

Tennessee crops are poorest ever reported in July. Rains, however, swell hopes for yields nearer to normal. Big corn belt bakes for 14th day. Crop disaster exceeding 1934 levels. Deaths maintain a 300 daily average. Now total 4,200.

July 19: Nazidom plots ambitious scheme to "colonize" entire world.

July 20 and 21: Showers pour new life into U. S. corn crop. Rains restore hope for crop in corn states—promise farmers good price in midwest. Drought considered a boon, destroying bumper crop evils.

August 1936: Jessie Owens, a black man, wins four gold medals in Berlin Olympics: 100 meters, 200 meters, relay race, and broad jump.

September: Nazis march on Nuremberg for crusade on Communism. Severe restrictions on non-Aryan businessmen.

Bob Feller, 17-year-old rookie speed ball artist, set new record when he whiffed 17 Philadelphia Athletics in the first game of a double header in Cleveland.

Van Meter, Iowa farm boy gets $75,000 bonus. Bob Feller got a clause in his 1936 contract with the Cleveland Indians baseball team, that gave him a bonus of five cents for each paid admission in excess of 1,000,000 during the 1936 season. Because of the enthusiasm his pitching feats aroused among the fans, admissions more than doubled, giving him this huge bonus, which far exceeded his original salary. Feller negotiated his own contract without the help of an agent.

November 4, 1936: GOP crushed in worst defeat. FDR wins easily.

Big Bill Thompson, political boss, "After a dead man has voted three times, he ought to be retired."

December 8, 1936: Wallis Warfield Simpson offered to give Edward up to save his crown, but Edward refused. King Edward tells Prime Minister Stanley Baldwin he means to keep both his love and his throne.

December 12: Former king sails from England. "I have found it impossible to carry the heavy burden without the help of the woman I love." (Wallis weeps.)

December 13: Britain proclaims George VI king today, while Edward VIII sought in a foreign land the solace of the love that cost him the throne.

December 27, 1936: Al Smith, " The Supreme Court is working overtime, throwing the alphabet out the window, three letters at a time."

"Why do some movie stars marry ugly men?" someone asked Vicky Vann of Hollywood. "Filmdom's lovely lasses want to mother the men they love," she replied. "Handsome men don't need mothering; ugly do."

Quotations authorized by the *Washington Post*.

CHAPTER TEN

In March, I started the first cultivation with a turning plow pulled by both mules. I couldn't start earlier because the ground was too wet, and the dirt would have come up in big slabs and chunks instead of crumbling as it should. The plow was a No. 12 Oliver, and it cut a furrow six inches wide and five inches deep. The wing was solid and curved, so it threw the dirt to the right and turned it upside down. I plowed in the same direction and just to the left of the previous furrow, so the dirt from the new furrow filled the previous furrow. One or more killdees (killdeers) followed me all day, picking at bugs and worms they found in the freshly plowed ground. They kept the mules and me company as we worked.

We turned the land each year to bury the dead grass, leaves, and old stalks from the previous year's crop, so they would rot and form humus to improve the soil. The plowing also loosened the soil and made it easier to cultivate. In Agriculture class, Mr. South called this bare fallowing. The better way would have been to turn the land in the fall and give the material a few more months to decompose, but we never got around to it in time.

After turning the land we pulled a drag over it to smooth the dirt and break up the remaining clods. To make a drag, we put two two-by-four boards on the ground about three feet apart. Then we placed other boards, either one-by-fours or one-by-sixes, across these boards and nailed them to the two-by-fours. The whole thing was perhaps six feet wide and four feet from front to back. Then we cut the front ends of the two-by-fours on an angle so the first board in the front would slant upward and not dig into the soft dirt that we were trying to smooth. Then we turned it over so the boards were down against the dirt and the 2 by 4's were up. This provided a smooth surface to drag over the freshly plowed ground.

We took a short piece of chain and fastened the two ends to the two by fours. That gave us a place to attach the doubletree for the mules to pull. I then stood on the drag, near the back, and held the reins in both hands while the two mules pulled it around. We followed in the general pattern that we used in plowing the land, and dragged the freshly plowed ground the same day. If we waited too long the clods of dirt got dry and hard, and would not crumble under the drag.

When I plowed, I tied the ends of the reins together and hung them around my neck—or sometimes around my waist, or over one shoulder and under the other arm, so I had both hands free to control the plow. The mules responded to voice commands. Gee turned them right, and Haw turned them left.

Terraces prevented the rain from washing the topsoil away. They were two feet high, forty or fifty feet apart, and laid out with a gradual drop in elevation so rainwater flowed slowly along the terrace and into one of the ditches. The rows of crops were parallel to the terraces, so they had the same gradual drop in elevation along the rows.

Ernest Roberts, Aunt Annis's husband, had brought a transit to the farm years before and he helped Dad lay out the locations of the terraces. He stood in one spot with the transit on a tripod while Dad went along the proposed route for the terrace with a six-foot rod that had an aiming target on the top end. Dad stood the rod on the ground and moved it around in the direction that my uncle signaled, until he found a spot that was the proper elevation. When my uncle extended both arms parallel to the ground as a signal to mark that spot, Dad dug a hole there. Then he moved out another twenty feet or so, where they went through the same routine until they found another spot with the elevation he wanted. Eventually they had a row of markers all across the field, which was then the path for the new terrace.

First we plowed a furrow along the row of markers with a two-horse turning plow. (Two horse is a generic term. In our case it always means two mules.) The plow threw the dirt to the right, and there was no other furrow there at the time, so it left a continuous line of dirt piled up by the plow. At the end of the field we turned around and plowed in the other direction, keeping to the left of the first furrow, thus throwing a continuous line of dirt on top of the dirt from the first furrow.

We plowed four or five more furrows in each direction, always throwing the dirt toward the top of the new terrace. After the newly plowed ground became firm again, we started in the middle and did it again. This time we were careful to plow the first furrow to one side of the top of the terrace. This threw the row of dirt to the top of the terrace, building it higher. After we did this two or three times we had a terrace. When we planted our corn or cotton, we planted one row on top of each terrace.

Land settles during the winter, so each spring we had to throw up the terraces again before turning the land. My father came in from the field one night and said he was so sick he had been throwing up terraces all day.

When we turned the land in the Spring, we first plowed a furrow next to a terrace, throwing the dirt to the right toward the terrace. When we reached the end we turned left and plowed along the edge of the field until we reached the next terrace. Then we plowed a furrow along the left side of that terrace, throwing the dirt to the right toward that terrace. At the end we turned left again and plowed along that edge of the field until we reached the starting point at the first terrace. This gave us a continuous furrow around the parcel of land between the two terraces. We then followed these furrows, with the dirt from each new furrow thrown to the right and filling up the previous furrow.

The roll of the land was uneven and the terraces were never parallel, so the new furrows met where the terraces were closer together and left unplowed places where the terraces were farther apart. We just plowed around the unplowed part until we finished it.

The pattern of the plowing threw the dirt toward the terraces, so there was an area halfway between the terraces without much loose dirt. We improvised a dirt mover by leaning the plow all the way over on its right side so the wing acted as a rake to drag some of the loose dirt toward the middle where it was needed.

After we ran the drag over the freshly plowed land and allowed it to settle for a week or two, we laid off the rows for planting. We used one mule and a Georgia-Stock plow, which had a little wing on each side and threw dirt in both directions. We started next to one of the terraces and plowed a row a constant distance from the terrace all the way to the end. Then we plowed another row in the other direction, keeping the same distance between rows. We had to fill in with short rows when we came to the second terrace, because the terraces were never the same distance apart all the way to the end.

Now and then I had to plow a first furrow all the way across a field with nothing nearby for a reference. Dad taught me to pick something on the other side of the field to use as a guide and concentrate on going straight toward it. It could be a tree, an old stump, or a bush. This helped me to keep the furrow straight. He said this is a good philosophy in life as well: Identify your important goal, keep it in view, and let it guide your actions.

A Ledbetter planter, pulled by one mule, put the seed and fertilizer into the furrow. It had a hopper in front for fertilizer and another hopper in back for seed. We planted corn between April 10 and April 15, with Dad plowing the furrows while I ran the planter. We planted corn in the bottom of the furrow and didn't apply fertilizer because of the cost. We spaced the corn rows three feet apart and put one grain of corn every eight or ten inches. After the young stalks were up and growing, we thinned them with a hoe, leaving one or two stalks every two feet. If we left the stalks too close together the soil we had would not support full growth for all of them, and production would suffer. Bottom land would support many more stalks to the row and would produce much more corn to the acre, but we didn't have any land like that. That is where floods over hundreds of years have deposited silt to make the topsoil very thick and rich. That brings up another problem, however, because crops sometimes are damaged or ruined by more floods.

Everybody liked fresh corn and ate roasting ears in the summer. The farm folk called them roe-sneers. We planted a row of corn in the garden ten days before planting the main crop, and another row ten days after the main crop. This gave us fresh corn for several weeks.

We planted cotton seeds in a bed. We laid off the row with the Georgia stock plow and then we used a one-horse turning plow, going in one direction to throw the dirt into the furrow and then in the other direction to throw that dirt on top of the other dirt. Sometimes we scattered manure(as long as it lasted) into the furrow before preparing the bed.

Then we pulled the drag lengthwise over these beds to make a level surface on top. The rows of cotton were closer together than the rows of corn, and there wasn't much dirt left in the valley between the beds. We then ran the planter on top of each bed, in the middle of the level part, thus assuring adequate drainage for the baby cotton plants. An adjustment on the back wheel let us control the amount of dirt over the seed.

We considered the danger of frost to be over by May 1, so we started planting cotton that day. We had planted the corn two or three weeks earlier because corn plants can withstand cold weather better than cotton.

We planted almost everything else soon after the cotton. It took longer to plant ten acres of cotton than it had taken to plant twenty acres of corn, because of the extra preparation that cotton required.

We adjusted the planter to spread 100 pounds of fertilizer to the acre and to put down a single row of cottonseeds ½ inch apart. Some of our neighbors used Avery planters, and they couldn't put down one seed at a time. Consequently, it took more seed to plant an acre and they had more thinning to do if all the seed germinated.

The fertilizer came in sacks secured by stitching across the top. It used two threads interwoven, braided at the end of the stitching to form a little roll about an inch long. If I got it started right I could pull the thread out with ease, and the sack came open all the way across with no effort. It worked well about one time out of five, but most of the time I had a problem getting the unraveling process started. I didn't want to cut the sack open with a knife because Mama needed to salvage the cloth from the sacks to make work shirts and sheets.

The bags of fertilizer weighed 100 pounds each, and the fertilizer hopper held less than fifty. I lifted the bag to fill the hopper and then to refill it when needed. At the rate of 100 pounds to the acre, I didn't have to refill it often.

The land in our area was not rich enough to support rows closer together or more plants in the row. Having too many plants in a row made them compete for soil nutrients and prevented them from reaching full growth. Not all the seed germinated, so we planted more than we needed. It was better to thin out the excess plants than not to have enough. We called this thinning the corn and chopping the cotton. For the cotton we used the width of a hoe as the spacer, leaving one or two plants on each side of the hoe.

We planted Irish potatoes, spuds, early in the spring or late in the fall, because they did better in cooler weather. This year we planted them in early April. Compared to corn and cotton, spuds had a short growing season. The plants did not spread out into vines like sweet potatoes, watermelons, and cucumbers, so it was no problem to cultivate around the growing plants.

Spuds saved from the previous year's crop served as seed for planting. They were shriveled and wrinkled, but that was no problem. We had kept them cool, but unfrozen, during the winter so they had not sprouted yet. We cut each potato into pieces, making sure there was an eye (bud) on each piece. Then we placed these pieces by hand in the bottom of a furrow, with the bud on the top side. Next we plowed dirt over them, and the new potato plants grew from the buds.

Sweet potatoes required a different procedure. Very early in the spring we framed off an area on the ground with 2 x 4 boards. First we put a layer of manure on the ground and covered it with a thick layer of sawdust. Next we placed sweet potatoes from the previous year's crop in the sawdust. We put them on their sides in the sawdust with about half of each potato buried in the sawdust and the other half out of it.

After watering it thoroughly, we put a glass cover over it and left it there until there was no longer a danger of frost. The manure and water generated heat, and the potatoes put out many little slips with roots growing on them. Where a new plant came out of the parent potato, it grew in one direction and the new root grew in the opposite direction. Eventually we pulled the potato slips off and planted them by hand. The root was firmly attached to the new plant and came off the parent potato with it.

For sweet potatoes we made a planting bed similar to a cotton row and poked a row of holes into it a couple of feet apart and four or five inches deep. All of a root and about half of a slip went into each hole, followed by a cupful of water. Finally we pushed dirt into the hole to fill around the root and the potato slip. We planted them in May, after we planted the cotton.

We plowed around the rows of sweet potatoes at least twice during the growing season. The first time it was fairly simple because the plants were still small and the vines had not grown long. By the second plowing the vines were so long we had to move them to plow one side, and then move them the other way to plow the other side. We had to put them back where they were after the plowing. We harvested sweet potatoes and spuds the same way, by plowing them up and then digging through the dirt with our hands to pick them out and put them in hampers.

We planted watermelon or cantaloupe seeds in beds with a mixture of barnyard manure and dirt. They were six feet apart with four or five seeds in each bed, topped off with a generous portion of water and another layer of dirt. The plants put out long runners fairly soon, and we had to move those runners temporarily to plow around the plants. Once the runners started to blossom, we didn't move them again. Many of the blooms eventually became watermelons or cantaloupes, and we didn't want to disturb them.

We had different ways to estimate when a watermelon was ripe, but none of them was infallible. If it gave off a dull hollow sound when thumped it might be ready to eat. Each one had a short curly tendril on the vine next to the watermelon. If this curl was dead, the watermelon was certainly ripe. If the curl was still alive and green, the melon might or might not be fully ripe. Also, if the bottom of the watermelon was creamy yellow it was likely to be ripe.

If you pull a watermelon too soon, it may be red inside but not sweet. If you pull it too late, it will be red and ripe, but mushy and not very good. Later in life, when I bought a whole watermelon at a store I always looked first at the ones they had cut up to be sold as halves and quarters. Usually all the watermelons in the store came from the same field at the same time. Therefore, if most of the cut ones didn't look very ripe, I tried to pick one that thumped ripe and looked the ripest of the bunch. However, if most of the cut ones looked too ripe and mushy, I picked a whole one that looked and thumped green. It was more likely to be a good one.

When a watermelon was especially good we saved the seeds for planting another year, because we believed the seeds would produce similar melons in the future. We dried the seeds so they would keep well through the winter.

I heard a story once about a Women's Christian Temperance Union convention being held in the same hotel as a Bartenders' Convention. As luck would have it, they assigned them to adjoining dining rooms. They served watermelon for dessert to both parties, but the bartenders had arranged for the caterers to inject a fifth of vodka into each of their watermelons with a syringe before it was cut into individual servings. At the end of the meal an assistant came to the manager and confessed that they had made a mistake and served the vodka-laced watermelon to the WCTU women instead of to the bartenders.

"Did any of the ladies complain? He asked.

"No, but I saw some of them putting the seeds into their purses."

Everybody liked good watermelons. Grandpa got a good laugh when he heard about a man who was selling watermelons in Lawrenceburg. He offered to sell a big one for a dollar and give the customer his money back if he could eat it all within 10 minutes. One man said he had to go home first and would give him his answer when he got back. He came back a half hour later, paid the man the dollar, and proceeded to eat the entire watermelon in eight minutes and scrape all the red off the rind.

The seller returned the dollar and asked the man why he had to go home first. "I had me one at home that same size, and I went home and eat it first," he said. "I knowed if I could eat that-un, I could eat this-un."

Watermelons, apples, pears, cantaloupes, grapes, and similar fruits have an effective way of propagating themselves. The fruit is good to eat, and the small seeds are in the fruit. Wild animals and earlier humans have eaten the fruits, seeds and all, for centuries; and the seeds simply passed through the animals without being digested. Eventually these seeds wound up on the ground a long way from the mother plant, and nature provided that the fertilizer needed to nourish the new growth was deposited right there with the seed. Soon there was another tree or vine to produce more fruit.

The best tasting watermelons grew during a sunny summer with just the right amount of rain. We had good and not-so-good watermelon years, just as wine makers had similar years in Europe. Too much rain and not enough sun made watermelons that were big but not sweet.

Cool and wet summers in Europe also made wine grapes that were not sweet enough. That's why the quality of European wine varied from year to year and why consumers wanted to see the year of the vintage on the bottle. In some places in California they always had sun and depended on irrigation water rather than rain. That gave them the control they needed to make wine of a consistent quality from year to year. That's why many of the California wine makers don't put the vintage year on the bottles.

We grew peanuts for our use and not for sale. Grandpa White called them ground peas. That made sense, because the peanut is a member of the pea family and the nuts grow underground. We planted them in a furrow by hand, with dried, shelled nuts and fertilizer in the row.

The branches of the peanut plant grow horizontally and the yellow flowers hang down on stems toward the ground. The flowers turn into brittle pods hanging down, and eventually they enter the ground where they develop into peanuts. After all the flowers had turned into pods, we shoveled a small amount of dirt over the middle of each plant. This covered the pods and made sure they got under the ground.

We harvested peanuts by using a shovel to dig out the plant with the peanuts attached. Then we shook the dirt off the peanuts, turned the plant upside down, and left it in the sun for the nuts to dry. Later we removed the peanuts and stored then in sacks.

* * * * *

Sometimes we planted our hay by broadcasting the seeds by hand, and other times we rented a drill from Mr. Voss. Two mules pulled the drill, and it planted a dozen rows at a time, very close together. Disk-like attachments rolled over the ground, cut a trench, dropped seed into it, and covered them with dirt. The seed came down from the hopper through tubes. Some years we planted Mung beans, but this year we planted Soybeans. We never cultivated these rows because they were too close together. Rabbits loved the young Soybean plants and the mature beans, and they came out of the woods to eat them along the edge of the field.

One of our staple foods was whippoorwill peas. They were common field peas, but we called them whippoorwills because they had brown specks, the same color as the bird by that name. In August, just before we cultivated the corn for the last time, we scattered those seed peas between the rows of corn. They had a shorter growing season and would mature along with the corn.

While cultivating around the rows of corn, the scratcher did not reach halfway to the next row and left a little ridge of soil between the rows. The last plowing of the corn we called busting out the middles. We set the scratcher with five teeth in an inverted V shape, so it threw dirt in both directions. With it, we made one last plowing on top of the middle ridge. That loosening the dirt between the rows, spread it in both directions toward the rows of corn, and covered the seed peas at the same time. By then the corn plants were three feet high, and any further cultivation would have damaged the roots, doing more harm than good.

Joe White, District Director, US Immigration Service, 1963 (Photo courtesy of Birdsong Photography, Lawrenceburg, Tennessee.)

Joe White, age 18, in front of country home (Photo courtesy of Eunice White Curtis.)

Joe White age 26, coming out of the outhouse behind the Taylor home in Auburndale Florida. (Candid camera shot by Othaniel (Giant) Taylor)

Seven cousins, circa 1926. Front row, Left to right: Quinton White, Eunice White, Lucy Robinson. Back row: Noah Robinson, R. B. Reeve, Jr., J. C. White, Jr., Eugene Robinson.(Photo courtesy of Wanda Stahl.)

Ida Reeve White, author's mother, with Eunice on her lap and J. C. Jr. standing. (Photo courtesy of Judy Bagett, Eunice White's daughter)

Eunice White Thompson, with daughters Janice, left, and Judy right.(Photo courtesy of Judy Baggett.)

Corporal Joseph C White, SR., my father, in France during World War One.

Left to right: Quinton White, Joe White Sr. Edgar White. My father is showing the effects of the cancer that caused his death the following year.(Photo Courtesy of Joseph D. White.)

Billie Gene White at an early age. He had Cerebral Palsy since birth and died at age 61. His twin brother, Bobbie, died at age five.

Quinton White and his wife, Beverly.(Photo courtesy of Joseph D. White.)

Oland Bruce White and his wife Kristin —center of picture. (Photo courtesy of Kristin White.)

Paternal grandparents, Monroe and Hester Ann White with their children and grandchildren: L-R: Leila White Canada, Virgil Canada; Dora White Wakefield, Henry Wakefield; Hester Ann White, Monroe White; Mrs. Arthur White, Arthur White; Back row: Joseph C. White, Thomas C. White, Buren White, Annis White.(Photos courtesy of William Newton White.)

Maternal grandparents, Noah Smith Reeve and Lucinda McCullar Reeve.
(Photo courtesy of Wanda Stahl.)

Mother's brother, Roy Bryan Reeve and family. L-R: R. B. Reeve, Jr., Bessie Lou Reeve, Lavene Reeve, Iris Prestige Reeve, Roy Reeve. (Photo courtesy of Wanda Stahl.)

My cousin Ray Abner and family. L-R: Front row, Millie Abner, William Ray Abner. Rear row: Ray Jr., Kelly, and Kirk Abner.(Photo courtesy of Kelly Abner.)

Stacy and Ruby Reeve Abner, with son Ray, upon his graduation from College.
(Photo courtesy of Kelly Abner.)

Tom and Eunice Bailey and their children. L-R Emily, Nelda, Betty, and Gerald.(Photo courtesy of Wanda Stahl.)

George and Alice Robinson and family. Front row: L-R Iva George, Pat, Alice, Charlie. Rear l-R Eugene, Lucy Jane, Evelyn, Pernie, Noah (Photo courtesy of Wanda Stahl, daughter of Lucy Robinson.)

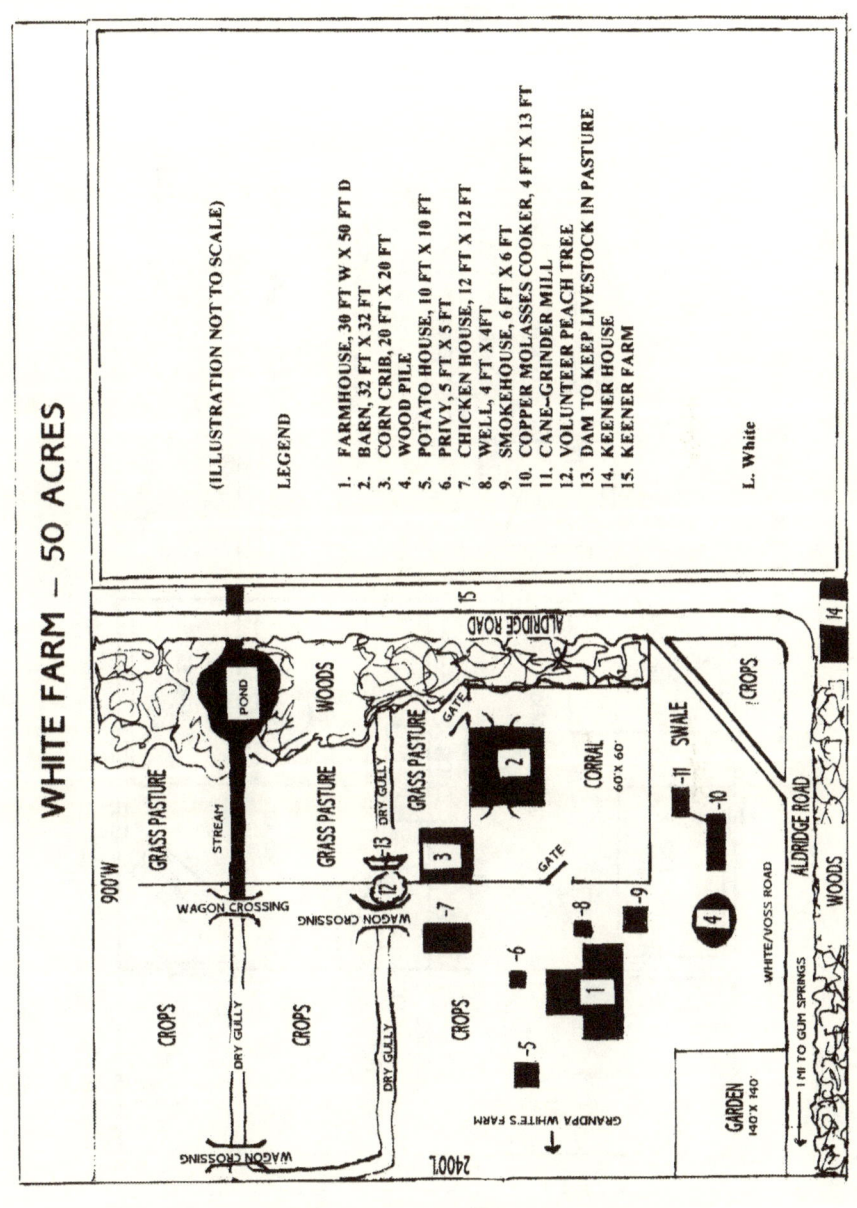

WHITE FARM – 50 ACRES

(ILLUSTRATION NOT TO SCALE)

LEGEND

1. FARMHOUSE, 30 FT W X 50 FT D
2. BARN, 32 FT X 32 FT
3. CORN CRIB, 20 FT X 20 FT
4. WOOD PILE
5. POTATO HOUSE, 10 FT X 10 FT
6. PRIVY, 5 FT X 5 FT
7. CHICKEN HOUSE, 12 FT X 12 FT
8. WELL, 4 FT X 4FT
9. SMOKEHOUSE, 6 FT X 6 FT
10. COPPER MOLASSES COOKER, 4 FT X 13 FT
11. CANE-GRINDER MILL
12. VOLUNTEER PEACH TREE
13. DAM TO KEEP LIVESTOCK IN PASTURE
14. KEENER HOUSE
15. KEENER FARM

L. White

Forged in a Country Crucible

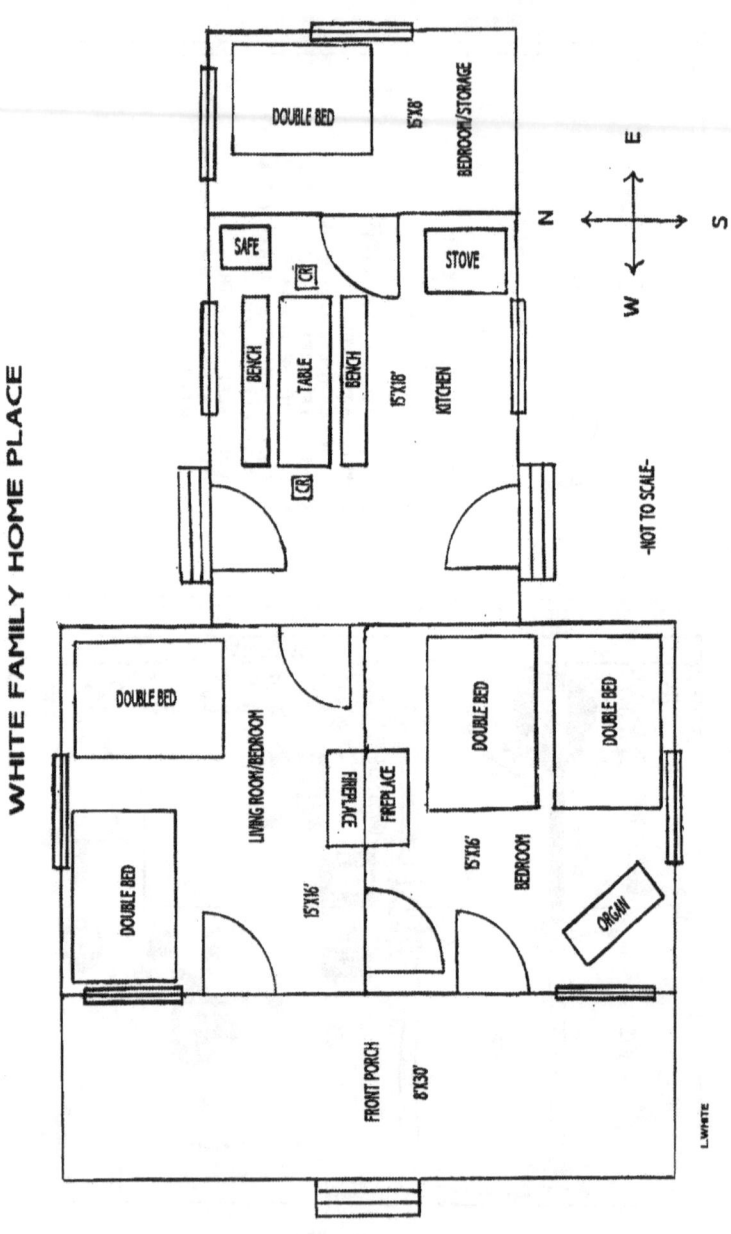

The farmhouse when Joe lived there. *Linda C. White*

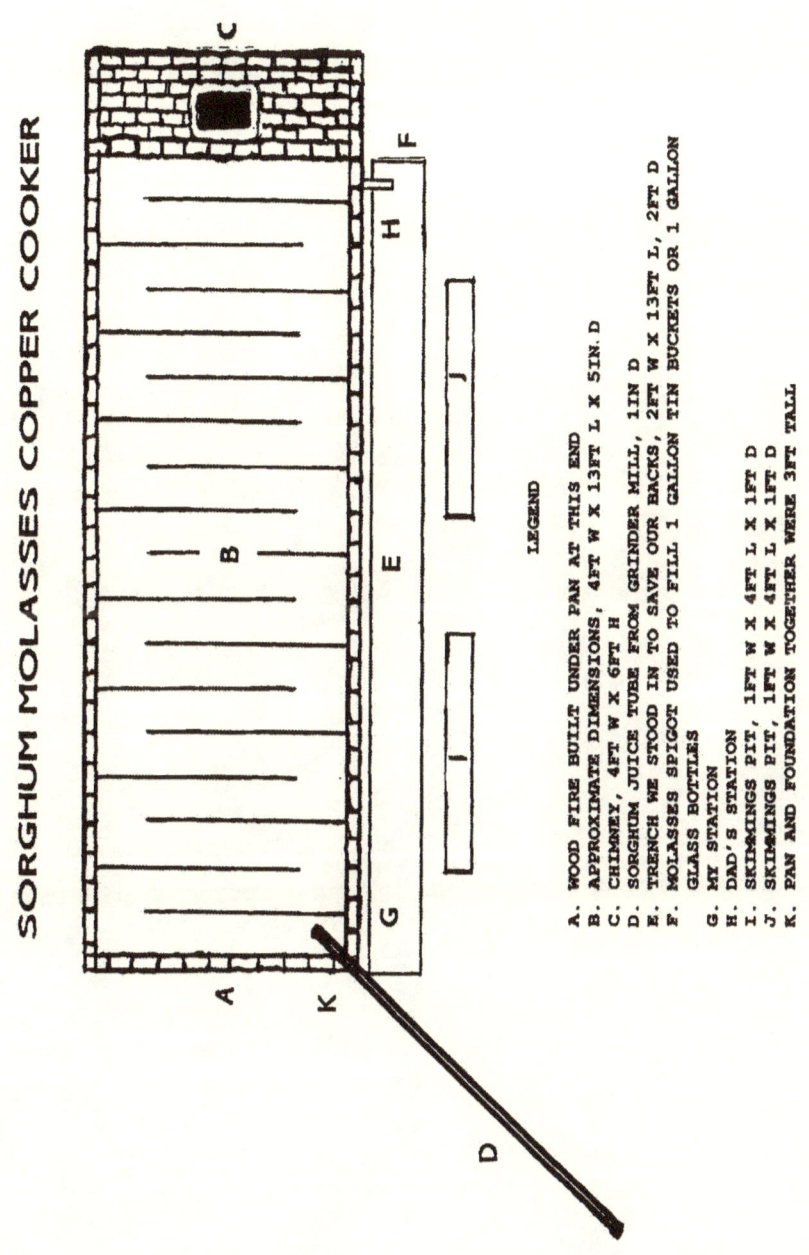

SORGHUM MOLASSES COPPER COOKER

LEGEND

A. WOOD FIRE BUILT UNDER PAN AT THIS END
B. APPROXIMATE DIMENSIONS, 4FT W X 13FT L X 5IN. D
C. CHIMNEY, 4FT W X 6FT H
D. SORGHUM JUICE TUBE FROM GRINDER MILL, 1IN D
E. TRENCH WE STOOD IN TO SAVE OUR BACKS, 2FT W X 13FT L, 2FT D
F. MOLASSES SPIGOT USED TO FILL 1 GALLON TIN BUCKETS OR 1 GALLON
   GLASS BOTTLES
G. MY STATION
H. DAD'S STATION
I. SKIMMINGS PIT, 1FT W X 4FT L X 1FT D
J. SKIMMINGS PIT, 1FT W X 4FT L X 1FT D
K. PAN AND FOUNDATION TOGETHER WERE 3FT TALL

The syrup making pan. *Linda W. White.*

CHAPTER ELEVEN

Our farming was labor intensive. We had to thin the corn and chop the cotton, and later had to go over the cotton at least twice with hoes to get out the crab grass and weeds that the plowing missed.

We planted in rows, and plowed every two weeks around them to loosen the soil. After a rain, the soil formed capillaries that let the moisture out of the ground. We plowed the ground around the new plants to break up these tiny tubes and keep the moisture in the ground. The plowing also destroyed most of the crabgrass that always tried to grow around our row crops. If left alone, it took over a row of cotton or corn and severely retarded the growth of the plants.

We plowed with a spring-toothed cultivator, called a scratcher. We could install three, four, or five teeth. Three worked better for breaking up new ground where there were too many stumps and grubs for the use of turning plow. Four was normal for cultivating around row crops. We put a metal defender on the right side next to the row, and adjusted it up or down to control the amount of dirt it threw toward the plants.

When we plowed young cotton the defender had to be low, but when plowing corn we raised it higher because the corn plants were bigger and could take more dirt. The second tooth of the scratcher was set to the left and behind the first tooth, the third tooth was set to the left and behind the second, and so on. This moved the dirt away from the row, with a controlled amount going toward the plants under the defender.

A scratcher tooth was a piece of steel an eighth of an inch thick and a little more than an inch wide, with two holes drilled near the front end, one behind the other. Two flat pieces of steel extended out from the stock of the cultivator, one behind the other. We bolted the scratcher teeth to these, through holes provided for the purpose.

The scratcher tooth extended straight backward about ten inches, then curved downward and then forward. The end of the tooth was flat, pointed, and sharp so it would dig into the ground. The teeth were stiff but had some flexibility, hence the name spring-toothed cultivator.

When we first cleared the ground of trees and bushes, we couldn't use a turning plow because it hung up on the stumps, grubs, and big roots. A grub is a baby stump attached to a bush. So for the first two years, we cultivated the new ground with a scratcher. When it hit roots or grubs the teeth sprang back and slid over the obstacles. For the first plowing in the spring we used only three teeth set with the left tooth in front, so the teeth went deeper into the ground and threw the dirt to the right like a turning plow.

We cleared two or three acres of new ground each winter by removing the trees and clearing out and burning all the underbrush. One winter, in the worst part of the depression, Uncle Virgil Canada offered to clear new ground for us for a bushel of corn for each day's work. His farm was nearby; and he needed the corn for food for his family and livestock, and for seed for the next year's crop. A neighbor told him he was foolish to work for that, because he could buy a bushel of corn for a quarter.

"Yeah, I know," responded Uncle Virgil, "but I ain't got no quarter."

Our double scratcher (spring-toothed cultivator) had four teeth on each side of the row, and needed only one trip to plow both sides. A double defender, with a metal blade on each side of the row, protected the young plants from too much dirt. One mule could have pulled it, but he would have walked on top of the row of plants. So we used two mules, one on each side of the row. It allowed one person to do the work of two, but the operator had to be careful not to step on the young plants as he walked behind it.

I realized much later that we damaged the roots of our corn plants by plowing too close to them. Eventually, corn farmers put down the corn seed, the fertilizer, and a herbicide at the same time. Grass and weeds couldn't grow, and the corn thrived with no cultivation. At harvest time a machine gathered the ears of corn and loaded them into a trailer towed behind the harvester. Some of the more advanced harvesters shucked and shelled the corn and even put it into bags. But farmers used them mostly in the mid-west, where they grew 150 bushels or more on an acre. We grew corn the hard way, but corn was critical to our survival.

* * * * *

At noon we had the main meal of the day, called dinner. We always had cornbread to eat with vegetables, fresh in the growing season and dried or canned in the winter. One favorite was mature green tomatoes, sliced, rolled in corn meal, and fried. Vegetable soup was another favorite, either freshly made in summer or canned in winter. We made the soup with okra, squash, tomatoes, fresh peas and beans, and anything else in season from the garden. We also canned sauerkraut, string beans, and black-eyed peas.

To make sauerkraut we packed 50 pounds of shredded cabbage in layers in a big crock vessel with 1 ½ pounds of salt, put a plate on top, and weighted it down with a large clean rock. After it sat and fermented for six weeks, we cooked it to a full rolling boil and sealed it in glass mason (fruit) jars.

Those fruit jars had many uses. People have said a man from Tennessee can be identified by the dent across the bridge of his nose that he got from drinking moonshine whisky from a fruit jar. One of the country bands that performed on the Grand Ole Opry called itself the Fruit Jar Drinkers, and Gid Tanner had a band called the Skillet Lickers.

We preferred biscuits for breakfast, but we had to buy flour since we didn't grow wheat. The most common brands were Yukon's Best and Yukon's Queen of the West. Yukon's Best was whiter and more expensive, but we bought Queen of the West, either because it was cheaper or because we liked it better. It came packaged in 24, 48, and 96 pound bags. They also sold it by the barrel, which was 192 pounds, but we never bought that much at one time. When we didn't have flour we had to eat cornbread for breakfast. We liked it at noon and at night, but not in the morning.

The stores also sold lard. The most popular container was an eight pound bucket, and the most popular brand was Swift's Silverleaf. A bigger size came in a fifty-pound metal container, called a stand. Having a barrel of flour and a stand of lard in the house was like having money in the bank. Lard did not require refrigeration.

* * * * *

It didn't rain for a long time that summer, and the corn leaves twisted themselves into tight rolls. This was nature's way of keeping the plants from dying from heat and thirst. We knew if they survived the leaves would spread out again when rain came. We needed a soaking rain to restore the cornfield to normal, because the roots went deep into the ground.

The farms in the Midwest and along the Mississippi River Valley have topsoil several feet thick. But our topsoil was only three or four inches thick, except for a few places where silt settled from flood water. We would have been overjoyed if we got a yield of forty bushels of corn to the acre, but we rarely did. This year there had not been enough rain, and some kind of a corn weevil or worm got into the tip ends of the ears and ate about a fourth of each ear, leaving droppings in the form of a powdery dust. Also, because of the dry weather, some of the ears of corn did nor develop fully and were no more than half the size of a normal ear. We called them nubbins. A neighbor asked Dad later in the year how much corn he made. "About twenty bushels to the acre," he replied, "and most of it was worm shit and shucks."

* * * * *

We expected to see the first cotton blooms by the Fourth of July, and they were right on schedule. The first ones appeared, as always, on the bottom branches near the ground, and they were white at first. After a day or two they turned red and a few days later fell off, leaving little squares with tiny cotton bolls inside. The plants bloomed for four or five weeks, gradually progressing to the top branches. Then over the next several weeks the cotton bolls grew bigger, until they started to open in September.

Soon after the squares appeared on the plants, some of them started to fall off. Nature was reacting to the extreme heat and lack of moisture, because the plants could not support all the squares under those conditions. Luckily we had a shower before we lost too many. The root system of a cotton plant is nearer the surface than the roots of a corn plant, and it can benefit from a brief rain, which we farmers called a cotton shower.

Grandpa planted sunflowers so he could feed the seeds to his chickens. The big flowers turned east toward the sunrise and followed the sun around all day until they faced west at sunset. The plants fascinated me with the way they reacted to the sun.

* * * * *

Men rolled their own smokes, usually with brown paper. Some of the more affluent bought OCB cigarette papers that were thin and white and just the right size for rolling a cigarette. They bought them in little packets of twenty papers to the packet. Some even bought a little mechanical device that would assist in rolling a cigarette with the OCB papers. One man joked that he used OCB cigarette paper, and then pulled a brown paper bag out of his pocket and said, "OCB—Old Coffee Bag."

Country Gentleman cigarette tobacco came in little cloth bags, closed with a drawstring. I found one of those empty bags and used it as a purse to store my coins, when I had any. A country store always had an open box of shotgun shells and an open box of .22-short rifle cartridges. I could buy one shotgun shell for three cents, and three .22 cartridges for a penny. One of my fantasies in those days was to buy an entire box of 25 shotgun shells at one time. I never had any money, at least not for long, because I was quick to spend it on ammunition. My sister was more frugal, and this trait served her well in later life.

When the corn and cotton plants were tall enough to cultivate, Dad came down with Malaria. He could walk around, but was too sick to work. He got up every morning, outlined what I needed to do that day, and made sure I had right equipment. Then he went back into the house and I followed the mules all day with the double scratcher up and down the rows of corn and cotton.

About a week later someone came from the Gum Springs Baptist Church and said several members had volunteered to come out every week or ten days with their mules and equipment and do all our cultivating. They did that when members were sick and unable to do for themselves. Dad thanked them but said he didn't think it would be necessary. He told them I would do the plowing and Eunice and Quinton would do the hoeing, but he promised to let them know if we found we couldn't handle it ourselves.

This went on for a month and a half before Dad was well enough to do much work. But we got through it, and it did wonders for my self-esteem. I learned that no matter how hot, sweaty, dirty, and tired I might be, that was no excuse to quit when work had to be done. If I stopped for an hour, that hour could never be recaptured. I developed an inner drive and persistence that summer that contributed to whatever success I enjoyed in later life.

Early in the spring of 1936, Dad had sent me with the mules and the turning plow to do a three-day job for Grandpa, turning the land for his cotton crop. We usually didn't charge for helping him, but this time he paid me three dollars, and Dad told me to keep it. I went straight to Richardson's Hardware store in Lawrenceburg and put the three dollars on the layaway plan for a Remington, bolt-action, single-shot, .22 rifle. Then on my 16th birthday, July 6, he went into town and came back with my rifle, together with a box of 50 long rifle cartridges. It cost him three dollars to pay the balance on the rifle and another quarter for the bullets, and I was happier than any lark in the county.

As usual, Mama made me a chocolate meringue pie for my birthday. She made a second one for the rest of the family, because they let me eat my whole pie myself. That was my birthday gift. Dad said paying off my layaway balance on the rifle was to show his appreciation for the hard work I did while he was sick.

* * * * *

We had less rain than average that summer. Occasionally while working in the fields I saw a black cloud in the distance with streaks going from the cloud to the ground. Those streaks indicated sheets of rain falling from the cloud. They came straight down from the clouds to the ground, unless the wind caused them to slant to one side. If the sun happened to be in the right position the reflection produced a rainbow.

Those streaks of rain were different from rays of the sun that sometimes streamed down through the clouds. Those rays started from the sun, and came toward the ground through the clouds at various angles. They looked like a folding Japanese fan opened to a quarter circle, with the pin at the sun and the wooden slats pointing to the ground at different angles.

Sometimes the rain came close but never reached us. I watched eagerly, hoping for the cool damp breeze to start blowing from the direction of the rain, indicating the rain might get to me eventually. Sometimes the air felt slightly damp and still, and the rain crows started to call. We never heard them unless it felt like rain. A rain crow is a little bigger than a robin, and I seldom saw one. The call sounded like a hoarse aaaoop!, aaaoop!, and always came from a wooded area. Webster's dictionary says a rain crow is a species of Cuckoo, the cries of which are supposed to presage rain. But this dry summer we didn't hear them many times, and when we did they were usually wrong.

When a rainstorm came we ran to the house, and sometimes we waited too long and got drenched before we got there. I didn't mind because I put the mules in the barn and took their harness off. Then I stayed out in the rain. When the ground got soaked we couldn't cultivate until it dried out. If plowed wet, dirt forms hard clods that are difficult to break up. Too wet to plow was a common comment to describe a bad situation.

When we had a warm rain I walked up and down the road barefooted. It usually brought lightning and thunder, and I knew it was dangerous, but I did it anyway. Like most teenagers, I thought I was immortal. The branches of the trees swayed in the wind, and birds went off somewhere to hide from the rain.

Winter rains usually lasted several hours, and in some cases even longer. Summer rains were different, because most of them were local storms. The sun heated the ground and the ground in turn heated the air above it. Hot air rose, and the cooler air from surrounding areas moved in to replace the rising hot air. Soon a column of air was rising, while cooler air came in from surrounding areas. The hot land surface then heated the cooler air, and it also rose. Hot air can hold more moisture than cool air, and the air temperature dropped three degrees for every thousand feet of elevation. As the column of air rose it cooled because of the higher elevation, and as it cooled, moisture was squeezed out of the air and formed thunderclouds.

Dad liked to sit on the front porch and watch the summer storms, unless the wind blew the rain in on him. Sometimes we heard the crack of lightning striking a tree in the woods. When a tree was severely damaged we cut it down and used it for firewood.

* * * * *

I enjoyed the sounds of the nights: katydids in the trees, whippoorwills and mocking birds going on and on without ever seeming to stop, hoot owls in far-off trees, crickets, frogs in ponds, and even the screech owl that once scared me half to death when he let loose in a little tree just outside my bedroom window. There were other sounds I could not identify, but nothing gave me more pleasure than the sound of a hard rain on the tin roof.

We had bluebirds, wrens, doves, bob white quail, crows, hawks, red-headed woodpeckers, sapsuckers, yellowhammers, robins, English sparrows, rain crows, jorees, (so called because of the sound of their call,) hoot owls, screech owls, mocking birds (nightingales), snowbirds, and jaybirds (bluejays). Once in a great while I saw a shrike. That was a miniature hawk about the size of a robin, and it preyed on sparrows and other small birds.

Red-headed woodpeckers—we called them peckerwoods—and yellow hammers (flickers) drummed their beaks against dead trees and dug holes in them to make nests. The holes went straight in for a few inches and then down, enabling the mother bird to be on the nest and look out at the same time.

Crows ate baby chickens, baby birds, birds eggs from nests, and corn from cornfields. Blue jays were almost as bad. When a grain of corn started to germinate, the new plant grew from the pointed end of the seed. The baby corn plant used all the nutrients from the seed eventually, and while doing so it grew roots to sustain itself later. But when the plant first emerged from the ground, most of the corn seed was still there. Crows pulled young corn plants out of the ground to get the corn seeds attached to the plants. One of my elementary school textbooks showed a picture of a crow sitting on a fence post and looking across the field at a man following a mule. Under the picture was this poem:

"Caw, caw, called the crow, Spring has come again, I know.
Just as sure as I am born, there's a farmer planting corn."

CHAPTER TWELVE

Poke Weed grew wild. When it was young and tender some farmers boiled the leaves and ate them as garden greens—they called it poke sallit (not salad). I couldn't stand the smell and we never ate it. The plant grew to be six feet tall and had smooth leaves, white flowers, and red berries. The roots and berry seeds were poisonous, but some claimed Poke Weed had medicinal properties. We experimented with it once, to our sorrow.

We had an epidemic of the itch (scabes) at Gum Springs School. The country people pronounced it the each. It was highly contagious, and almost everyone got it. We had never heard of a dermatologist; so we tried a home remedy a neighbor told us about, a lotion made by boiling roots of poke weed. It did nothing to cure the itch, but it burned and raised little blisters on our skin. We finally got rid of the itch after rubbing on a smelly mixture of sulfur and lard.

The rabbit tobacco plant had long silvery-gray leaves and grew to be two feet tall. It was plentiful in the woods and in uncultivated fields, and many kids and some adults made cigarettes with the leaves and smoked them. The dictionary called it Life Everlasting.

Nobody in our neighborhood had a lawn. Front yards were nothing but dirt, and we swept them with brush brooms made from small branches and twigs. We swept our floors with brooms made at home from a tough heavy grass we called sage. It was about three feet tall and brownish yellow when mature. It grew wild in open fields and in open spaces in the woods, where it provided hiding places for small animals and birds. Good brooms were available, but they were expensive for farm families, and few bought them.

Mama grew flowers in the yard: Roses, dahlias, flags, gladiolas, petunias, and something she called Easter lilies. She also brought from Alabama three seedling pine trees and planted them in our back yard. The first three or four plantings died. Finally she brought a wash tub full of sandy soil from Alabama and planted the pine seedlings in that. It got them over the initial shock of being transplanted, and they thrived. Pine trees were rare in that area, but she took care of them and they grew to be huge trees.

Our garden was next to the road and on the opposite side of the house from the barn. We fenced it with small-mesh wire to try to keep the rabbits from eating our small plants. We grew tomatoes, butter beans, English peas, pole beans, okra, cabbage, collards, turnips, onions, radishes, mustard, bell peppers, red peppers, and probably other things I can't remember. We had a row of grape vines supported by wire running from the front of the garden to the rear. Half were early-maturing pink grapes and the others were later-maturing black ones. I remember eating those sweet pink grapes until I felt I couldn't swallow another one. Then I would break them open in my mouth, one at a time, and savor the taste of the juice for a moment before spitting them out on the ground. In the far right-hand corner, outside the fence, we had a huge thicket of raspberry bushes.

We also grew sweet potatoes, Irish potatoes, and peanuts; but we grew them in the fields and not in the garden. We always had a patch of cantaloupes and muskmelons, we called them mushmelons, that were bigger than cantaloupes but not as sweet. The Encyclopedia Encarta says true cantaloupes come from Europe and take their name from Cantaloupa, a village near Rome, Italy. What we call cantaloupes are really Muskmelons, and there are several varieties.

Many farmers grew long-necked gourds to use as nests for Purple Martins and as dippers for water buckets. They grew to be more than a foot long. The neck of the gourd was not much bigger than a broomstick, but it had a round knob at the end bigger than a softball. After the gourds were completely mature and dried out, people carved holes in the knobs the right size for a Purple Martin's nest. Then they made little holes through the opposite ends and ran wires through them.

Finally, they prepared a pole ten or fifteen feet long and nailed a thin, six-foot board across the top. They fastened the wires from six gourds to this board and raised the pole into the air. That accommodated six pairs of nesting Martins, three on each side.

Martins sent out scouts early in the year to look for likely nesting sites. They liked to nest in groups, and martins looked for appealing accommodations like these. They came back year after year once they established the location. Most farmers installed the pole so they could take it down in the winter to clean out the nests, so the martins could build them fresh the next year.

Farmers liked purple martins because they caught and ate mosquitoes and other insects on the wing, and because they chased away hawks and crows. They were much smaller than either, but they were so fast they could get behind hawks or crows and peck them on the back just ahead of the tail feathers. Nobody worried about hawks stealing chickens if they had a colony of martins around. Sometimes in the evening we saw martins coming to their nests so fast they looked like purple streaks. The farm people described a swift and direct trip by saying it was like a Martin going to its gourd.

When we made water dippers from gourds we cut bigger openings in the knobs, about half the size of the knob. After we cleaned out all the seeds it made a fairly convenient dipper for drinking, with the neck of the gourd serving as a handle. Most gourd dippers could hold as much water as an eight-ounce glass.

Every farm had a well, protected by a square wooden curb around it. These curbs were four feet high and flat on the top, with hinged hatches that provided entry for drawing water. Each one had a windlass mounted on one side, with a crank at one end and with a rope fastened to the round windlass. The rope went up and through a pulley hanging from a scaffold built for the purpose, then down to a galvanized water bucket tied to the end of the rope. The bucket had a small iron weight attached to one side so it would tip over and sink when it reached the water.

Turning the crank pulled the rope through the pulley as it wrapped around the windlass. The weight of the water held the bucket upright as it came up to the top of the well curb. The operator then held the windlass crank with one hand, pulled the water bucket over to the side with the other hand, and set it on top of the curb. Then he closed the top hatch, reached for the gourd dipper, and helped himself to a drink of fresh well water.

Most of the time the rope was wound around the windlass, the hatch was shut, and the water bucket was sitting on top of the curb. A store-bought metal dipper or a home-made gourd dipper usually hung from a nail on the side of the curb for the convenience of anyone who was thirsty. Turning the crank counterclockwise allowed the rope to unwind and let the bucket down into the well, and turning it clockwise re-wound the rope and pulled the bucket back to the top. It would have worked equally well turning the crank the other way, but this was more convenient for right-handed people.

Our water came from a limestone aquifer and the quality was excellent. Dad always wanted his water fresh. If a bucket of water was more than five or ten minutes old, he threw it out and drew a fresh bucket.

CHAPTER THIRTEEN

Wagon wheels were made of wood and had iron bands around the circumference. The installers heated the iron bands until they expanded enough to slip on over the wooden wheel. Then as the iron band cooled, it shrank enough to make a very tight fit on the wheel so it wouldn't come off. They also had smaller iron bands around the wooden hubs, eight or nine inches in diameter. If a kid could get one from an old junked wagon he could make a great toy. He flattened a metal Prince Albert tobacco can and nailed it to a flat narrow board. He bent the ends of the can upward, leaving a flat place in the middle about two inches wide. With this contraption, he could push the iron wheel and make it roll along the road for hours.

We played mumblety peg with a pocket knife. The player opened the big blade all the way and the little blade half way. Then he knelt down with the left knee on the ground and the right leg bent at right angles. He put the tip of the big blade on the right knee and his right hand on the very end of the handle. The game was to flip the knife end over end and make the blade stick into the ground. I don't recall how the game was scored or what one had to do to win. I just know that it was easy when the ground was damp and soft, and it was difficult when the ground was dry and hard. When describing someone who was awkward and inept, some would say, "He couldn't play mumblety peg on a rotten stump."

In the spring the sap rose in the hickory trees, and the kids made hickory whistles. They took a green hickory bush and cut out a piece about three inches long and a little less than an inch in diameter. Then they rubbed the bark all around, pressing down with the back of a pocket knife until the bark came loose from the wood. Next they cut a notch in the stick about an inch from one end, and then slipped the bark off and made the notch in the wood bigger than the notch in the bark. They trimmed the wood down slightly along the top, from the notch to the back end of the stick. This made a passageway between the bark and the wood through which to blow air into the notch. Finally, they slipped the bark back on and cut the back end of the stick on a bevel, so the top part was thin enough to put easily into the mouth. That was a working whistle.

People made checkerboards out of old pieces of cardboard, and they played with coca cola caps. One player turned the caps upside down and the other had them right side up. We played another game called foxes and geese with two coca cola caps (foxes) on one side and with many grains of corn (geese) on the other. I can't remember the rules, except that the foxes could capture the geese; but all the geese could do was surround the foxes until they couldn't move.

Another game involved hitting a tin can off a stump with a stick. The one hitting the can had to run to a designated spot and return before the other player could retrieve the can and bring it back to the stump.

When we found a tree stump about three feet high that was smooth on top, we sometimes made a flying jenny. We drove an iron stake into the middle of the top of the stump and left about three or four inches sticking up to hold the board. Then we got a two-inch by eight-inch board about ten feet long and bored a hole in the middle. We centered the board on the stump with the iron stake coming up through the hole in the middle of the board. With one kid on each end of the board, another kid could push the board and spin it around. If only two kids were present, they ran around with the board and got it to spinning and then jumped on and rode it until it stopped. In that case, they leaned over the board, face down, and picked up their feet to ride the board around. If one kid was heavier than the other he sat nearer the stump on his end and the lighter kid sat nearer the end of the board on his end.

Another toy we made with a large button and a long piece of string. We ran the string through one of the holes of a button and then from the other side put it through the opposite hole. The string needed to at least two feet long, and the ends evened up and tied together after being threaded through the two holes in the button. Now we relocated the button so that it was halfway between the ends of the doubled string.

With thumbs through the two ends of the string (on either side of the button) we then rotated both hands rapidly forward and down then back and up, swinging the button and twisting the string as we did it. The trick was to continue until the string was fully wound up, and then pull the ends of the string in opposite directions. That caused the string to unwind and spin the button in the process. As the string unwound, the inertia caused the button to continue spinning and wound the string in the opposite direction. By first pulling and then releasing the tension on the string, we could keep the button spinning indefinitely. The noise the button made as it was spinning gave the toy its name, zizz wheel. If all this sounds simple and childlike, remember we had no television, no radio, no bicycles, and very few toys.

* * * * *

I don't recall ever hearing my parents yell at each other, or even argue. They must have had disagreements, but they kept them private. We never had any doubt that they loved us kids. We didn't think much about how poor we were. We had the same tin roof over our heads year after year, and we always had something to eat and wear.

Our parents always stressed telling the truth, and they were usually lenient when we messed up, so long as we didn't lie about it. If they ever caught a kid in a lie, he got serious lecture. I tried to follow the same practice in later years with my own children.

Children are more likely to follow what their parents do than what they say. When we returned from a trip and found a hotel or motel towel mixed in with our laundry, I always made it a practice to take or send it back and made sure the kids knew it. I never wrote a note to excuse a child from school because of a doctor's appointment unless it was true. Telling small lies leads to telling big lies, and telling big lies destroys self-respect and makes the liar untrustworthy.

Nevertheless, it is a kindness sometimes to tell a little white lie to avoid hurting someone's feelings. When a friend asks how do you like his new suit, does her new dress make her look fat, or do you think her new hairdo is becoming, they are looking for support and approval—-not criticism. But some people use total honesty in those situations as an excuse to hurt people. I think that is a greater wrong than telling a little white lie to make them feel good.

CHAPTER FOURTEEN

We finished cultivating the crop in August. Dad said the other work could wait a few days, so he let me go to Alabama to visit my grandparents and my cousins in Winston County. Two of the Hunter boys, Wesley and Harley, drove to Alabama to visit relatives for a week, and they gave me a ride as far as Haleyville, where they turned left to go east to Addison. They drove a 1931 Model A Ford, an elegant car for the time. From Haleyville, I set out to walk the 10 miles to Double Springs and another two miles to my destination. After walking a mile or two, I got a ride to Double Springs and then walked the rest of the way, carrying a small suitcase and my new .22-caliber rifle.

My roots are in Winston County. When Alabama withdrew from the Union over the Civil War, citizens there held a meeting and proposed withdrawing from the state of Alabama. During the meeting someone yelled, "Free State of Winston." In the end they did not withdraw, but the term became a nickname for Winston County. That was Alabama hill country, and many hard-headed people lived there. Some have accused me of inheriting those genes.

I was born July 6, 1920, in a wooden house in the middle of a cotton field in Natural Bridge, a tiny mining town in northern Alabama. It got its name from a rock formation in the shape of a short bridge. It later became a tourist attraction, but the local people referred to it as the rock bridge and didn't think it was all that special.

My father was Joseph Clark White, and my mother was Ida Lewellyn Reeve (no s.) He was a farmer both before and after he was a coal miner, and she was a school teacher. I carried the Jr. after my name for many years, but dropped it a few years after my father died at age 67 of Melanoma cancer. My mother died at age 44 of Typhoid Fever. Somewhere in my ancestry there was a Cherokee Indian on my father's side of the family. I don't know whether it was a man or a woman, but I am one sixty-fourth Cherokee Indian.

Dad eventually quit mining because his body could no longer stand the strain. The miners had to go far underground and dig the coal with picks and shovels. Often the seam of coal was not thick enough to permit them to stand erect, so they had to work either on their knees or stooped. They brought the coal out in small cars that ran on narrow rails from the mine.

Their only light was from carbide lamps mounted on their caps. A lamp had two compartments. The one on the bottom held dry lumps of carbide and the top compartment held water. An exterior adjustment on top controlled the amount of water it released slowly to drip into the dry carbide. The mixture of carbide and water caused a flammable gas to form and be forced out through a small nozzle in the middle of a little round reflector in front. A small wheel near the nozzle had notches all around the circumference and rubbed against a little piece of flint when turned. Spinning that wheel with the thumb produced a spark that ignited the gas coming out of the nozzle and produced the flame that created the light for the miners. Increasing the flow of water made more gas and made the lamp burn brighter, and shutting the water off completely turned off the lamp.

They blasted with dynamite to loosen the coal so they could take it out with picks and shovels. First they drilled a hole in the coal big enough and deep enough to hold a stick of dynamite. Next they fitted a dynamite cap on the end of a long fuse and stuck the cap into a little hole in the stick of dynamite. Then they put the dynamite deep into the drilled hole. Finally they lit the fuse from the flame of a carbide lamp and huurried out of the tunnel before the fire traveled down the fuse and reached the cap. The flame from the burning fuse set off the cap, and the exploding cap detonated the dynamite. Dad said the smoke from the dynamite gave him headaches.

Visiting Winston County brought back memories of my childhood. The first thing I can remember is sitting with Dad on the front edge of the porch of a country store. We sat on the floor with our feet resting on the steps below. I asked him to buy me some candy, but he said he had only a nickel and asked me if I wanted him to spend his last nickel. I remember thinking about it a while and finally telling him to save it.

I also remember riding in a wagon loaded with furniture when we were moving from Natural Bridge to Nauvoo, Alabama. We lived there a year, and then moved to Lawrence County, Tennessee, where Grandpa White's sister and her family lived. She was married to Bob Rooker, who had a big house and farm on Fall River Road between Gum Springs and Lawrenceburg. I was five years old, and I'm told that we moved in an old borrowed truck that broke down on the way. We made the rest of the trip in a wagon.

William N. White, of Henagar, Alabama, has studied the history of the White Clan. He told me Bob Rooker was convicted in Alabama for making moonshine whiskey, and served a year in jail. After that he couldn't face his neighbors, so he sold his house and moved to Lawrence County, Tennessee, where he was not well known. Then my grandparents and my parents followed him to Tennessee, because of our relationship to his wife. We had another connection on my mother's side, because Mr. George Roberts, of New Prospect, was married to my mother's aunt

* * * * *

My maternal grandfather was English and my grandmother was Scots-Irish. They always lived near Double Springs, the county seat. Their names were Noah and Lucy Reeve, and they were farmers and schoolteachers. By the time of my visit he was in his seventies but still working his farm.

A sandy dirt road ran in front of their house, and a weather-beaten, wooden barn sat on the other side of the road and faced the house. Wooden double doors opened the middle to a hallway running through the barn. The doors were wide enough and tall enough to accommodate a two-horse wagon loaded with hay, or with enough seed cotton to make a bale.

Inside the barn, doors on each side led from the hallway into stalls and stables for the livestock. The first stall on the right had a wooden floor and served as a storage place for harness for the mules and for various pieces of equipment and small tools. All the other stalls and stables had dirt floors.

The ridgeline ran from front to back, and the tin roof formed an A when viewed from the road. The loft held hay, fodder, and corn tops for livestock feed. A built-in ladder provided access.

Two huge black walnut trees stood between the barn and the road. The walnuts had thick, shiny-green hulls at first, and when they matured they softened and turned dark brown, almost black. Once the hull was off, the nut was slightly smaller than an English walnut, and was harder to crack. Removing the hulls was a messy chore because of the dark stain that came from inside the hulls. That stain was almost impossible to remove, and Grandma Reeve sometimes used the hulls to make a dark brown dye.

The chunks of walnut meat were bigger than those in hickory nuts, and they were easier to get out of the nuts. They also had a heartier flavor than hickory nut meat, and you could fill up on walnuts fairly soon.

English ivy covered most of the house, and English sparrows nested in the ivy. The house resembled an upside down T, with the stem of the T extending to the rear of the two rooms across the front. An open porch ran across the front, and another open porch along the T in the rear. It was on the right side as you faced the house from the front.

Fifty feet straight out from the side porch Grandpa had built a springhouse that covered a good spring. It furnished all the water for the household, and it kept milk and butter cool in the summer. A pipe ran from the spring to a wooden trough where Grandpa watered the mules when he brought them in from working in the fields and before he took them out to work. The spring flowed constantly, so the trough was always full of fresh, cool water.

Along the outside edge of the back porch he had built a long bench about three feet high. He cut holes to fit two porcelain washbowls and a water pitcher, and they held the vessels in place on the bench. A community dipper rested in the water pitcher. It had a handle long enough to stick out above the top of the pitcher when the dipper was on the bottom.

The front, back, and side yards were sand. Mixed with the sand were hundreds of small stones, so smooth and shiny they looked almost glazed. Grandma had many flowerbeds and several small plants, but no grass for a lawn.

Grandpa Reeve had built the two front rooms with a puncheon floor—split logs with the flat sides up—and he built a fireplace of large flat rocks that he picked up on the farm. He prepared the house to have a place to bring his bride, and they had lived there ever since. She had been one of his students when he was a teacher, and every member of that family except Roy had been a teacher at one time or another. A high school graduate could teach in elementary schools then, and often a teacher would be only five or six years older than a student.

I liked the kitchen best. Rows of shelves held jars of jellies, jams, and preserves, plus many cans of assorted vegetables. I remembered earlier visits when Uncle Roy parched (roasted) peanuts in grandma's oven in the kitchen, with his kids and our kids sitting around asking him every few minutes how much longer before they would be ready to eat.

Roy Reeve was the only boy in the family. The girls were Alice, Eunice, Ruby, and Ida (my mother).Twin boys died when they were babies, and another girl, Pernie, died in childhood. Alice married George Robinson and later moved to Giles County, Tennessee. Eunice married Tom Bailey and lived near Jasper, Alabama. Ruby married Stacey Abner, who earned his living singing and writing gospel songs. He was a gifted singer and composer.

Ida Reeve married my father and later moved to Tennessee. They had seven children, six boys and one girl, and I was the first. My sister and I are the only ones still living in 2006.

Roy married Iris Prestige and built a home two hundred yards up the road from grandpa's house. It was square, with a wide porch on all sides. He used wooden shingles for the siding and never painted them. They had three children: R. B. Jr., Lavene, and Bessie Lou.

Uncle Roy and R. B. were avid hunters, and they had a liver-and-white Pointer named Queen. She responded to whistle and arm signals and went anywhere they directed her. She was an outstanding bird dog, and paid no attention to squirrels or rabbits when they were hunting birds. But when they left the fields and went into the tall pines, Uncle Roy gave her a signal and she switched to hunting squirrels.

When she ran a squirrel up a tree, she stood there and barked until he came and shot the squirrel. She also watched the squirrel if it jumped to another tree, and always barked at the base of the tree where the squirrel was. They could depend on her never to bark up the wrong tree, as the saying goes.

Uncle Roy hunted with a twelve-gauge, Winchester Model 12 pump shotgun. He hunted mostly quail, squirrels, and turkeys. When R. B. was a teenager, Uncle Roy bought him a gun exactly like his dad's, except it was twenty gauge instead of twelve gauge. It was considerably smaller than Uncle Roy's gun and shot a smaller shotgun shell, but they were alike in every other respect. Winchester also made a sixteen-gauge gun, but the twenty gauge was popular with women and young boys. It was light, easy to carry, and more comfortable to shoot.

I took my new rifle and went squirrel hunting with them at first light one morning. They got two or three with their shotguns, but I got nothing with my rifle. About eight o'clock Uncle Roy suggested we go back to the house before it was too late for dough biscuits. He and R. B. liked to eat biscuits before they were done, when the dough was still sticky in the middle.

About three hundred yards in front of Uncle Roy's house, across an open field, past several big trees, and across a little creek, the Overton family had an operating grist mill. A dam created a mill pond, a waterway made of wooden boards guided a stream of water from the pond to an overshot water wheel, and the turning of the wheel provided the power to turn the grindstones. As needed, Uncle Roy—or sometimes R. B.— brought a bushel of shelled corn on his shoulder and waited while Mr. Overton ground it into meal. He kept a portion of the meal as payment for the grinding.

At the appointed time, I met the Hunter brothers and rode with them back to Tennessee.

CHAPTER FIFTEEN

From the earliest greens from the garden and the first crop of spuds in late spring, to the last of the corn and peas in December, we were harvesting something most of the time. We took greens, vegetables, and fruits from the garden almost daily; and we had peanuts, apples, peaches, watermelons, cantaloupes, and roasting ears of corn from the fields. But the big jobs were cutting the sorghum cane, making the syrup, and getting in the hay, sweet potatoes, cotton, and corn.

Sweet potatoes matured in late summer. They grew in the ground, and we plowed them out with a Georgia stock plow or a one-horse turning plow. When we fished them out of the dirt, juice from the raw potatoes got all over our hands. It hardened when it dried, and soap and water would not remove it. Only hard, continuous scrubbing with coal oil eventually got it off.

When digging Irish potatoes we got our hands equally dirty, but they didn't give off the sticky juice.

We built a curing house between our home and the field, and during the winter we stored the sweet potatoes there, in one-bushel hampers. The hampers were light weight and made of slats of thin wood running up and down. The slats were about four inches wide and they didn't touch each other. Strands of thin wire encircled the hampers and held the slats in place. The hamper was round and at the bottom was about eight inches in diameter. It gradually got larger toward the top, which was 12 or 14 inches across. The design of the hamper allowed air to circulate around the stored potatoes, and that helped in the curing process.

We filled the space under the floor and inside the walls with sawdust for insulation. A fire in a small wood stove kept the potatoes from freezing

149

when it was cold outside. The potatoes dried out and cured within a couple of months, and we could then keep them several months if we made sure they didn't freeze. The insulation was so effective it had to be very cold outside before anything in the building would freeze. Next to cotton, sweet potatoes provided our best source of cash income.

We liked the sweet potatoes baked, and usually had a few in the warming closet of the stove for snacks between meals. The long skinny ones came out almost like candied potatoes if they had been cured first. Baking usually made the skin pull loose from the inside of the potato. When they were raw, we peeled and sliced the biggest ones and fried them in a skillet. Both when they were raw and after they were cured we also cut them up with a knife and ate them, as you might eat an apple.

* * * * *

When I returned from Alabama the sorghum cane was ready to harvest. We always planted a couple of acres, from which we made molasses. We called it surp or 'lasses, as did most of our neighbors. Nobody pronounced it searip except the very precise Mrs. Annie Williams, the mother of my friend Lacy Williams.

It was it a hot and disagreeable job that came at a hot and disagreeable time, the dog days of August. The cane stalks gave off a dusty white powder, and it stuck to our arms, got down our necks, and irritated our skin. We first stripped and discarded the leaf blades from the stalks and cut off the seed heads. Since the seed heads were higher than we could reach, we walked along the row with the left arm around the stalks, pulling them forward and down as we moved along the row. As we bent the cane stalks down, the heads came within reach; and we cut them off and let them fall to the ground. We later retrieved them and used them for chicken feed and for planting the following year. A seed head was a little bigger than an ear of corn, but not as long. It was dark red in color and had hundreds of little seeds on it. Thereafter, we cut the cane off at the ground and laid the stalks out in piles. Finally, we loaded the stalks into a wagon and hauled them to the sorghum mill.

We cooked the juice in a long copper pan, as we made syrup for ourselves and for other farmers. They brought their sorghum cane and stacked it near our mill in separate piles, and we made it into syrup when we got to it. We processed the cane in the order we received it, and our charge for this was a share of the syrup.

To produce the juice, we ran the cane stalks through a mill, which consisted of three iron rollers about one foot high, one big one and two smaller ones. A long pole attached to a gear turned the big roller. One end of the pole extended five or six feet from the mill in one direction, and the other end extended about fifteen feet the other way. The pole sloped downward until the long end was two feet off the ground. We hitched a mule to the low end and tied a rope from his bridle to a two by four sticking out at right angles from the high end. When we started him walking in a counter-clockwise direction, the rope led him around in a circle as he pulled the pole that turned the big roller.

An operator, usually my brother Quinton, sat at the mill and fed the cane stalks between the rollers, with the big roller on the right and the two smaller rollers on the left. When the operator placed a stalk of cane between the big roller and the front small roller, the inward rotation of the two rollers pulled the cane into the space between them. The first small roller allowed enough space to accept the big ends, and the second small roller was close enough to squeeze any remaining juice out of the canes. By the time the first stalk was well into the rollers he started another one, so he always had several stalks going through at the same time. Grooves about a quarter of an inch deep ran around all the rollers and covered the entire surfaces.

The canes were big at the bottom, up to 1 ½ inches thick. They tapered off gradually until they were the size of a pencil at the top. The operator fed new cane stalks into the rollers fast enough to keep them full.

The rollers squeezed the juice out, and the crushed cane stalks came out of the other side of the mill. From time to time the operator had to stop the mule to bring up more cane stalks and to carry off the crushings. The operator had to remember to lower his head when the low end of the pole came around, or else it hit him on the head. The pole moved slowly enough that the bump wasn't serious, but it did hurt.

Yellow jackets hung around the mill, drawn by the sweet cane juice. We tried to ignore them, and they seldom stung us. When it did happen, we put wet baking soda on the sting and it helped.

The cooking pan was about fifty feet away and downhill from the mill, so gravity took the juice to the cooking pan. It came out of the bottom of the grinder and flowed down to a collection basin. From there it went through an iron pipe to the pan, where the pipe extended about six inches over the edge of the cooker at the very end. I peeled a short section of a cane stalk and used it to plug the pipe to prevent any juice from coming out until we were ready for it.

A homemade, wood-burning furnace provided the heat to cook the syrup. It consisted of two walls three feet high and the same length as the cooking pan. The walls were as far apart as the pan was wide. The cooking pan sat on top of these two walls, leaving three feet between the ground and the bottom of the pan. A brick chimney was at one end of the furnace, and the other end was open. When the cooking pan was in place, it formed a seal between the pan and the tops of the walls and between the end of the pan and the chimney. Therefore, the firebox under the cooking pan was reasonably airtight. After the wood fire was burning well at one end of the pan, the chimney drew the heat out through the flue. On its way from the burning wood to the chimney the heat passed along the bottom of the cooking pan and kept the cane juice boiling.

Standing at the open end of the furnace and looking toward the chimney, Dad and I were on the right side doing our work. I was at the end away from the chimney, and the grinder was behind me and uphill. The raw juice came into the pan at my end, and that was where most of the fire was. We dug a trench to stand in so we wouldn't have to bend over all day.

The cooking pan was about twelve feet long, five or six feet wide, and five inches deep. It was made of thin copper, and when the pan was empty two people could move it from one place to another. Copper partitions ran from one side of the pan to within six inches of the other. The first partition was open at one side of the pan, and the next partition was open on the opposite side of the pan, and so on to the end.

The raw juice came into the pan at my end, and after it cooked a while I pushed it with a paddle to the other side of the pan. The paddle was nothing more than a piece of one inch by four inch wooden board. It had a hole bored through it in the middle near the top and slanting downward. The operator controlled the paddle with a three-foot handle inserted in the hole and anchored so it wouldn't come out. The paddle was about eight inches wide, enough to fill the width of the channels the juice followed across the cooking pan.

I placed my paddle in the first channel and pushed the juice to the other side of the pan. There was nowhere the juice could go except around the opening at the end and into the second channel, which led back across the pan toward me. Then I put my paddle at the other side of the pan in the second channel and pulled the juice back to my side of the pan. Once again there was nowhere for the juice to go except around the opening and into the third channel. By the time it came out as syrup, it had made about a dozen trips across the cooking pan.

When the juice reached the halfway point to the other end, Dad took over and kept moving it along. It took ten or fifteen minutes for the raw juice to travel up the pan and come out the other end as syrup He had a small round hole at his end of the last channel, and that's where the syrup came out. He peeled a stalk of cane, wrapped a clean cloth around it, and stuck it in the hole until he was ready to draw off more syrup. Then he got another jug, or bucket as the case might be, put his funnel in it, and filled the container

The raw juice was pale green, so at my end of the cooking pan I had to skim off an ugly green scum and throw it into a pit that we had dug for that purpose. As the juice moved up the pan—cooking all the while—the skimmings got progressively lighter in color, until at the very end they were white. Dad always worked the upper end of the cooking pan and drew off the syrup when it was ready. I worked the lower end of the pan and kept the fire going to provide the heat. He tested the syrup by holding his skimmer up and letting the cooked juice drip back into the cooker. When it ran very slowly and formed a little rope as it dripped off, he knew it was ready for the buckets or the jugs.

When he drew off the syrup in the two last compartments, he drew the juice from the adjoining compartments to replace it. At the same time, I released the raw juice into the lower end of the cooking pan and started pushing it along toward the upper end.

The skimmers had three-foot handles and were metal scoops the same width as the compartments. They had little holes in the bottom to allow the juice to go through, but not the green scum. The sides and backs of the skimmers were two inches high, and were open only in the front. In addition, my father and I each had a paddle as previously described. Dad drew off the finished syrup, either into one-gallon, amber-colored, glass jugs or into tin buckets holding one gallon each. He made good syrup and sold it during the depression for fifty cents a gallon.

The farmers used molasses mixed with sulfur as medicine. They thought this combination would cure almost anything. If we had an open wound, we soaked it in coal oil. For many other ailments, we took either castor oil or sulfur and molasses.

Sometimes we boiled molasses to make it thicker and then mixed it with popcorn to make popcorn balls, and at other times we mixed it with roasted peanuts to make peanut brittle. If we boiled it still more it formed molasses candy, but when it cooled it got so hard it was difficult to chew. When we were out of sugar we used molasses as a substitute sweetener, but it was not as good.

Most farmers dropped the mo and called it simply 'lasses.

In some areas they use a simpler method. They simply put the cane juice into a big pot and boil it until it becomes molasses, removing the "skimmings" from time to time as it boils. I saw them do that once on one episode of the Waltons television series. I suppose that would be less labor intensive, but I wouldn't know about the comparative quality of the molasses.

From time to time the subject of blackstrap molasses comes up (as compared to sorghum molasses.) I didn't know what it was, so I looked it up on the Internet and found it comes from sugar cane. The following is quoted from Yahoo, on Internet explorer.

"Blackstrap molasses is the residual liquid food obtained in the manufacturing of raw sugar. The cane juice, or mother liquor, after having been purified, is concentrated into a thick mass. As the sugar crystallizes, this mass is passed through a centrifuge which allows the mother liquor to pass through but retains the crystallized sugar. The resulting molasses is very dark and has a robust, somewhat bitter-tart flavor"

(It is) "Used in a variety of baked goods, particularly meat and vegetable dishes, as a sweetener and cooking agent. It is also widely accepted as a 'health food'. When blended with fancy molasses, it produces a cooking molasses which can be used in a number of recipies and is particularly suitable for ginger snaps, soy based sauces, licorice, canned baked beans, and fermentation systems."

I read somewhere else that it is also used as an additive to feed for cattle.

* * * * *

We planted soybeans or mung beans for hay, and occasionally we had a crop of lespedeza. Rufus (anything for a laugh) Hunter called it Leslie's deezer. We mowed it with a machine pulled by two mules, then let it lie in the sun until it wilted. Then we used a riding hay rake pulled by mules to put the hay into windrows. After drying two or three more days in the sun, we piled it up into haystacks to cure for two or three more weeks. If it rained much after we cut the hay and before we stacked it, it damaged the new hay and possibly ruined it. To a farmer, make hay while the sun shines was a meaningful expression.

The frame for a haystack was a 2 by 4 six or seven feet long sticking up into the air, with four shorter 2 by 4s nailed to it at the bottom. They stuck out in four directions and provided a foundation to hold the pole upright. We stacked the hay on and around these bottom boards and piled it higher than the pole. Once we had the hay in these stacks, the rains did less damage.

When the hay was dry enough, we loaded it into a wagon, hauled it to the barn, and stored it in the loft. We removed the frames and saved them for use another year. Sometimes we hired a hay-baling machine to pack the hay into bales. They set up the machine in the middle of the hay field and we brought the haystacks to it with the wagon.

A gasoline engine powered the baling machine. The operator packed hay into a cubicle of the machine until it was full, then stepped on a treadle that caused the compress to push the hay into the compression channel. After he repeated this process ten or twelve times there was enough hay compressed to make a bale. Each compression of the machine formed a section (hand) of hay within the bale. We could then take hay from the bale in sections and could better estimate how much hay we were feeding to the livestock at any one time. The operator put wooden blocks into the compression channel to separate the bales, adding blocks at appropriate times to make bales of uniform size. These blocks had two grooves on each side, one about 1/3 of the way down from the top and the other about the same distance from the bottom.

When a bale was compressed and another one started, an assistant inserted a strand of hay-bailing wire through the top groove in the wooden block at one end of the bale, brought it around the bale and put it through the top groove in the block at the other end. Then he pulled the two ends of the wire together and used wire pliers to twist the two ends securely together. He then took another strand of wire and tied it around the bale using the bottom grooves in the blocks.

By the time someone tied a new bale with wire, the machine was already compressing another one; and the new bale eventually pushed the old one out of the compression channel. As the bales came out the hay tried to expand, and the bailing wire got tight around the bale. The wire did not go around the blocks, so they fell away at the end and the operator reused them. At the end of the day we loaded the bales into the wagon and took them to the barn for storage.

Baled hay took less room in the barn. Whether we baled it or not depended on how much hay we had that year and how much money we could spare for the baling operation. I don't recall what it cost to have the machine do the baling, but any cash outlay was significant.

The hay-baling wire was light and strong, and we saved the used wire for many repair jobs around the farm. Some said the old Model T Ford was so easy to work on a mechanic could take a strand of hay-baling wire and a pair of wire pliers and make it climb a tree. That was an obvious exaggeration, but baling wire did serve for many temporary repairs to farm machinery, furniture, and cars.

Soybeans and Mung beans required annual planting, but a good crop of Lespedeza lasted two or three years from one seeding. All three crops took nitrogen out of the air and stored it in their roots, so the crops that followed did better than usual. Alfalfa would have been even better, but our County Agent had run tests and determined that most soils in Lawrence County were not suitable for Alfalfa.

* * * * *

I didn't remember much about the stock market crash of 1929, because I was only nine years old at the time and because we never owned any stocks. But I did remember some of the years that followed when cotton sold for four cents a pound, and when dry weather cut production to a half bale to the acre. The cheapest fertilizer cost a dollar for a 100-pound bag, and we applied only one bag to the acre because of the cost. Hired labor got four dollars for picking 1200 pounds of seed cotton, which it took to make a 500 pound bale after it was ginned.

I remember picking cotton when I was ten, in 1930. Eunice was not yet nine, Quinton was seven, Edgar was four, and Bruce was a baby. Dad and Mama had their big pick sacks, we kids had our little pick sacks, and Mama had spread a quilt on the ground in the cotton field and put Bruce on it. Mama picked all the cotton in the area near the quilt, and then moved the quilt and the baby to a new spot. She never got out of sight of the baby on the quilt, and now and then she had to stop picking to let him nurse or to change his diaper.

The cotton bolls kept opening in September and October over a period of seven or eight weeks, and we went through the field and picked the cotton three times. The cotton was whiter, fluffier, and more valuable soon after it opened. If we waited too long and rain fell on it, the cotton lost its fluffiness and bright white color, and it brought a lower price at the gin. We often had a couple of neighbors helping us pick, and Dad paid them 33 1/3 cents per hundred pounds. They usually earned 65 or 70 cents a day.

At four cents a pound, a 500 pound bale sold for twenty dollars in 1930. The fertilizer to grow it cost two dollars, the picking cost four dollars, and the ginning cost two dollars. That left twelve dollars for the cotton from two acres, or six dollars an acre. At that rate, a ten-acre cotton field produced sixty dollars in cash. We saved enough of the cottonseed to plant next year's crop and fed the rest of it to the cows. Ads in the paper offered apples for five cents a pound and cigarettes for $1.59 a carton, tax paid. A new Plymouth business coupe sold for $485, and a 2-door sedan for $510.00. A subscription to the local weekly newspaper cost a dollar a year, and the daily Nashville Tennessean cost ten dollars a year. We didn't get the Sunday edition because there was no mail delivery that day.

One day about this time a man and a woman came walking up the road toward Gum Springs. They saw Mama working in the front yard and asked her for money for food. She didn't have any money to give them but she gave them half of the cornbread she had cooked for our supper, together with a pint jar of blackeyed peas. Later we saw it all in a ditch about a hundred yards up the road where they had thrown it away. Mama was furious.

Now, in 1936, times were better. In Lawrenceburg they had started installing sewers, and things were looking up for the plumbing industry. There were public rest rooms in the basement of the court house, but many of the homes still had privies in the back yard, especially on the roads leading out of town. Now they were connecting some of these houses to sewers, local plumbers had plenty of work, and plumbers were coming from other places to work in Lawrenceburg.

One local plumber, who was the husband of a relative of ours, did so well financially that he bought a new car and took three musicians (guitar, fiddle, and accordion) on a whirlwind tour of several towns where they played for groups in restaurants and in town squares. They passed the hat to collect spending money to pay for their food and illegal booze, and they were gone three or four days. A niece of the plumber's wife went with them to sing with the band, and every time he started to talk about getting back home to his wife and kids, she plied him with more moonshine until he changed the subject. "I know not what the truth may be, I tell the tale as 'twas told to me."

The Tennessean of December 31, 1935, had a cartoon headlined, "Retiring in a blaze of glory." It showed a man labeled 1935, with a long white beard and holding boxing gloves over his head. Another man, also wearing boxing gloves, was lying on the floor. On his belly was the legend, "The depression pronounced definitely out." The price of a first-class postage stamp was up from two cents to three cents, and cotton sold for ten cents a pound.

Dad told a story about a man who was walking home from Lawrenceburg when he felt an urgent call of nature. He walked fast, hoping to make it to the woods at the edge of town. Finally he got so desperate he asked a woman working in her yard if he could use her privy in the back yard. She said yes, and he sprinted around the house toward the privy. About halfway there, her clothes' line caught him just under his chin and he landed on his back with a heavy thud.

"Oh, I'm sorry sir, I forgot to warn you about the clothes line."

"It doesn't matter, Maam. I don't think I would have made it anyway."

But farmers didn't feel the financial gains enjoyed by the plumbers and the storekeepers in town. Once again, we estimated a yield of only one half bale to the acre—five bales from our ten-acre field. Three quarters of a bale would have been an excellent yield. We started picking in early September and didn't finish until early November. The twins were eighteen months old, but both had Cerebral Palsy and needed constant attention. They took all of Mama's time, with additional help from Dad and Eunice, and this reduced our family's cotton picking potential.

Our parents didn't want us to skip school to work in the fields. But by working after school, on Saturdays, and on school holidays, and with the help of some hired pickers, we finally got it all in.

* * * * *

Picking cotton was agonizing work. The cotton bolls opened into four sections, and each section had a sharp thorn on the end. If I took the time and care to avoid the thorns I got very little done, and if I snatched the cotton out quickly the thorns pricked my fingers to above the first joint.

My fingers were raw and sore from the beginning of cotton-picking time to the end. A good cotton picker must have nimble fingers, and wearing gloves was not a practical option. We could have pulled off the bolls and let the gin separate the cotton, but the finished product would have been full of trash and the sale price would have been too low.

Our soil was poor and fertilizer was expensive, so our cotton plants were relatively short. That meant the cotton grew close to the ground, and after a while my back ached from the constant bending to reach it. When I dropped to my knees and picked from that position for a while my knees started to hurt. All day I alternated between going on my knees and stooping. Some bought leather kneepads, but they were expensive and nobody in our family ever had them. I usually picked two rows at a time to avoid dragging my sack so far. I picked with both hands on one row for a couple of feet and switched to the other row before moving on. Later in life, when I faced a tiring and difficult task, I remembered my years on the farm and kept going by thinking that any job I had to do was easier than picking cotton.

One machine at the gin removed the seeds from the cotton and another compressed the lint cotton into a bale. They wrapped each bale with burlap and secured it with steel bands. They left the burlap off the sides of the bale so the buyer could judge the quality of the cotton. All the bales were the same size, because they all went through the same compress. When there was more cotton in a bale it looked the same but they packed it tighter and it weighed more. A bale weighed approximately 500 pounds, depending on how much seed cotton the grower put through the gin. They weighed the compressed bale with a huge scale when it arrived at the platform, and that was the official weight for purposes of selling the cotton.

The brand of cotton we planted was Half-and-Half, meaning it was supposed to be half seed and half lint cotton. We never found that to be true as to weight, because we usually got 700 pounds of seed for every 500 pound bale of lint cotton.

We put sideboards on the wagon so it would hold twelve hundred pounds of seed cotton and left the wagon in the field so we could unload our pick sacks into it. We took the wagon tongue out of its socket and passed it through the spokes of a wheel and then down to the ground, with the other end extending up into the air. This gave us a place to hang the scales we used for weighing the cotton sacks.

All the pickers wanted to know how much cotton they had picked, and we needed to know when we had enough to take to the gin. So we kept an account book and a pencil by the scales, and entered the weight of each sackful that went into the wagon. We deducted the weight of the sack each time, so the cotton weights would be accurate.

The pick sacks were made of a heavy white cloth, almost as tough as canvas. Each one had a broad strap fastened to the sack in two places. A right-handed picker got into it by putting his head, right arm, and right shoulder through the opening and letting the left shoulder carry the weight. That put the right hand near the opening in the sack. Most pickers used both hands to pick and then transferred the cotton in the left hand to the right to stuff it into the sack. A left-handed picker reversed the procedure.

The part of the sack that dragged on the ground finally wore out, and we had to patch it with canvas or some other tough, long-wearing material. Just about everybody picked cotton. Little kids had small sacks, adults had six-foot sacks, and the serious pickers had nine-foot sacks.

It took fast hands to pick much cotton, and it helped to be short, so you didn't have to stoop so low to reach the cotton. In the Mississippi Delta country the cotton grew five feet tall and produced two or more bales to the acre. I have heard of people picking four hundred and fifty pounds a day in those conditions. But our cotton grew about two feet tall, and a big crop was three quarters of a bale to the acre. We couldn't afford heavy applications of fertilizer and had no way to irrigate, so we were at the mercy of the weather.

Ten years later I picked 357 pounds in one day. That was the year I was 26 years old, after I came home from the war. I was picking close to the house, the cotton was especially good, and I wanted to see how much I could do. I started at sunrise, took only fifteen minutes for lunch, and picked until dark. Alford Keener was a 250-pound-a-day man on his good days, and he was proud of it. He said 357 pounds was the most he had ever heard of in our kind of cotton. I believe all that hard physical labor when I was young helped me to be healthier in later life.

I never felt degraded because I picked cotton, cleaned out stables, or lived in a house with no indoor plumbing. My work didn't pay much, but it was as honorable as any other line. Someone wrote a song titled "I Never Picked Cotton." The song continued, "But my mama did and my daddy did and my brother did and my sister did." He took pride in refusing to do such degrading work. People who say they couldn't live like that might benefit from the experience.

The elementary schools started early in the county and then vacated for a month or six weeks during cotton-picking time. That was not long enough to get all the cotton picked, but it helped. High school started in September and went straight through until the Christmas break, except for Federal holidays. I got home from high school each day around 3:30 PM and went to the field and picked cotton until dark.

* * * * *

When we had twelve hundred pounds of seed cotton on the wagon we hauled it to the gin, but usually there was a long line of wagons and we had to wait for our turn. When we reached the head of the line, we drove the wagon under a suction arm and moved the arm around over our cotton until the suction pulled it all up into the innards of the gin. If we had packed the cotton tight by walking on it, we had to loosen it before the suction would pick it up. After they ginned the bale, we took the wagon under another chute and they dumped our cottonseed into the wagon. During the busy season it might be an all-day chore.

There were always cotton buyers at the gin. They cut a small sample out of the bale and examined it for color, cleanliness, and length of fiber. Cotton with longer fiber was more valuable and brought a higher price per pound. You could sell the cottonseed if you wished, but not many did. If you didn't want to sell the bale, you could arrange with the gin company to leave the bale there to be sold later.

Farmers depended mostly on the cotton crop and sweet potatoes for cash. They ran lines of credit for feed, seed, and fertilizer, and paid the bills when they sold the cotton. "If I have any money left this fall, " Loid Voss told me, "I'm a-gonna buy me a rifle." He wanted a Winchester single-shot .22, and it cost $5.10 from Sears Roebuck. He didn't get it that year.

* * * * *

When the ears of corn were fully mature and the corn stalk and leaves were still green, we used a sharp knife and cut the stalk off just above the top ear. We called this cutting tops. We tied them into bundles with twine, and combined the bundles to make shocks, which we left standing upright to cure in the field. After they cured, we hauled them to the barn and stored them in the loft Later we stripped the blades from the bottom part of the stalk and tied them into hands and hung the hands on the stalk just above the ear. A hand is ten or twelve leaves tied together with another leaf. We called this pulling fodder. We fed the cured fodder and tops to the mules and cows.

After it cured, fodder was too dry to handle during the day, so we worked at night to gather the hands, combine them into bundles, and haul them to the barn. The fodder usually was moist enough at night from dew so it didn't shatter when handled. We consulted the Farmer's Almanac to look for a night with a full moon

After the ears of corn were completely dry, usually in late November, we pulled the corn. This was easier than picking cotton because we could stand straighter, it went faster, and we had to go over the field only once. We drove a wagon, straddling two rows, across the cornfield. One of us went on one side and just behind, pulling the ears from two rows, one row the wagon had pushed down and the row beside it. The other one went on the other side pulling the ears from two other rows. We threw the ears of corn into the wagon as we pulled them, and when the wagon bed was full we drove to the barn and unloaded it all into the corncrib. Pulling corn required little finesse, so we usually wore gloves to protect our hands.

The easiest way to remove the ear from the stalk was to grab the ear with one hand and whack down between the ear and the stalk with the other. Our soil was thin and we couldn't afford to put fertilizer on the corn crop, so twenty-five bushels to the acre was a reasonable yield. It took only a few days to gather the corn. We took the shucks (husks) off only when we were ready to use the corn.

Peas grew and matured much faster than corn, and they were ready to harvest by the time the corn was ready. When the hulls were completely dead and dry we gathered the peas in a cotton sack and pounded them with something heavy to break up the hulls and release the peas. To do the final separation of the peas from the dead hulls, we winnowed them when a brisk wind was blowing. We poured the peas and shattered hulls from a height of five or six feet into a washtub. The wind blew the chaff away, and the heavier peas fell into the tub. We then put the peas into bags and stored them in the corncrib. Mr. Voss had a pea-thrasher machine that simplified this procedure. Since we didn't have one, we did it the hard way.

I had many noon meals of corn bread and peas. Some chopped raw onion and hot pepper sauce made it even better. We made our pepper sauce by filling a jar with red peppers and pouring vinegar into the jar. After this soaked for a few weeks, it was ready.

Peas would grow almost anywhere. The worst thing you could say about an old run-down farm was that the land was so poor it wouldn't sprout peas.

"They feed me on corn bread and peas, and I ain't a-gonna be treated this a-way," is a line from an old song about life in prison. I'm sure many prison meals consisted mainly of cornbread and peas. For the evening meal we never ate anything except corn bread and milk. Some farm families ate the cornbread with buttermilk, but I never liked it that way.

We also raised Great Northern (white) beans and blackeyed peas and stored them dry during the winter months. But we usually raised them in much smaller quantities than the whippoorwill peas that we planted between the corn rows.

Many years later when I worked in Washington for the Immigration Service I went to lunch with my boss, Don Coppock, at the Senate Cafeteria. When we sat down at the table with our trays he started to laugh and said, "Look at your tray." I had two pieces of cornbread, two cartons of milk, a slice of watermelon, and a piece of chocolate meringue pie. I told him those were my favorite foods, and when I go to a cafeteria I get what I like. He laughed some more and told me he had practically lived on corn meal mush when he was young. He was from Oklahoma.

In early December we went over the cotton field one more time to get the small bolls that opened too late to pick with the other cotton. This time we pulled the bolls off and put them in the sack and let the gin separate the bolls from the cotton and then the cotton from the seed. There wasn't enough to make a bale, and the quality was inferior anyway, so we kept that cotton for spinning thread and stuffing quilts and mattresses. Pulling the bolls required very little finesse, so we often wore gloves for that picking.

* * * * *

When the weather turned cold, one or two neighbors came to help us kill hogs. For their help, it was customary to give them a generous supply of spare ribs. I never liked this necessary chore. Killing and eating is a natural part of nature, and it happens all the time on the farm. But I always felt sorry for the animals; and I hated even to wring a chicken's neck, which was the customary way to kill one. Accordingly, I prefer not to go into the details of killing and dressing a hog. Preserving meat without refrigeration was always a problem, so we had to wait for cold weather.

We salted and smoked the hams, shoulders, and bacon in a small smoke house in the back yard. We usually sold the hams and shoulders because we couldn't afford to eat them ourselves. We made the sausage with plenty of sage and hot peppers, and cooked it and preserved it in glass fruit (mason) jars. Gravy was especially good when made after cooking country sausage.

Sometimes we had red-eye gravy. That came from cooking lean bacon in the frying pan. Mama poured a little coffee into it to give it some color on the bottom, and we didn't put in the flour and milk. We ate this with fruit and biscuits in the morning, and with dried beans or peas and cornbread at noon.

When we killed hogs, we took all the pieces of pure fat and cooked them in a big iron pot. The pot stood on three legs and we built the fire on the ground under the pot. After we rendered the lard from the fat, the remains were dry and shriveled. We called them cracklin's, and many farmers put these in corn bread to make cracklin' bread. I never liked it because it was too greasy for my taste. We saved the lard and used it during the year for making soap, for cooking, and as an ingredient in Hoover gravy.

We used the same iron pot to boil our clothes on washday. After boiling them we put them into a washtub with hot soapy water and scrubbed them against the metal ridges on a washboard. We usually made the soap at home, and it was yellow and very strong. I don't remember the exact ingredients, but hog fat, Red Devil lye, and water were the main ones. My sister recalls that the fat for soap making was usually taken from the area of the hog's entrails, and that the distasteful chore of removing this fat without cutting into an intestine was women's work. We also used Red Devil lye to add to the water for soaking grains of corn in the process of making hominy. It helped to get the hard husks off the grains and it softened the dry corn. Naturally we had to rinse it well afterwards. If we didn't have any lye, we made a substitute by draining water through wood ashes. It was weaker, but it was better than nothing.

Many years later, my friend John Giles told me a story about a man who was visiting a farmer and saw a three-legged pig walking around the yard. He asked the farmer why the pig was missing a leg, and the farmer started raving about what a fine pig it was.

"That pig saved my life twice. Once my house caught on fire and he woke me up in time to put the fire out. Another time I fell into the creek and he pulled me out. Yes sir, that is just about the finest pig I ever did see."

"But what about the missing leg?"

"Well now, when a pig is as fine as that pig is, you wouldn't want to eat him all at once."

* * * * *

After the crops were harvested we rented a riding stalk cutter from Mr. Voss and chopped up the old dead stalks of corn and cotton. That machine had two big wheels and a rotating drum between them that rolled along over the ground. The drum had several blades, so as it rolled along the row of dead stalks it pushed down the dead stalks and chopped them into pieces eight inches long. That made the stalks decay faster over the winter and made it easier to plow them under the next spring when we turned the land. We paid him fifty cents a day to rent the stalk cutter.

We spent the rest of December cutting, hauling, and splitting firewood and cook wood, mending fences, and doing repairs around the house and barn.

* * * * *

Each kid hung up a sock for Santa Claus, but we all knew in advance what we would get. When a neighbor asked one of us what we expected for Christmas, we answered, "Apples and oranges and candy." That was the standard stocking stuffer for years: two apples, two oranges, and a few pieces of candy. Yet Christmas morning was a treat for us. We were thankful for what we got, and we looked forward to it with eager anticipation. We needed no names on the socks: A kid could take any sock and get exactly the same as the others, and none of our neighbors' kids fared much better.

The Hunters and the Keeners usually made a Christmas gun, some loud bang, for the Fourth of July and for Christmas. Sometimes they placed a stick of dynamite in the top of a tree and exploded it by shooting a rifle bullet into it. I never saw them do it, but heard them tell about it.

* * * * *

We had no parties, no celebrations, and no rituals for New Year's eve, but it was an occasion to look back over the year. The crop had been poor because of the prolonged dry spell, but the price of cotton was up and Dad had finally received his World War I Veteran's bonus. President Roosevelt vetoed the legislation, citing budget problems. But congress passed it over his veto, probably looking forward to the next election. I never knew how much Dad got, but it was probably close to the minimum, which was reported to be sixty dollars. Most of the money had gone to pay the annual interest on the mortgage and to pay off medical debts incurred because of the problems the twins had. I got my new .22 rifle out of layaway on my sixteenth birthday, and that made my year.

My brother Bruce told me a story many years later that illustrated the life of a farmer during the depression:

"A man farmed most of his life and finally retired when he was 75 years old. He sat around the country store for weeks, whittling and chewing tobacco, until he became bored. Finally the storekeeper said he had too many hammer handles in stock and suggested the retiree buy a dozen and try to re-sell them to some of his friends. He sold them all the first day and came back and bought another dozen. He sold them all again the second day and told the storekeeper he wanted to buy another dozen."

"What are you charging for them?"

"Fifty cents."

"But you pay me seventy-five cents. It costs you a quarter every time you sell one."

"Yeah, I know. But it beats farmin'."

* * * * *

CHAPTER SIXTEEN

I knocked on the door of the tiny house near the Gum Springs Baptist Church. Several years had gone by since I lived in the neighborhood, and I had come back for a short visit. I had always admired Mr. Joe Voss, and had learned from neighbors that he sold his big farm and divided the money among his twelve children. He kept only enough to buy this modest home for himself and his second wife, Lessie. He had been taking an afternoon nap, but he got up quickly and greeted me warmly. Lessie was ordinary looking, a little heavy, and at least 20 years younger than her husband. But she seemed devoted to him and content with her situation.

He was seventy-something years old, six feet tall, and 180 pounds. With his close-cropped gray hair, gray-blue eyes, and intelligent look, he could have put a black robe over his blue overalls and passed as a federal judge. Looking at him reminded me of the old law-school joke that a judge should have gray hair and hemorrhoids: The gray hair to give him a look of distinction, and the hemorrhoids to give him a look of concern.

He was friendly as usual, and we had a pleasant visit for two hours. I told him I had admired him more than any other man in the community, except for my own father and grandfather. His children all called him Paw and their mother Maw. He lived to be 85, and Lessie lived 15 or 20 years after he died. I don't think she ever re-married.

This visit brought back memories of the Voss family and of my other friends and neighbors in the community.

Mr. Voss had always been quietly proud, but never pompous—-self assured, but never arrogant. He married Della Stancil at a young age, and they raised twelve children. Della died in 1939, and he married Lessie a couple of years later. He had one of the largest farms in the neighborhood and more farm equipment than anyone else.

He was a Jack of All Trades: farmer, blacksmith, barber, brick mason, musician. When some part of one of his machines broke he made a new part to replace it.

Neighbors brought their horses and mules to his blacksmith shop for shoes. When I was younger I watched in wonder as he put new shoes on a mule. He pumped the overhead bellows to make the fire hotter until a piece of iron in the forge became fiery red. He hammered the iron on the anvil until he shaped it into a shoe, then heated it red again and punched holes in it for the horseshoe nails. He trimmed a hoof with a drawing knife and shaped the new shoe until it fit. He cooled the new shoe in water, and nailed it on the hoof. He set the horseshoe nails so they went into the hoof about an inch and then came out the side before reaching the tender part, then he crimped them so they wouldn't pull out later.

He kept a set of barber's tools and gave haircuts to all of his boys, as well as to some of his neighbors. He built the brick fireplace and chimney for our house and for one or two others. He owned a fiddle and played simple country tunes for pleasure.

The Voss farm consisted of more than a hundred acres, and it joined Grandpa's farm on the North. Some years, when his older boys were still at home, he rented more acreage from Old Man Crum, about a half mile away. They had a big barn a hundred yards behind the house, with a long shed on each side. They had a drill for planting hay seed, a corn shelling machine, a cream separator, a hay rake, a hay bailer, a stalk cutter, a pea thresher, and a scythe with a cradle for harvesting wheat, which they took to be ground into flour. They always ate biscuits for breakfast, and with fourteen mouths to feed, they used a lot of flour. They all wanted butter for breakfast with their biscuits and syrup, so Mrs. Voss spent many hours on the back porch churning for butter.

Sometimes Mr. Voss helped her churn when he was not working in the fields. They usually churned three times a day, and in the summer when houseflies were everywhere she held a small branch in her hand as she churned. The leaves on the branch moved the air enough to help shoo the flies away from the churn. Because of the nearness of the barn and the number of livestock, houseflies were always a problem.

My mother died of Typhoid Fever at age 44, no doubt infected by disease-carrying houseflies. They were so numerous it was impossible to keep them out of the house. All the farm families had the same problem because of the proximity of the barns. When we got ready to eat, we took towels and tried to shoo as many as possible out of the kitchen before we sat down. We had screens on our doors but they usually had holes in them the flies could easily get through. After the noon meal (dinner) we usually rested a half hour before going back into the fields. I used to crawl under the bed to take a short nap, because the flies wouldn't go under there.

Every farm family had a churn, usually made of some kind of crockery or of wood. It held four or five gallons, and it had a lid with a hole in the middle and a stick that looked something like the handle of a broom with a dasher on the bottom. That was made of two thin wood slats crossing each other and both attached to the end of the stick. First they put the clabber milk into the churn, then the dasher. Finally they put the round stick through the hole in the lid and fitted the lid on top of the churn. The operator then churned the milk by pounding the dasher up and down, using the handle that stuck out of the top of the churn.

The milk had to form into curds, or clabber, before they could churn it to make butter. After twenty or thirty minutes of churning, butter formed on top of the milk, leaving buttermilk in the churn. Buttermilk is low in fat, because the butter has been churned out of it. Most families had butter presses to shape the loose butter into round cakes. Some presses made a design on the cakes of butter, such as a star or a cloverleaf.

They needed plenty of butter for fourteen people, and had to use all their sweet milk to make butter I think they had buttermilk with their cornbread at night because that's all they had left. Mr. and Mrs. Voss spent many hours on the back porch each week pounding that clabber milk in the churn.

The cream separator was like a round metal tub standing on four legs. It was two feet in diameter, and the action part was a spinning cone that filled the tub at the bottom and tapered down to a point at the top. They turned this cone with a crank and a gear. When the cone was spinning fast they poured milk on the tip and allowed it to run down the sides, a distance of perhaps eighteen inches from top to bottom. The centrifugal force of the spinning cone threw the lightest part of the milk outward, and caused it to come out first.

Since the cream and the whey didn't weigh the same, one stayed on the cone longer before being thrown off, and the whey and the cream came out of different spouts. They fed the whey to the hogs. I'm not sure what they did with the cream. I suppose they either sold it to the creamery in Lawrenceburg or put it in the churn with the clabber milk and churned it into butter.

* * * * *

Mr. Voss raised wheat and cut it himself. The scythe had a sharp blade four or five feet long that curved forward from the back to the tip. It had a round, curved wooden handle five feet long, with a 90 degree hand hold at the end and another about halfway to the blade. A cradle mounted on the blade consisted of horizontal wooden slats running above the blade and parallel to it. Mr. Voss swung the blade parallel to the ground and cut a swath of wheat as wide as the blade was long.

The force of the swing held the stalks of wheat in place on the cradle, and he completed the swing by turning the tip of the blade upward. This motion caused the stalks of wheat to fall together to the bottom. He then took this little sheaf of wheat stalks and put it on the ground. Before nightfall someone collected these, bound them into larger sheaves, and stacked them with the heads of wheat pointing away from the ground. He left them that way until they were dry enough, then separated the wheat kernels from the stalks and had them ground into flour.

On the farms where they have huge wheat fields they have machines to mow the fields, remove the wheat from the stalks, and sometimes put the wheat into bags and compress the straw into bales. But none of the farms in our area planted enough wheat to afford machinery like that.

* * * * *

In front and just to the left of the house he had an orchard of perhaps twenty fruit trees. There were early and late bearing peaches, three or four kinds of apples, and two or three kinds of plums. Mr. Voss told the neighbors to take anything they wanted, so long as they could eat it all at the time. But he didn't want anybody taking it away by the basketful without making prior arrangements.

Of the twelve Voss kids, only two were girls. From the oldest down they were: Eunice, Elbert, Ollie, Alvin, Loid,(sic) Roy, Ezra, Allen, Lorene, Howard, Dennis, and Ottis. Ollie and Lorene were girls, and all the others were boys. Eunice Voss was the only man I ever knew with that name.

They had beds in just about every room, and the parents slept in a double bed in the living room. The upstairs was one big room, with several beds for most of the boys.

Allen was a few months younger than I was, and Ezra was a year or two older. My sister said that the youngest, Ottis, had no official name until he was almost of school age. A common superstition was that no new babies would be born until after the last one was named. After twelve kids I suppose Mrs. Voss was ready to try almost anything.

Allen was the Don Juan of the family, and most girls liked him. He parted his hair in the middle, took pride in his appearance, and was a good athlete in high school. He never cared much for hard work and usually looked for ways to make money without sweating too much. After the war, he bought a clean, 4-door 1941 Plymouth and operated his own taxicab in Lawrenceburg.

Allen spent six years, off and on, in high school. His three passions were basketball, football, and girls, not necessarily in that order. His two extra years in school probably were to milk the last possible semester of athletic eligibility out of the rules.

His graduating class voted him most athletic. He played forward on the basketball team, but the football coach assigned him to play blocking back instead of running back, and he usually had to block for Bill Willard or some other runner instead of carrying the ball himself. He got to catch a pass occasionally, but he didn't get as much publicity and glory as the regular ball carrier got.

He was popular with girls, and it may have been partially because he liked them so much. He had even features but not pretty-boy good looks, and women were fascinated by his natural arrogance and self confidence. He never had any doubt that he would win, no matter what the game or the competition.

Allen first married one of the Tucker girls, but she died of leukemia while he was away in the army. I think he had a couple of marriages later. I heard he had one child, a boy, and that his older brother Alvin raised him. Alvin and Anna adopted him after the boy reached legal age.

A few years earlier, Alvin and Anna had a son named Kinnard, who died of Diphtheria before he was old enough to go to school. They were devastated by his death and almost lost interest in living. They had no other children until they adopted Allen's boy. Alvin later worked for years as a barber in a shop in Lawrenceburg. He was probably the most handsome of the Voss boys, and I considered Roy and Allen to be second and third.

The most unusual member of the family was Ezra. He was six feet two and thin. His pants had a thirty-two inch waist and a thirty-two inch inseam. In his late teens he got an expensive ($18), three-piece, custom-made suit with an extra pair of pants. From a small sample of material, he selected a thick gray plaid, but when the suit was delivered, it turned out to be suitable for the coldest weather but too hot for warm weather. It cost too much to leave at home, however, so he wore it even when it was too warm.

He had a hump in his back near the base of his neck, and nobody knew what caused it. His face bulged slightly on both sides of the bridge of his nose, perhaps because of some glandular condition. His hair was black, and he wet it with water and combed it straight back.

Ezra's eyes were white on the outside and black in the middle, with no Iris; and they moved from side to side like a metronome ticking off one-second intervals. The left eye was almost blind; and when he read a book he held it within six inches of his face and turned his head to the left, so his right eye looked straight at the print.

David Hunter told me years later that he and Ezra bought a young steer from Dad once and planned to butcher it and sell the meat in Lawrenceburg. Ezra was going to "knock it in the head" with a sledge hammer, which was as humane a way as any other. David was holding a rope on one side and Dad was holding a rope on the other side to keep the steer's head still so Ezra could make a well-placed blow. Ezra had his head cocked to the left as usual so he could look straight at the steer with his better right eye.

"Do you always hit where you look? Dad asked him. "I shore do," replied Ezra. "Then you better get somebody else to hold this rope", Dad replied, "'cause you're lookin' straight at me."

He graduated from high school, but he couldn't see well enough to drive a car or make the high school basketball team, two great disappointments in his life.

"I'm a-gonna git my diploma," he told me once, "and then when I ask for work can say I'm a high school graduate. Then I can git me a job whur all I hafta do is put a pencil behind my year." He demonstrated by putting his forefinger next to his head over his right ear.

He pronounced his name Ez' ruh, and so did his mother. Everybody else called him Ezry, including his father. He always called me White.

One day he was standing in front of a mirror combing his hair. "White," he said to me, "if you could saw a couple of inches off of my height, take this hump out of my back, and give me two good eyes, I'd be a damn good lookin' man." I wasn't going to argue with him.

Ezra thought I was his best friend, probably because I treated him better than anybody else except his mother. He did and said some things that annoyed me, but I considered his handicap and tried to conceal my irritation. When someone lit a cigarette in his presence, Ezra was quick to say "Gimme a smoke." He rarely saw anyone smoking a ready roll, which is what we called a factory-made cigarette. But he could roll Country Gentleman tobacco in brown paper as well as anyone. He licked the edges of the paper to make it stick together and twisted the end so the tobacco wouldn't spill out. He struck a match on the outside right leg of his pants, held it between his right thumb and forefinger, and cupped his hands around the flame to protect it from the wind while he lit the cigarette. He did that routinely, whether the wind was blowing or not. When he smoked he twisted his face around to the right so the cigarette was pointing to the right and up.

He liked Coca Cola, and he always tilted the bottle up and pressed his lips together so he had to suck hard on the bottle to get out a small amount. Sometimes he put peanuts into the bottle and sucked them out with the coke. I asked him once why he did that, and he said he just loved to suck it out of the bottle.

Ezra had strong opinions even when he had limited knowledge of a subject. I knew how to pronounce "was" as well as the next person, but when I stressed it at the end of a sentence it was natural for me to say he wuz, she wuz, or I wuz. Most of the other people I knew said it the same way. Ezra told me one day I shouldn't say I wuz. He said the correct word is I were. He wasn't talking about the subjunctive either, because at that time neither of us had ever heard of it. I didn't argue with him, because it would have been a waste of time. Crawford James once said he would just as soon argue with a signpost as with Ezra. I assumed that some English teacher would set him straight later in school.

Ezra didn't get that tendency from either parent, because they were not that way. But Roy also had some of it in him. One day I heard him explaining the difference between the Navy and the Marines to his younger brother Ottis. "The Navy goes on top of the water, Ottis," Roy said, holding his hand palm down and moving it up, over, and down to illustrate. "The

Marines go under the water, Ottis," he continued, moving his hand down, across, and up. As ignorant as I was, I knew the difference between a marine and a submarine, but Roy was older, and I didn't want to start an argument.

During the early years of World War II, Ezra married Doris Keener, one of Dal Keener's daughters. She was beautiful, and most people were surprised when she married Ezra. But they say when the gods close a door they always open a window. They closed a door on Ezra when they robbed him of the good looks he craved, but they opened a window when they gave him extraordinary male endowments.

They had two children, first a beautiful little girl and then a boy who had eyes exactly like Ezra's. In 1947 they moved to Auburndale, Florida, and she worked at night in a restaurant in Winter Haven while Ezra worked in the orange groves during the day. They lived in a big canvas tent that he bought for $100 and set up on a vacant lot owned by Shirley Taylor, a friend from Tennessee.

One night after work Doris got a ride home with a co-worker who went too fast around a sharp curve, lost control of the car, and crashed into a telephone pole. The impact broke her neck, and she died a few days later.

Soon after that I loaned Ezra fifty dollars. I was married by then, and my wife was not thrilled, because she didn't like him. She said I would never get my money back, and she was right. About two months later, Ezra called me from a nearby town and wanted to borrow three hundred dollars more so he could buy a heating oil business. I told him I didn't have three hundred dollars, but he asked me to borrow it so I could loan it to him. I told him I wouldn't go into debt to finance a venture that neither of us knew anything about. He was obviously annoyed, and never called or saw me again.

Many years later Ezra ran a concession stand in Jasper, Alabama, sponsored by an organization to assist the visually impaired. David Hunter told me this in 1995 when I visited a Hunter-Keener family reunion in Lawrenceburg. I don't know what happened to his children, except that my brother Quinton said he heard the boy became a professional wrestler. A few years ago I heard that Ezra had died.

* * * * *

Eunice Voss married Nellie Hunter and had several children. He was chubby, to say the least, and lost his teeth by age forty. Their oldest son, Neil, was a handsome young man and made a lot of money selling aluminum ware at home parties. He married a daughter of the minister of the local Church of the Nazarene. They built a beautiful home, with much marble and slate, on Fall River Road a mile from Lawrenceburg. Neil died at an early age, and Alvin Voss bought the house and lived there until he died.

Elbert Voss was thin and frail, and I don't know what happened to him. His sister Ollie moved away and we lost track of her.

In the late 30's Mr. Voss bought a new International pickup truck, and Loid used it to visit a girl who lived on the other side of Lawrenceburg. Loid was also small and thin. They finally married and moved to a little farm a couple of miles away. He worked at one time at the Manhattan Project at Oak Ridge, Tennessee. I don't think they ever had any children, and he died before he was fifty.

Roy Voss used his share of the sale of the home place to buy farm land on the other side of Fall River Road from the Gum Springs school and church. He became a brick mason and built a brick home there. I suppose he learned the trade from his father. Roy also died at a comparatively young age.

I don't know much more about Lorene, Howard, Dennis, or Ottis, except that Howard had an impediment in his speech, and I had to listen carefully sometimes to understand everything he said.

* * * * *

The Voss family had a Victrola and several records. The needles were designed to play only one record, because they were so soft they wore out. But they turned the needle around and played one more, to wear out the other side of the needle and get the maximum use from it. They couldn't sharpen them again, because there wasn't enough metal left. The sound was tinny because it was not electric, but it was better than nothing at all. The thing I remember best about that Victrola was Uncle Dave Macon and his son Doris playing the banjo and singing On the Dixie Bee Line, a song about driving a Henry Ford car on a new highway. They had a couple of other records that we thought were funny, but it would be politically incorrect to describe them.

Mr. Voss called Dad Joe Cephas, and sometimes just Cephas, possibly because he printed Joe C. White on our mail box. Mr. Voss never asked where Dad was. Instead he asked, "Whur's ole Cephas at?" How he came up with Cephas I don't know. Webster's Dictionary mentions a Cephas from Greek Mythology, who was King of Ethiopia and placed among the stars after his death. There is a constellation by that name in the Northern Hemisphere, but I'm sure Mr. Voss knew nothing about Astronomy or Greek Mythology.

There is a reference to a Josephas in the bible, but I never saw Mr. Voss in church, and I never saw a Bible in his home, although he had strong moral principles. He sometimes referred to The Almighty, but never to God or Jesus. I suppose Mr. Voss had known someone named Cephas at one time, and the name stayed with him.

My sister is serious about religion, and once when I was at her home I looked for the name in her Dictionary of the Bible. According to that book, Cephas was the name first given to Simon, or Simon-Peter, who was one of the Apostles. Cephas means stone in the Aramaic language, one of the languages in the original writings that later became the Bible. The Ancient Greek language was also used extensively in those writings, and in Ancient Greek, Peter means stone. That Apostle eventually became known simply as Peter.

The Vosses came from Winston County, they were republicans, and they hated Franklin D. Roosevelt. They grumbled when the New Deal program caused them to plow up some of their cotton if they had planted more than their allotment. But they still accepted the money from the subsidy. They also resented the "high falutin" way Roosevelt spoke on the radio and the jaunty way he tilted his long cigarette holder up into the air. Eunice Voss always called him Rosie. "I'm tellin' you," he said, "Rosie's gonna 'clare war so he can git elected agin."

CHAPTER SEVENTEEN

The James family worshipped FDR as much as the Voss family hated him, and Crawford James often needled Ezra by saying he wished they would make FDR King. The Jameses gave him credit for every good thing that ever happened, and the Vosses blamed him for everything that went wrong.

In the mid-30's, Frank and Frances James lived on a hilltop across a little valley from Oak Hill Baptist Church. The church had no well on the property, and when they had all-day programs people walked down one hill and up the other to get water from the well on the James place. The house was big and unpainted and, like most of the houses in the neighborhood, had seen better days. They had an underground storm cellar by the road in front of their house, and they went into it at any sign of a storm. It served also as a storage place for turnips, apples, and canned goods of all kinds.

All the James children were thin like their father and tall like their mother. The oldest was Malcolm, who was twenty-something and had a tendency at that time to drink and get belligerent on occasion. Next came Fausner, a girl, and then Crawford. Donna was next after Crawford, and Mrs. James insisted that Crawford go everywhere with Fausner and Donna as a protector and chaperone. Two younger boys, Solon and Edsel, rounded out the family.

Mr. James planted his rows of cotton closer together than any other farmer in the neighborhood. I asked him once why he did that.

"If ye put yer rows clost," he told me, "ye git more cotton."

Solon James married P. D. Webb, the twin sister of D. R. Webb from Revilo. They never had any children, and the marriage lasted only a few years. They went to Detroit and worked for a while, and I have no idea why they separated. I don't think either of them ever remarried. After P. D. became an adult she started calling herself Pansy.

During World War II Mr. & Mrs. James sold the farm and moved to a big house near Lawrenceburg in the Crowder Field subdivision, so named for a Dr. Crowder, who once owned the land. Several of the adult children lived with them. Fausner married Charley Price, and they had a small store on the edge of the development. It had a minimum of shelf space and not much merchandise, so I doubt that it was profitable. They had living accommodations in the back, however, and that saved them rent.

Crawford and Malcolm worked for a long time at a Consumer's Service gasoline station nearby. Their primary duties were changing tires, cleaning windshields, checking oil, and pumping gas. "I'd like to try my luck someplace else," Crawford told me once, "but I can't leave my job."

* * * * *

Mrs. Hunter was already a widow when I first knew the family in the early 30s. Her children were Wesley, Harley, Nellie, Rufus, David, Alford, and Eunice. There may have been another girl, Euvie, but I never knew her. Another boy, Charlie, had died earlier. The family came from Addison, Alabama, not far from Double Springs, where my maternal grandparents lived.

The Hunters lived west of us, about a quarter of a mile in front of our house. An old wagon road went from Grandpa White's house through the woods to the Hunter place. It may have been a logging road at one time. When the Hunters had occasion to go into Lawrenceburg, they went on a more direct route from their house west to Prosser Road and turned right past the Rush Beard farm and Brother Speakman's farm. Prosser Road intersected Highway 43 near the Doctor Leo Harris mansion just south of Lawrenceburg.

Harvey Keener's house was two hundred yards farther down the road from ours. There was another wagon trail that started from beside his house and ran between his field and the woods to a point about even with the Hunter place. At that point you could turn right and follow along between the woods and the field until you reached the Hunter home. Just after you turned right the trail crossed a little stream; and just beyond the stream the Hunters had built a small weaner house on the left, for a child to live in temporarily when he or she married. The newlyweds usually lived in the weaner house only until they could do better.

The Hunters had a Model A Ford car, their only outward sign of prosperity except for a big, battery-powered Philco radio. One year Wesley and Harley were going to Addison to visit relatives, and Dad paid them to take Mama and a couple of us kids to Double Springs to visit our grandparents. I had never ridden in a finer car. Wesley and Harley soon married and moved out of the household. Nellie married Eunice, the oldest Voss boy, and Rufus married Estella Sisk. That left David, Alford, and Eunice at home.

Alford was overweight. I once saw him cut raw onions into bite-sized pieces and pile as many on his plate as it would hold. Then he poured red-eye gravy over them and ate the whole thing with nothing to go with them, not even bread. He liked to eat all kinds of wild game, and especially doves.

In the spring only one person at a time could run the turning plow because they had only one team of mules, so David and Alford alternated. When Alford was plowing David went out to hunt doves. Dave usually brought home the meat, and both of them were happy.

David could put a blade of grass or a straw to his lips and whistle just like a hen quail. He used this ability to call up and shoot male Bob Whites in the spring during mating season. We all thought the male was like a rooster who mated once with the hen and that was all that was necessary to hatch out a brood of babies. I learned later that the male Bob White relieves the hen on the nest to give her a chance to eat. Nobody worried much about the game laws or closed seasons then.

A wooded area extended from the road in front of our house to the Hunter place. When the breeze was from that direction, we could sit on our porch at night and hear Rufus playing a banjo on his front porch. Nobody seemed to know who owned that wooded property, and we all thought it was somebody "up north." The Keener twins, Wesley and Leslie (Hig and Buck) eventually bought it.

* * * * *

When I was fourteen or fifteen, David and Rufus hunter, Norman Keener, and I went to a big creek about five miles away to seine for fish. We didn't have a regular seine, which would have been made of cotton cords; so we took a roll of chicken wire instead. It got heavy after a couple of miles, but nobody else wanted to carry it. I finally agreed to lug it all the way there if they would bring it back.

When we got to the creek, we learned it had been raining upstream and the creek was out of its banks with rushing, muddy water. We stood around a few minutes trying to decide what to do. Finally Rufus said he didn't want to come all this way for nothing, so why didn't we try it on the side of the creek, in the eddy water. David and Norman said no, but I finally agreed to try it with him, since it took at least two to handle the seine. So we took the wire and stepped off into the eddy water, and it was up to our noses. That ended the fishing trip.

I didn't have to carry the wire back, but they didn't either. They hid it behind a big log in the woods, and never went back for it. For years after that Rufus mentioned eddy water from time to time, and we had a big laugh.

Alford eventually moved to Lawrenceburg to live, David married Helen Wilson, and Eunice married Hig Keener. They built a house across the road from Grandpa White's farm on the land that Hig and Buck bought. David worked in Birmingham, Alabama during the war, and worked in Detroit, Michigan, many years afterwards. They moved back to Lawrence County when he retired. They have a son, Ronnie, who is a doctor, and had a married daughter, Debbie Calvert, who lived near them, but who is now deceased.

Debbie had one son, Lee, who is the apple of David's eye. Lee also loves to hunt and fish, and he is a crack shot with a rifle and pistol. He is married now and lives north of Lawrenceburg between Ethridge and Summertown.

David was the most active hunter in the neighborhood, and he especially liked to hunt squirrels with a 22 rifle. Squirrels were not so plentiful then as they are now, but he knew a place in the Dunn hills where there were many hickory trees and where he usually found squirrels. I once saw a half dozen squirrels hanging on the Hunter back porch, and they all had 22 bullet holes through the heads. Squirrels are tough to kill, and if you shoot one through the body it will run off and hide before it dies. David would never shoot one unless he thought he could put the bullet in the head.

David told me years later that once in Birmingham during World War II he and a friend stood in line an hour to each buy their limit of one box of rifle cartridges. That was a bonanza for them, because ammunition was hard to find and the merchant was spreading his supply among his customers. David went squirrel hunting with those two boxes and in one day killed 51 squirrels with 91 shots. He and his friend had squirrel meat in their freezers for a long time.

Some people object to eating squirrels or other animals. Our nephew-in-law, Jeff Black, and his wife own four restaurants and he has the answer to that argument: "If God hadn't intended for us to eat animals, he wouldn't have made them out of meat."

Estella Sisk married her husband, Rufus Hunter, when she was sixteen years old and he was twenty one. She always called him Roefus, and he called her Stellar, as did most of the neighbors. They had two children, lived together sixty years, and obviously had a great marriage. They had another baby later in life, but it died. Once I heard Mrs. Hunter say Rufus borrowed and wasted twenty-five dollars to take Stella to Nashville on their honeymoon.

Rufus and Stella Hunter lived in the weaner house after they married and before they had children. The house had a living room, a kitchen, and a bedroom. They never painted it. The siding was 1 by 6 wooden boards running vertically, and they sealed the siding by nailing 1 by 2 slats over the cracks between the boards. I believe they call that board-and-batten construction. As usual, the bathroom was out the back door. Rufus referred to Diarrhea as the back-door trots.

Early in their marriage, Rufus and Stella bought a farm a half mile behind the Harvey Keener house. They named their two children Willard and Sibyl. After he grew up, Willard went to Mississippi to live, married, sired two children, and eventually died before he was fifty. Sibyl married an agriculture major at Ohio State University who later taught at a college in Ohio.

In addition to his corn and cotton, Rufus planted a small plot of tobacco one year. Tobacco was labor intensive, and Rufus spent many hours hoeing and weeding and pulling suckers off the plants. He also had to pick tobacco worms off the plants every day. "I made me some good money offen that little patch uv t'baccer," he said later, laughing. "They wuzn't much uv it, but it shore wuz good."

He had an old mule that was as slow as molasses. Always looking for a laugh, Rufus named him Lightning. One day he was leading him along the road in front of our house, going to have Mr. Voss put new shoes on him. Rufus was in front pulling on the rope, trying to get him to go faster, and Lightning was holding back. "Hey Rufus!" my brother Quinton yelled at him, "If you would lay him down on his side he would drag easier."

Rufus and Stella sold that farm in the early 50's and bought thirty acres on the Fall River Road, about a mile toward Lawrenceburg from Gum Springs. It was across the road from the farm owned by Bob Rooker, who was married to Grandpa White's sister. They built a little red-brick house with indoor plumbing for $6,000.00. They farmed the land for a while, then Rufus worked in a gas station long enough to retire on Social Security.

They raised hogs for extra income. Once or twice a week he took a couple of empty barrels to Lawrenceburg in his pickup truck and the creamery filled them with whey, which was a by-product of the butter-making process. It didn't cost him much, and his hogs grew fat on it, along with some other feed.

In the mid-eighties they sold that thirty acres and moved into a 2-bedroom apartment in a big complex in Lawrenceburg that Wesley Hayes had built. Wesley and Stella had been classmates in elementary school, and he gave them first choice of all the apartments when he was ready to accept tenants. They spent much of their time at the local Senior Center in Lawrenceburg and helped with the Center's activities. Rufus died in 1989 at the age of eighty-one. Stella continues to live there and work with the Senior Center. They both were sweet, loving people, and I don't know anyone who had anything against them.

Rufus could see humor in almost any situation. One day when I was about 14 we were watching a small plane fly over, a rare occurrence in our neighborhood. Air mail was something new at the time, and I dreamed of becoming an air-mail pilot. As the plane went by I asked Rufus if he thought it was a mail plane.

"Don't think so," he said with a grin. "That's just the wheels a-hangin' down."

CHAPTER EIGHTEEN

Mrs. Hunter and Mrs. Keener were sisters. Ortons before they married. The Keener children were Dal, Callie, Harvey, Alford, and the twin boys, Wesley and Leslie. They were all first cousins to the Hunter kids. Dal married a Kobeck, and they had eleven children. Callie married Dallas Flippo, and Harvey married Pearl Sisk, an older sister of Stella Hunter. Wesley (Hig) married Eunice Hunter and Leslie (Buck) married one of the Whittaker girls.

Dal Keener and his wife had eleven children. He was tall and lean, and bent his body forward from the hips when he stood or walked. I could recognize him as far as I could see him, just from the way he bent forward. I have no idea why he did that, because he didn't seem to have any physical disabilities. His son Jim Keener looked like a clone of Dal and walked the same way. His brother Alford had a similar mannerism, but not so pronounced.

Dal liked honey. If a swarm of bees flew by, he followed them and tried to find where they landed so he could collect the bees in a hive. He often stood around watching bees gather nectar and pollen and trying to see which way they went when they took off for the hive.

A worker bee can go directly from the last flower to the hive with no turns or detours, and a bee line meant the shortest route between two points. The term was so commonplace that when they named a new highway the Dixie Highway, it was so long and straight many people referred to it as the Dixie Bee-Line highway.

When Dal saw a bee head for the hive he looked for landmarks and followed them, looking for signs of a beehive in a hollow tree. Sometimes he put out sugared water to entice bees and followed them when they left for the hive. When he found a bee tree, he put on protective netting and either cut the tree down or climbed the tree to get the honey.

Dal also liked chili, and now and then the Keeners and the Hunters got together and cooked a big pot of it. Dal called it a chili run. They put one of the kids on a mule and sent him to the store to get a big box of soda crackers, and it was a family social event. I never had a chance to eat any of it, but I understand it was mostly beans, canned pork sausage, and chili powder. David Hunter told me years later that it wasn't as good as what he made later, because back then they didn't have the money for the good ingredients

Two of Dal's daughters married during the war. Dorothy married A. C. Springer, from Fall River, and Doris married Ezra Voss. Ezra couldn't go to war because of his eyes, and A. C. couldn't go because one leg was shorter than the other, causing him to bob up and down when he walked.

Before the war, A. C. had a job measuring cotton fields for one of the New Deal Agencies. Each farmer had an allotment limiting the number of acres he could plant in cotton. If he stayed within his limitation the government gave him a subsidy payment. If he planted too many acres the government paid him nothing. A. C. went to a farm, measured the cotton field, and certified that the farmer had not planted too much. If he had, A. C. showed him exactly how much of his crop he had to destroy to be certified for his subsidy payment.

When I came home from the war in late 1945, A. C. and Dorothy were living in the weaner house on the Hunter farm, and they lived there several years. They never had any children. He had two strokes not far apart and died in the mid-nineties.

* * * * *

The big tract of woods in front of our house extended a half mile up the road. It went two hundred yards beyond the Voss house and all the way to the Abercrumbie home, which was on the left side of the road next to a small stream. We used to find Indian arrowheads in a little valley a hundred yards from our front porch.

Every winter someone set fire to the woods. The fire cleared the small underbrush and the grass and weeds, leaving a few islands of grass that happened to escape the fire. These made good places for rabbits and quail to hide. The wild grass grew back in the Spring, and some of the neighbors let their cattle run free and graze on it.

One summer some disease killed most of those cattle. We didn't lose any, because ours were in our pasture and had no contact with the others. We never knew what caused the deaths, but buzzards came from miles around to clean up the carcasses. Buzzards filled the trees at night, and I saw as many as 15 roosting in a single tree.

When the Keener twins finally bought this woodland, Buck took the northern half and Hig took the southern half. Hig built a house a hundred yards from the road and directly in front of Grandpa White's house. Buck built a house on the same side of the road as Hig's but a couple of hundred yards farther up the road, about halfway to the Voss house. They were thirty-five years old at the time. They cleared several acres near each house to start farming.

I was away when it happened, but I heard that Buck Keener came home one day from hunting rabbits and found his wife with another man. He had his double-barreled shotgun with him at the time, and he emptied one barrel into his wife and the other one into the man. I never saw Buck again, and I never found out what happened to him. Hig Keener died years later after working for many years at the Murray Bicycle plant in Lawrenceburg. He fathered seven children, and his widow gave the land to her children but kept the house. The county named her road Keener Road and extended it through the woods to join Prosser road near the old Rush Beard place.

After Harvey Keener moved out of the house near us, his brother Alford lived there several years. Eunice Voss and Harley Hunter also lived there at one time or another, but I don't remember exactly when.

Alford Keener was a gentle person and spoke with a soft, slightly hoarse voice. He qualified most of his opinions, as if he expected a challenge and wanted to cover himself. Words like in a way, more or less, and I heard tell were sprinkled through his conversation. The front half of his head was bald, and he often complained about "stummick troubles." He was shy, and was the only person I ever knew who found his wife through a personal ad in the newspaper.

Ruby Horton, who lived in Alabama, answered his ad, or else he answered hers; I was never sure which. She had a pretty face and was a fine woman, but was substantially overweight. Soon they were married, and they seemed to be happy. They never had any children.

They attended the Church of the Nazarene in Lawrenceburg and were quietly religious. Alford was afraid of windstorms, and kept looking at the clouds in the sky when a rainstorm was imminent. He had heard the predictions that the world would end in 1936, and when he saw something unusual in the clouds, he was afraid it was about to happen.

He thought I was foolish for walking up and down the road in the pouring rain. He was right of course; but only because of danger from lightning strikes, not because of danger from wind. If a tornado came through, it wouldn't help much to be in our old frame house."If you keep on a-doin' that," he told me once, "you'll be ridin' on the clouds with your lord." He was referring to a popular gospel song.

Alford hunted often when he was not working his crops, and they ate almost any kind of wild game. He got mostly squirrels and rabbits; but in the spring he took his .22 rifle and followed the flocks of robins that appeared in the burned-off woods. When he shot one, the others flew only a short distance and started feeding again. They always let him come within shooting range, so he usually came back with a full game sack. I never wanted to eat a robin, but they ate every one they could get. A pigeon came to his farm once and lit on the ridgepole of his barn roof. He shot it, and they ate it.

A little valley ran behind his house, and the county built a dirt dam across it to form a pond to provide water for livestock. He got them to stock it with fish, and they had many meals from that pond. If a migrating wild duck happened to stop to rest there he was in trouble. Alford took his rifle and went out his front door, around his barn, and down into the valley below the dam, where the duck could'nt see him. Then he crept up behind the dam, still out of sight of the duck, until he reached the dam. He then rose carefully with his rifle pointing toward the duck, and before the duck knew he was there it was too late. He kept hoping a big Canada goose would pay him a visit, but that never happened.

Alf had a shotgun, but he preferred to hunt with his rifle because the ammunition was much less expensive. Fifteen cents for a box of 50 .22-short cartridges was the going price. The .22- long cartridges had a longer metal case than the .22 short and sold for twenty cents, but the bullet weighed the same. The .22-long-rifle cartridges had a longer case and a longer and heavier bullet, and they sold for 25 cents a box. Most .22 rifles would handle either of the three cartridges, but most of us bought the .22 shorts because they were cheaper and good enough at short range.

For years Alf paid seventy-five cents for a box of twenty-five shotgun shells, and he was careful not to waste them on doubtful shots. When I came home from the war, ammunition was more expensive and shotgun shells were hard to find. When a friend from his church offered to get Alford a box he jumped at the chance. He almost fainted when the friend delivered them and told him he owed two dollars and a quarter.

"I paid him the two and a quarter," he told me later, "but I won't shoot nary one of 'em in the air." That was exactly three times what he had been paying, and he didn't intend to risk a nine-cent shell on a bird flying through the air.

A few days later I saw Alford hunting with his .22 rifle in the woods where a little stream ran from our farm into his pasture. I went over to visit a few minutes, and while we were talking I saw a rabbit sitting in some grass about thirty feet away. I didn't have a gun with me, so I tried to show the rabbit to Alford. It was the same color as the dead grass, and he couldn't see it. I even took his rifle and pointed it at the rabbit and let Alford look over the sights, but he still couldn't see it. He finally asked me to shoot it for him.

When the rifle fired, the rabbit jumped about a foot straight up and fell dead, as they usually do when shot through the head. Alford ran over and held it up by the hind legs. "Boy, ain't that a big 'un," he said, his eyes shining. "I can taste 'im already." He stuffed it into his game sack, and was still smiling when I left a few minutes later.

Apart from the wood burning space heater, a battery-powered Philco radio had the most prominent place in their living room. It was the classical model like the one used years later in The Waltons TV series, with a big knob for dialing the stations, and a little knob in the middle of the big knob for fine tuning. I thought it had the finest sound I had ever heard. One of their favorite programs was the soap opera Stella Dallas.

They kept White Leghorn hens, the only ones of that breed in the neighborhood. They laid big white eggs, but didn't have much meat on their bones. He fed them both corn and commercial egg mash, but he didn't make much money from selling eggs. He told me he did well in the summer when the hens were laying plenty of eggs, but he had to spend all his profits to feed them during the winter when egg production was low.

Most farmers kept bigger and heavier breeds of chickens. We called them Domineckers and Wyandottes, and some were white and some had blue-gray speckles. Their eggs were not as big and they didn't lay as many as the White Leghorns, but the young chickens grew faster and bigger and were better for the fryer market.

* * * * *

Harvey Keener sometimes dug wells, and had to blast with dynamite when he hit a layer of rock. He used the same method as the coal miners, with a fuse and a dynamite cap. If he was deep in the well he had to use a long fuse to allow him time to get out before the blast. He kept his dynamite in a secure place, but was not as careful with the dynamite caps. One day his oldest son, Norman, found the caps and decided to make one go pop. He held the cap in his left hand and stuck a flaming kitchen match into it with his right. He was nine or ten years old at the time. The explosion blew off the thumb and first two fingers of his left hand all the way to the knuckles.

Harvey and Pearl Keener had six children: Norman, Gladys, Roy, Juanita, Talmadge, and Herbert. Norman was the oldest, and was a little younger than I was. He often boasted of telling lies and getting people to believe them. Perhaps he did it just for the practice. He said he always tried to mix a little truth with his lies, and that made them easier to believe.

He didn't lie to hurt anyone or to cause trouble. It was usually just an exaggeration of something he had done or had seen. He also had a habit of laughing a loud HAHAHAHA laugh, without smiling, when he was telling a story and when nothing was funny. I think it was a nervous habit that had nothing to do with humor.

He was extremely interested in girls, and to hear him tell it, he was the Casanova of Lawrence County. We didn't take his word for it, but there was enough evidence otherwise to support his stories. He walked around Lawrenceburg on Saturday and had no trouble starting conversations with girls he met. He had big blue-green eyes and full sensuous lips and he radiated warmth and energy. Many girls were drawn to him like bees to honeysuckle.

He joined the National Guard and went with us to Fort Jackson, South Carolina, when the National Guard became the Army of the United States in September 1940. They accepted him in spite of his three stubs on his left hand. I asked him later how he passed the physical with his crippled hand. "They didn't worry about my hand," he said, laughing. "They ast me if I could see lightnin' and hear thunder, and I told 'em yeah. Then one doctor looked in one ear and another doctor looked in the other'n. They couldn't see each other, so they said I wuz O. K. for duty."

Passes for trips off the post were limited, but Norman found a hole in the high fence around Fort Jackson and got out through that hole almost every night to see a girl who lived a few blocks away.

Later he was in nearby Columbia and saw a slender young waitress in a restaurant. The name on her uniform was Ann, and Norman was smitten. They were married before he left Fort Jackson to go to Europe to fight. She later went to Baltimore and worked at Martin-Marietta during most of the time while he was overseas during the war. I left Fort Jackson to go to the Army Air Corps before they met, and I first knew her after the war, when they lived in a little house near Lawrenceburg and she was pregnant with their first child. She told me Norman had said his family owned big farms in Tennessee and had plenty of money, but she would have married him even if she had known he was dirt poor.

She was new on the job and had been wearing a uniform borrowed from a girl named Ann. Her name was Omia Lee Franklin, and she was from Spruce Pine, North Carolina. Omia was pronounced Omy, but it didn't matter, because Norman never called her anything but Ann. Her father's name was Deck Franklin, and he lived with his wife in a little frame house perched on a steep hillside near Spruce Pine. They had two acres on which they raised potatoes and various vegetables.

They also had a son named Steve and a younger daughter named Coria, pronounced Corey. I understand they had an even younger daughter who had died previously. Norman's brother Talmadge married Coria after the war, and they later moved to Hickory, N. C., not far from the old home place near Spruce Pine. Talmadge was in an airborne unit during World War II.

Humpback Mountain was within walking distance. Nobody seemed to know who owned it, but it was covered with mountain laurel. Deck Franklin, his son Steve, and several others made most of their cash income by digging up the young laurel plants with a generous ball of dirt, wrapping the root balls in burlap, and selling them in Spruce Pine to a wholesale place by the railroad tracks.

The buyer shipped them all over the country to nurseries, to be sold at retail. The mountain was so big and the laurel so plentiful there was never a shortage, and people around there earned a living for many years by digging plants.

The back yard of the Franklin house continued uphill, and about twenty-five yards farther back a year-round spring flowed out of the hill. They had dug it out and contained it with rocks and cement, and planted a pipe in it through which all the water came. Then they built a wooden trough ten feet long, two feet wide, and a foot deep, and the water pipe emptied from the spring into the upper end of this trough. It provided clean mountain water, clear and cold. They had no electricity, and this trough full of cold water served as their refrigerator.

At the lower end of the trough another pipe, near the top, let the excess water pour onto the ground. It formed a little stream that continued down the hill to a ditch by the road. Thereafter, it turned right and followed the ditch to a creek that was a few hundred yards away.

There was no bridge over the creek, but it was wide and shallow at that point, and had a rocky, gravely bottom. Fording the creek was easy for a wagon or a car unless the water was high from rain.

* * * * *

After the war Norman worked for a while at a grocery store in Lawrenceburg. One of his chores in that job was to deliver groceries when someone called in an order. He liked to boast to me about his amorous exploits while on these errands. He claimed that one woman always ordered only half of what she needed, then waited a day or two and ordered the rest so he would have to make another trip to her house.

He and Talmadge later attended a school in Lawrenceburg, sponsored by General Motors, to prepare workers to take jobs in the auto industry in Detroit, Michigan. They then moved north, and eventually Roy and Herbert followed them. Finally, Norman and Talmadge bought a service station in Toledo, Ohio, and moved there.

They were aggressive with their merchandising and made plenty of money. A large storage space over the garage housed a huge assortment of belts and hoses, as well as most brands and grades of motor oil. Norman said he never wanted to lose a sale because he didn't have what the customer wanted.

I was at the station with Norman and Talmadge one afternoon when a little kid came in and said to Norman, "Mama wants you to come over to the house." Norman washed his face and hands, put on a clean shirt, and took off with a big grin on his face; returning in about 45 minutes. He told me the woman's husband had been in jail a long time. Norman's wife told me once that Norman couldn't help being the way he was. She preferred to have him that way than not at all. They had several children together.

After several years they sold the station and moved to Hickory, North Carolina. Both Norman and Talmadge bought service stations; but each handled a different brand of gas, and the stations were not near each other.

Norman was in his fifties when he died suddenly of a massive heart attack. He liked to keep large amounts of cash on hand, and his wife heard he had ten thousand dollars in his pockets when he died. She thought she knew who took it; but couldn't prove anything and the money was never found. She later sold the service station and went into the used car business with one or more of her sons. She was doing well the last time I saw her, around 1980.

Talmadge was even more successful with his station than Norman was. He bought a big wrecker and did a thriving business towing broken-down cars and trucks. He eventually got a wrecker big enough to tow a Greyhound bus, and thereafter he got all the Greyhound business in that area.

Talmadge bought a big vacant lot directly across the street from his service station. He said he had no use for it, but he wanted to be sure nobody put another service station there to compete with his. He eventually put a gravel surface on it, put a high security fence around it, and built a big metal building in the middle. He made it into a successful, low-overhead business renting secure storage space for cars, trucks, and other equipment.

Talmadge and Coria had a son named Sidney, who became a nuclear physicist. Neither of the parents went to high school. Talmadge and Herbert always attend the Hunter-Keener reunion at Lawrenceburg that occurs on the last Saturday in August of each year, and Roy attends on occasion. Roy and Herbert live in Toledo. I have no idea where the girls are.

CHAPTER NINETEEN

Arthur Wilson and his family rented a farm one year on the Jim Moses place. Then they moved to a bigger place on Fall River Road at Aldridge Road, just east of Gum Springs School and Church. Their children were Helen, Herbert, Hewitt, Harold, and Hoover. Arthur took a nip now and then, but none of his children drank.

Herbert Wilson was a handsome young man with broad shoulders and slim hips and legs. He had big green eyes, like all the Wilson kids, and girls liked him. His father bought a horse and saddle when Herbert was seventeen years old. He wore riding boots and pants, and looked sharp on that horse on weekends around the community. The first time Arras Webb saw him she was on the bus that stopped on Fall River Road to pick up high school students. Herbert came by just then, driving a team of mules pulling a wagon. He was wearing overalls, standing up in the wagon, and holding the reins in both hands. Arras was sitting on the side of the bus near the wagon, and she couldn't stop looking at him. I don't know how the word got around so fast, but he was soon going to Revilo to see her on Sunday afternoons.

Herbert usually rode his horse and tied him to a post nearby while he visited Arras. One day her younger sister Avo got on the horse and fell off and broke her arm. Finally, Mr. Wilson sold the horse for financial reasons, and it almost broke Herbert's heart. The Wilsons moved to Alabama after a few years, and I lost track of them.

I saw Helen Wilson Hunter many years later at the Hunter-Keener reunion in Lawrenceburg. She told me Herbert had sworn that someday he would have a horse again and would never get rid of it. She said he had show horses later in life and won several prizes with them. He died of a sudden heart attack while riding in a horse show. He collapsed and fell off the horse and was dead when they got to him. The horse nuzzled him and pushed his body with its nose, as if trying to get Herbert to get up off the ground. Harold Wilson lives in Lawrence County. David and Helen have since sold their place near Lawrenceburg and moved to East Tennessee to be near their son, Ronnie, the doctor.

After the Wilsons moved to Alabama, a Mr. Whittaker and his family moved to that farm. They had two daughters and no sons, and the girls ran the plows in the fields like men. Mr. Whittaker liked to turn his land in the fall, as soon as the crops were off. This got the old stalks and grass under ground sooner and saved him time the following spring, when he would run a disc harrow over the ground and then plant it. The disc cut a wide swath, and he could disc the ground eight or ten times faster than he could turn it with a turning plow.

Many farmers in Lawrence County had given mortgages to The Metropolitan Life Insurance Company and then lost their land during the depression when they couldn't make the payments. Met Life then rented the farms to tenants. I learned much later that Met Life required all their farm tenants to grow a certain amount of Hairy Vetch and plow it under as a source of green manure for the land. Since Mr. Whittaker did that, I assume he was renting from Met Life. I had learned in Agriculture class this would improve the land, but I hadn't seen anybody do it before.

* * * * *

The Hunts were sharecroppers. They lived on one farm for a year, giving a share of what they harvested to the landowner. Then either they were dissatisfied or the owner was, and they moved again during the winter to another farm. Moving was no big deal, because one or two trips with a wagon took all their possessions. Many of the sharecroppers played musical chairs with the available farms each winter. Nobody had to worry about having to change the billing on the utility bills because there were no utilities and no bills. One winter Dad asked Grady Hunt when they were going to move. He said they would move when the Smiths got out, the Smiths would move when the next family got out, and so on and so on.

"When the movin' chain starts draggin'," he said, "we will drag right along with it."

Grady was the oldest boy in the Hunt family, perhaps twenty-five years old, and he was so thin he looked like six o'clock when standing. Most of the family looked pretty much the same. Grady had a good bass voice and liked to hum religious songs to himself. Dad sometimes referred to him as hummin' Jesus. Once he got into a fight with his neighbor Clive Mattox and hit him on the head with a rock, inflicting a fatal injury. I don't know how the matter was settled, and I have no idea why they were fighting; although Mattox was a womanizer, according to neighborhood gossip. I don't think Grady ever went to jail. There must have been serious provocation, because I was surprised to hear of him fighting.

* * * * *

From the Fall River Road south toward our farm, the first house on the right (west) side of the road was the Grover Aldridge home. The road later became known as Aldridge Road. There were fourteen living children in the Aldridge family, and I don't remember all the names. Allen was the oldest living, and an older brother, Stanley, died before they moved there from Summertown, a little village a few miles north and west of Lawrenceburg. Stanley was cutting firewood and a tree fell on him.

Allen told my brother Quinton he once had to submit an application, and was asked to name all of his brothers and sisters and give the year of birth for each. He knew when he was born and the order of birth of the others, but didn't remember the years. So he started listing them in order, allowing two years between births; but when he came to the current year there were two kids left. That meant his mother had fifteen children in approximately twenty-six years. Mrs. Aldridge was a Spear before she married, and her sister was Mrs. Brock The Spears and the Brocks were prominent in the James D. Vaughan gospel-music business in Lawrenceburg. They wrote and sang gospel songs and published song books used in the churches in the area. They also conducted singing schools at various times at some of the local churches.

Brock Spear and his younger sister Rosemary sang as a duet in the churches and at singing conventions, and his mother and father joined with them to form the Spear Quartet. Brock played the guitar for the duet, and for the quartet when they didn't have a pianist or an organist. His guitar was a National brand all-metal model, but it was not electronically amplified.

When this beautiful young girl from the Spear family married Grover Cleveland Aldridge, her parents may have been disappointed. He was not more than five feet six inches tall and probably weighed less than 150 pounds. Moreover, he was a farmer with no observable interest in either gospel music or the church. They had fifteen children, five girls and ten boys, and she didn't weigh much more after fifteen kids than she did when she married. She was usually pregnant while still carrying a baby around who was too young to walk. To borrow Dolly Parton's comment, "She always had one on 'er and one in 'er." If she ever regretted her lot in life she never let it show.

Mr. Aldridge built a one-room house on his farm for his mother, about a hundred yards down the road from his house. She lived there many years. He hauled farm produce to various markets in a pickup truck, and he sold more sweet potatoes than anything else.

I saw Vernon Aldridge in Lawrenceburg in 1992. He and his brother Allen and one or two of the other siblings were still living on the home place. The old house was not habitable, and most of it may have been destroyed by fire; so they were living in trailer homes. Allen had one in front of the old house; and there were two more near a little pond at the back of the farm, accessible by a narrow dirt road that ran down the property line.

Allen was small like his father, and he had an avid interest in girls. I don't think he ever married. Ola, the oldest girl, married Otho Farrington when she was still a teen-ager and had a baby about a year later. I heard that Ola eventually went blind. Mae, the next oldest girl, married Huey Tucker. They had three other girls, Ivalee, Norma, and Ruby Dean, but I don't know what happened to them. I heard in 1996 that Allen was in the Alvin C. York Veterans Hospital in Murfreesboro, Tennessee, and was not doing well.

* * * * *

If you follow the Fall River road to Crossroads, turn right and go a mile or two toward the Oak Hill Baptist Church, you will come to a Y in the road just after you pass the Jim Moses farm. The left fork is the Steadman Ridge road, so named for the Steadman family living a few miles down this ridge road. I understand they now call it Revilo Road. The Steadmans kept dairy cows and sold the milk to the creamery in Lawrenceburg. Each morning they drove into town in a pickup truck carrying six to ten cans of milk. They were big cans, holding about ten gallons of milk each. You could ride to Lawrenceburg and back on the back of that truck, going either direction, for a dime each way. I never knew much more about the Steadmans, except the family lived there many years.

A couple of miles down Steadman Ridge road were the Revilo school and Dave Webb's store. Revilo is Oliver spelled in reverse. Oliver was the brand name of a line of agricultural tools. Webb's store sold general merchandise, including seed, feed, and fertilizer.

One gas pump stood in front of the store, with a three-foot handle on the side for pumping the gas. A round glass storage compartment at the top of the pump was marked off in one gallon amounts, and it held a maximum of ten gallons. Rocking the handle back and forth pumped the gas up from the underground storage tank into this ten-gallon container, after which gravity brought the gas down to the car's tank through a hose. A thin little piece of metal extended from each one-gallon mark into the gasoline, so the operator could tell more precisely how much gasoline was left in the storage compartment. The attendant watched the marks on the container to judge how much gas went into the car. Gas was fifteen cents a gallon. A metal drum on the porch held motor oil. Turning a hand crank pumped the oil into a quart sized container that had an adjustable spout to help get the oil into the car engine. There was one kind of gas and one kind of oil, and all the cars that stopped there used the same. Besides the drum for motor oil, he had another drum on the back porch from which he sold coal oil (kerosene).

The store was twenty or twenty-five feet wide and perhaps fifty feet deep. An open front porch ran the full width of the store with double doors in the middle leading to the interior. Shelves on either side held groceries and canned goods of various kinds. Bags and barrels of flour were stored in the middle. Barrels stood on end so they wouldn't roll, and a barrel head made a convenient surface for counting out money to pay for a purchase. Therefore, cash on the barrel head was a colorful way of saying payment in full at the time of sale.

A soda pop dispenser sat in the aisle toward the back. It was a red metal box with a lift-up lid, and the necks of the bottles fit into grooves that held them by the tops and kept them from touching the bottom of the box. It offered an assortment of drinks, mostly Coca Cola, R. C. Cola, and Double Cola, a 12-ounce bottle. It was designed to hold ice and water to keep the drinks cold, but they never put ice or water in it. The nearest ice plant was in Lawrenceburg, at least ten miles away, and most of the customers never used ice anyway, except on the Fourth of July to make ice cream and lemonade.

A big sign in front said Feed, Seed, and Fertilizer, and that is what occupied the back one third of the store. A big back door and a back porch provided access to move goods into and out of the store. But if somebody needed huge amounts of seed, feed, or fertilizer he probably went to Lawrenceburg and bought it from Robert Hayes, who had a much bigger store and might beat Mr. Webb's prices.

The family home was a hundred yards behind the store. The Webbs had eight children, and most of them had unusual names. The oldest was a girl named Annis. They pronounced it Anus. Then there was a boy named Zenas, followed by a girl named Arras, pronounced "Are-ess." Next was a boy named Zirkle, then a girl named Annie Avo, followed by twins, a boy and a girl named D.R and P. D. They named them after the initials of the parents, David R. and Pearl D. Webb. Last was a girl named Buna, pronounced with a long U.

Mr. Webb's brother Mansfield Webb lived with his wife less than a half mile farther down the road. They had three sons named Fount and Felix and Flint, and two daughters named Faye and Fern.

Revilo had a Pentecostal Holiness Church, and Mrs. Webb went there regularly. She was Mr. Ed Taylor's sister, and he and some of his family went there also. Sometimes during their ceremonies they talked in an unknown tongue, and the preacher always mixed in something unintelligible with his sermon. I went there once or twice out of curiosity, and I still remember the preacher saying, "Halley secunimy seminey solo icee." He let that roll off his tongue every two or three minutes during his talk. They held the service in a tent rather than in a building.

The Taylors did not criticize other religious faiths. "You can get from New York to San Francisco by many different roads," Mr. Taylor once told me. "They will all get you there, and there are also different routes to get to Heaven."

Mr.Webb provisioned a truck with most of the staples needed by farm families, and he ran a peddling route once a week. We usually depended on him for sugar, coffee, salt, and similar staples. He sold salmon for ten cents a can, and sometimes three cans for a quarter. We often paid for these things with eggs, butter, or chickens. He also carried rifle cartridges and shotgun shells. A plant called Star root grew wild in the woods and we kids collected it, washed and dried the roots, and sold them to the peddler. I think it was processed and used for medicinal purposes. We seldom collected more than a few pennies, because it took so much of it to weigh a pound.

After a few years he turned the route over to the Weathers Brothers. He eventually sold his store and home at Revilo and moved to Auburndale, Florida. Before he moved there, he worked two or three winters in the citrus harvest. Some said he spent only ten dollars and three cents a week. He paid ten dollars for his room, board, and washing, and three cents for a stamp to write to his wife. "He gits his jollies," Ezra Voss once said, "out uv puttin' his money away."

He must have been fifty years old at the time, but he did as much work as anybody else in the crew. He averaged about $100 a week. That was at least three times what a worker could earn in Lawrence County at that time.

After he moved his family there, they lived in a house in town and he worked in a hardware store. He eventually bought a sawmill that included a contract on several acres of good cypress timber. He hired a crew to cut the trees and bring them to the sawmill and another crew to help him saw the logs into cypress boards. He stacked them and air dried them, and then used the lumber to build several frame houses for rental. They were simple and unpretentious, but they rented readily. They required no paint and needed little maintenance, because cypress boards are extremely durable and termites won't eat them.

He bought several acres near town on Highway 92, and built a big home for his family on the part that was high and dry, plus two smaller houses for his married kids. Part of this land was a wet marshy bog, just off the highway, about three acres in size. The water table in Florida is near the surface, and when you dig a hole it fills up with water. So he bought a used dragline and got someone to show him how to operate it. He then dug out the bog and made a lake, using the dirt from the digging to build up the land around it. After the land settled he built trailer pads around the lake and created a mobile home park. This venture was so successful he built another park a little farther west on the other side of Highway 92. He even opened a dealership to sell new and used trailer homes. Eventually he opened a third park at Carter's Corner, about halfway between Auburndale and Lakeland.

D. R. Webb married Pauline Castleberry, a local girl, and managed the park at Carter's Corner. D. R. died of cancer in November 2002. D.R.'s twin sister, Pansy, managed the original park by the lake. Zirkle, another brother, managed the second park.

Arras Webb married Barney Moses, who then worked for Mr.Webb a few years. Arras fell ill and died while quite young, also of cancer. Annis never remarried after her divorce from Howard Shultz. She lived with her daughter, Phyllis Shultz, in one of the houses Mr. Webb built.

* * * * *

Mr. Ed Taylor, Mrs. Webb's brother, moved with his wife and family from Tennessee to Florida in the mid-forties. They bought a building site on Route 92 just west of Auburndale and built a house out of concrete blocks. They had a bathroom space but no plumbing, so they still had a privy in the back yard. I lived with them a few weeks in 1947, and paid $10.00 a week for room and board. I slept upstairs dormitory style with the four boys: Othaniel, Gentry, Villard, and Johnny. The three girls, Shirley, Mildred, and Esther slept downstairs, as did the parents.

Othaniel was six feet three and a lean 250 pounds. His nickname was Giant, and he looked the part, with red hair and a freckled face. His mother called him OATH nul, but Giant insisted it was Ah THAN yul. Gentry was tall and soft spoken, but not so massive as Giant. Villard was average sized, but all man. He and I loaded fruit together for several weeks, and he was as tough as leather. Johnny was young, not yet a teenager. Later in life he became an accomplished musician and traveled widely, playing guitar as an opening act for the Platters. He died at an early age, and his widow, Dorothy, still lives in Auburndale.

Villard was handsome, but extremely shy with girls. He liked his beer and I watched out for him on weekends and tried to keep him out of trouble. One Saturday night I found him asleep beside the road about ten blocks from home. I managed to get him home slung across my back in a fireman's carry. Giant married Rosie Williams, a neighbor, and later became a Pentecostal Holiness preacher. He died of cancer at an early age. Gentry married a beautiful girl named Jeanette Allen, who was so tiny she was a foot shorter than her husband.

Shirley married a man I knew only as Slim, and Mildred married Harold Deese. Shirley was a wonderful cook, and Esther at age 17 had a figure to make any woman proud; but Mildred had the prettiest face. Esther died of ovarian cancer, and Othaniel, Villard, and Johnny all died of cancer also. Gentry, Mildred, and Shirley are the only ones still alive.

They still live in the area and seem to have done well. Lettie, the mother, lived until she was 98.

Mr. and Mrs. Taylor were gentle people. He was tall and rawboned, with a heavy shock of snow white hair. He had been a farmer in Tennessee, and at one time had owned a shoe repair shop. She was short and just a little heavy and had a sweet disposition. When they came to Florida they built the house with their own hands.

They built the privy in the back yard of unpainted scrap lumber, and one day Giant surprised me and took my picture as I was coming out of it. He said he gave me the picture so I could remember my humble beginnings in case I ever become famous.

* * * * *

Jim Moses was one of the more prosperous farmers in the area. His farm was on the road between Crossroads Church and Oak Hill Church, and just before the Steadman Ridge Road split off to the left to go to Revilo. His farm was so big it joined ours on the back, and he had many big trees in the woods. Most of the trees were around a creek that ran through the woods. He was famous for his frugality.

Someone quoted Mr. Moses as saying the only time he ever wasted any money was when he took a wagon load of cotton to the gin and had to wait all day to get to the head of the line. He said he got so hungry about five o'clock in the afternoon he spent fifteen cents for some cheese and crackers. Another story was that he gave his cows wheat straw and put green glasses on them so they would think it was hay and eat it. One more was that when he went to his spring to get a drink of water he always went down below the spring to get the water that was wasting. Perhaps people told these stories on Mr. Moses because they were jealous of him.

Billy Putman lived down the Steadman Ridge Road beyond Revilo, and he farmed and bought and sold timber. He bought the farm from Jim Moses for $8,000, giving him $1,000 in cash and a mortgage for the other $7,000 to be paid one year later. The farm was the sole security for the amount of the mortgage, and Putman allowed Moses to stay in the house and farm the land rent free until he was paid off in full, although Putman owned the farm. Putman cut and sold $8,000 worth of timber logs from the farm during that year; and then gave the farm back to Moses, never paying him another dime.

Some people would call that smart business. After all, Moses could have put a clause in the mortgage that Putman had to pay most of the timber money to him until the mortgage was paid off. But isn't that like saying you have a right to steal a man's horse if he doesn't know enough to lock his barn door?

Mr. Moses bought a new pickup truck just before the war; and when the war was over, somebody in Lawrenceburg offered him a couple of hundred dollars more than he had paid for it new. He grabbed the offer, only to find out too late that used car prices had gone up, and it would cost him more to replace it.

Barney and Charley Moses joined the Navy at the same time and served on the same ship during the war. The ship sank in a sea battle, and they escaped death only by swimming under water to avoid the burning oil on the surface near the ship. Then they swam around until a lifeboat rescued them. They had a younger brother named Willie, but I don't know what happened to him.

* * * * *

Lacy Williams was my best friend when I was 16, and he lived about a half mile south of us. He had one sister, Ruth, and two brothers, Mont and Paul. His parents were Lavado and Annie Williams, and their marriage was something short of blissful.

Lavado (Vader) Williams had been a semi-professional baseball player at one time, and he still had his catcher's mitt and a real baseball. I liked him very much. He played sometimes in the pickup games on weekends at Gum Springs, and people marveled at his hitting ability. He threw right handed and batted left handed, and usually hit the ball to right field to generate more power. In one game he drove three straight balls deep to right field, so when he next came to bat the opposing team shifted all three outfielders around to the right, leaving left field open. He then shifted his stance and drove the ball into left field, and nobody was within thirty feet of it. He said he didn't succeed in professional baseball because he could never learn to hit a curve ball.

He liked to play catch with me because he said I had a good arm and could throw hard. He told me not to try to throw a curve ball until I was older, so as not to hurt my arm. I heeded his advice, but I ruined my arm another way, trying to throw a hickory nut over a tall tree. Something popped, and I could never throw hard since.

Mrs. Williams was the only person in the neighborhood that I actively disliked. She had a shrill voice, and she spoke precisely and enunciated her words fully, unlike anybody else I knew at the time. She berated her husband and gave him orders in the presence of their children and their guests, and I often wondered how he could put up with it. When I spent the night with Lacy once, she made us account for everything we did all day. Every time we told her something we did, she asked, "And then what did you do? You haven't accounted for more than half the time, what else did you do?" It was not like a parent sharing with a child. It was more like an inquisition, and we had given her no reason to question us.

Dad and Mr. Williams were good friends. They talked often about politics and the possibility of getting the veteran's bonus, and he helped us at hog-killing time. He was mild mannered and not easily provoked. But one night Mr. Williams came to our house and he and Dad went outside to talk. He never went back home, and soon thereafter he sold the farm and built his wife a house on Steadman Ridge Road where she lived with the kids. I found out later he told Dad they had a big argument and she got up in his face and yelled at him over and over. He said he would never live with her again. He lived in a little one-room place the rest of his life.

My sister said she went to spend the night with Ruth after they moved so they could go to Revilo to the Friday night musical event. It would be a fairly short walk from there and Mrs. Williams had agreed to the arrangement. But when they were about ready to leave, Mrs. Williams changed her mind and wouldn't let them go.

Lacy married Evelyn Tankersly from Fall River and owned the country store at Crossroads the last time I saw him. Mont and Ruth were the only ones still living in 1996.

* * * * *

Mrs. Abercrumbie had her daughter Reba late in life; and Reba was somewhat chubby, as were her parents. Mr. Abercrumbie was feeble and could not farm his land, but he had a tenant house three hundred yards behind his home, in the edge of his field next to the woods. An old logging road ran from the house, through the woods, to the road in front of the Voss home. Harvey Keener lived there once and farmed the land on shares. That's where he lived when Norman blew his fingers off with a dynamite cap. Later, Alvin Voss lived there after he married, and one or more of the other Voss boys lived there still later.

Reba paid little attention to the local boys, and vice versa, but one day she turned up married to Wilburn Rogers, from Giles County. I never knew how or when she met him. He lived there with them, and a year or two later both of her parents died and Reba inherited the old house and farm.

Wilburn was as short and thin as Reba was big. His tousled brown hair hung out over his forehead, and his front teeth were usually visible. His father, Elsie Rogers, had been a semi-professional baseball player at one time. Wilburn enjoyed playing the game, but never was as good as his father had been.

Wilburn and Reba hosted a square dance at their home one Saturday night, and some of his relatives came from Giles County, including three young girls. I didn't want to dance, and didn't know how anyway, so I played the French harp to provide the beat. David Hunter and Lacy Williams learned the steps and Allen Voss hawked the new girls as he danced, like a lion circling a herd of zebras, looking for the most vulnerable.

Wilburn clapped his hands in time with the music and called the sets:

"Swang yer partner, Do Si Do, purty little gal ye ort t' know."

I played the French harp for rhythm. I switched from turkey in the straw to Eighth of January, or Old Molly Hare, or Sailors Hornpipe. The tune didn't matter so long as the beat was the same. Now and then I croaked out some words for variety:

"McGinty was dead and McGarrity didn't know it
McGarrity was dead and McGinty didn't know it
And there they lay side by side in the bed
And neither one knew that the other was dead."

When I came back from the war, Wilburn and Reba were gone and Ezra and Doris Voss were living in the old house.

CHAPTER TWENTY

Roy Bryan Reeve was Mama's only brother. He died many years ago, but his widow lived several more years in a little house next to a two-pump service station in the tiny town of Phil Campbell, Alabama. Roy owned and operated the station during the last few years of his life. Aunt Iris lived to her late nineties, and she needed someone with her the last few years. The last time I saw her, Lavene's son was staying with her.

My cousin R. B. Jr. was four months older than I was. He was an Air Force pilot in World War II and stayed in after the war. At one time he had the choice of being promoted from Captain to Major or transferring to the Strategic Air Command where he would fly jets. He passed up the promotion and went to the SAC, where he flew B-47's and later B-52's until he retired in California as a Lt. Colonel. I once saw pictures of him with other crew members standing in front of one of the SAC airplanes. He was a handsome man and a very impressive figure in his flying uniform.

His last assigned station was March Air Force Base near Riverside, California. He had a nice home in Riverside, where he lived with his wife, Edna, who had been his childhood sweetheart. They never had any children, because they always said they didn't want them. But after they were in their fifties, they changed their minds and adopted a little girl. They stayed there in their home after he retired.

The 20-guage, Winchester Model 12 shotgun his father had given him became a collector's item. He was so fond of it he sent it back to the factory years later and had them restore it to new condition. A few years later, someone broke into his house when he was gone and stole the gun, along with some other things. He never got it back, and it almost broke his heart. R. B. died in the middle 90's from Leukemia, and they brought him back to Alabama for burial.

His adopted daughter could not bear the thought of her father being put underground, so they delayed the burial five or six days until they could arrange for an above-ground mausoleum. That was so uncommon in Winston County they had to get someone from Atlanta, Georgia, to come and do the work.

R. B.'s sisters, Lavene and Bessie Lou, both married and had families, but beyond that I lost track of them.

Eunice Reeve married Tom Bailey. He had a deep melodious voice and a handsome Irish face and was always welcome to any choir or quartet in the local churches. They moved a short distance south to Jasper, and lived there the rest of their lives. Mama named my sister for Eunice .The Baileys had four children, Gerald, Emily, Nelda, and Betty.

Their son, Gerald, got his college degree at Auburn and became Field Operations Manager of Gold Kist Inc., the parent company of Gold Kist farms, producers of All Natural, Young'n Tender Chicken.

Nelda married Vaughn Hendon, who became a highly successful real estate developer and builder in and around Jasper. He had learned the business working with his brother in Florida.

Betty Bailey Law worked at SPC/Southern Living . They had a book division (Oxmoor House) that specialized in cookbooks, craft books, and various homes and home improvement/decorating. At times they did coffee- table books, but their bread and butter was from the cookbooks and craft books. Betty was involved on the front end, prior to publication and distribution in a mostly technical capacity. Her group took the manuscript from the author through the production process.

Emily is the oldest. She married Donald B. Hudson, and they have two boys (Barry and Keith). They were married in 1953, and Don has worked for more than 40 years for South Central Bell.

Ruby Reeve married Stacy Abner, a gospel singer and song writer, and they had four sons and a daughter: Stacy Jr., William Ray, Ronald Cole, and James Lowell. The baby girl was born after William Ray and lived only two weeks.

Stacy wrote 25 gospel songs, and some of them still appear in song books. He traveled extensively teaching singing schools at churches using the Vaughan method. He also had gospel quartets for many years. The Vaughan Four was the first. He later formed a quartet called the "Swanee

River Boys", and they sang on radio station WNOX in Knoxville, Tennessee on a program called the Mid-Day Merry Go Round. It was similar to the Grand Ole Opry, and a number of performers, Chet Atkins, Archie Campbell, and Bill Carlisle were on the same program. They made their money by going to churches and schools for personal appearances. Uncle Stacy paid Chet Atkins two dollars a night to appear with them. They were later on WSB Atlanta, and stations in Cincinnati, Indianapolis, and Dayton, Ohio.

Atkins later became rich from playing his guitar and selling his record albums. He said in an interview that none of his albums sold fewer than 50, 000 copies. He made dozens of them. It's too bad gospel singing and song writing didn't pay equally well. James D. Vaughan published a gospel song book in 1937 called Heavenly Choruses. It had a Manila binding and sold for 35 cents.

Once I saw Chet Atkins being interviewed on television in connection with a story of his life. He said Bill Carlisle had advertised for a fiddle player, so he went to KNOX in Knoxville and played the fiddle for him. He got the job. Some time later Carlisle heard him practicing on his guitar during his time off, and he immediately switched Atkins from the fiddle to the guitar. The rest, to use a cliche, is history.

Merle Travis was on that same Chet Atkins TV special, and he told a story about how Chet started singing along with his "pickin". Chet had recently signed with RCA to make instrumental record albums, and one of the RCA officials asked him if he could sing also. "No, sir," Chet replied, "I can't sing at all, not even a little bit." "That's too bad," commented the RCA official. "We had hoped that you could pick and sing too, like Merle Travis does." "Oh, I can sing as good as HE can",responded Chet.

Merle Travis was one of the pioneers of finger style guitar, but he probably was more famous for the songs he wrote. *Nine Pound Hammer*, *Roll on Buddy*, and *Dark as a Dungeon* were Kentucky coal country classics. His *Sixteen Tons* made him a fortune as a composer and brought Tennessee Ernie Ford international recognition as a singer, even as far away as Russia.

Chet Atkins was a virtuoso on the guitar, but his singing was just so-so. He wrote several songs and sang them on his guitar albums, but without the exceptional guitar artistry I don't think he could have made a living as a singer. That reminds me of a comment Ben Hogan made to Billy Casper when they were playing in an important golf match. Casper was one of the great putters of his day, but the other parts of his game were not so good. "If you couldn't putt like that" Hogan told him, "you would be selling hot dogs on the tenth tee."

Ray Abner worked 35 years for IBM and was involved with the early commercial computers. He was IBM account manager handling Tennessee state government and installed their first computer and many others over a 15 year period. He became Consulting industry specialist for government and traveled to every state and to Mexico, South America, and Thailand during his last 15 years there. His wife, Millie, and his daughter, Kelly, are involved in genealogy.

Kelly went to the University of Tennessee, and since has worked in Maryland and Virginia. She has been in restaurant management and is currently operating her own gourmet carry-out business south of Nashville.

She sent me a transcript of a letter written by Noah Van Reeve to his wife, Frances, August 13, 1862, during the Civil War. He was my great grandfather. She transcribed it from a copy of the original letter in Nashville, Tennessee, in 2002. She left all spelling, punctuation, and verbiage as written when possible to preserve the originality of the letter. She is the great, great, granddaughter of Noah Van Reeve:

"Hamilton Co. Tenn

"Dear companion I take my pen in hand to let you no that I am well at present. Hoping that these few lines may arrive safe at hand and find you and the children and all the friends enjoying the _____gods blessings. I received your kind and affectionate letter you sent by Lieutenant (McJenkins?)Monday night last which gave me great joy to hear from you all and to hear that you all was well. You note that George and Wm. Smith was in Tupelo. I want you to rite to me what regiment they are in if you no, for I don't no what (regiment?) they are in. If I knowed I might find them sometime. I would be glad to see the boys. Our regiment draud their comutation money twenty five dollars before we left (_altilor_) and I sent ten dollars by __ York. He got a discharge. Our regiment draud another uniform-a coat and pants and hat. I sent my old uniform coat and hat to Jasper by wagons that was passing from hear thare. I had more clothes than I wanted to toat for we do not no what day we will be ordered to march. I have no notion that we will stay hear long but where we will go I don't no. There is some talk of us going to Knoxville from hear but I pray god that we won't have to go many more places until we git to go home and that for good to stay for I long to come home one more time and see you and the blessed little children my dear companion do the very best you can and put your (trust?) in god who is able to save to the utmost all that come unto him. Rite to me how you are gitting along and if you need any more money for if you need any money I will try and send you some when I drau in of more. I (recon?) we will drau our wages before long. George F. Ballew has not draun his comutation money for he was in the hospitle when we draun our money and I will have to divide with him untill he draws his. We need more money than I had any notion we would need in the army to buy one little thing and another and they cost so (dogged much?) and they all cost money but I have made out with as little as possible and will make out without buying as little as possible. I want you to have the Negroes moved down home as soon as convenient if you can for I want them thare to help you for I no that you see a hard time of it for I don't know when I can git to come home and attend o it.. So rite to me as soon as you can and let me hear all the news in that country so I will bring my letter to a close. I pray god to bless you and the little children. I remain yours truly, N. V. Reeve to F. C. Reeve.

___direct your letter to Tyners Station
Hambleton, Co. Tenn."

Noah Van Reeve was killed August 23, 1864, before his son, Noah Smith Reeve (my grandfather) was born.

* * * * *

Alice Reeve married George Robinson in 1917 and moved to Tennessee in 1918, when most of the Robinson clan moved there. They lived at West Side, a community made up of people from both Giles and Lawrence Counties. Their house was in Lawrence County and their barn was across the road in Giles.

Nine children were born of this union.
Daniel Eugene 12 / 27 / 1917
Noah Washington 11 /16 / 1919 (died 7 / 21 / 1996)
Lucy Jane 11 / 4 / 1921 (died 8 / 13 / 1996)
Pernie Estelle 3 / 28 /1924
Evelyn Delene 7 / 31 / 1926
Rosemond 3 / 25 / 1929 (died June 1931)
William Charles 8 / 11 / 1931

Joseph C. White

Iva Nell 1 / 12 / 1935
Patricia Faye 10 / 23 / 1937

Pat married Joe Dodson in 1960, and they have lived most of their married life in the Chicago metropolitan area. In recent years she has worked in the personal banking area of a large bank in Chicago. They have a son, Brian Daniel, who is a physician, and a daughter, Suzanne Elizabeth, who is a clinical psychologist. They have two grandchildren.

Soon after the Robinsons arrived in Tennessee, the influenza epidemic hit and claimed the life of George's dad in January 1919. George took care of many of his family who were sick as well as many others in the community. Alice stayed home with baby Eugene and did laundry for all the sick folk. It was a difficult time for them since George was one of only a few who was not too terrified to care for the sick, and the house they were building had not been completed inside.

George Robinson died in 1966 in Wisner Louisiana, and Alice died in 1979 in Bloomingdale, Illinois. They are buried at West Side Cemetery in Giles County, along with their baby daughter Rosamond. I believe Noah is buried there also.

* * * * *

Uncle George had the reddest and toughest beard I had ever seen. The going rate for a shave at a barber shop was fifteen cents; but they usually charged him a quarter, at least if they had ever shaved him before. He shaved only once a week and sometimes once every two weeks. During the winter he sometimes let it grow for several weeks.

His brother, Jeff, owned a country store 200 yards from Uncle George's house. I don't remember what the brother looked like, and I don't remember much about the store. I do remember the candy case and the huge chocolate drops that he sold for one cent each.

Uncle George belonged to the Primitive Baptist Church at West Side, and my cousin Noah Robinson told me a story about one of their terminally-ill church members. He was ninety years old, and some of the other church members were at his home staying up with him, as was customary when death was near. The sick man asked to hear some gospel singing, so the others sang The Old Ship of Zion. Noah and a teen-aged friend were waiting on the front porch, and he asked his friend if he thought the sick man would make it.

"I don't think so," he replied. "I heard them in there singing the old shit's a-dyin'."

In 1964, George, Alice, Eugene and Noah Robinson moved with their families to Louisiana. Noah told me he went there and leased 500 acres of land and then came back to get his family. He said they had already changed to no-till farming in Tennessee before they moved, and that's how they farmed in Louisiana. They put the seed into the ground with a machine, along with the fertilizer and a herbicide to prevent the grass and weeds from growing. They didn't do anything else until harvest time. The yields were much greater because the topsoil was so thick and they didn't disturb the root systems of the plants by plowing through them.

In 1970 Noah was written up in the Progressive Farmer magazine as the Farmer of the Year, and he and his wife were offered a free trip to Europe as his award for the honor. They declined because his wife didn't want to go, and Noah didn't care.

They were farming in the Red River Valley, not far from Natchez, Mississippi. The last year Noah farmed was 1973, and that year he grew 500 acres of cotton, 500 acres of soybeans, and 1,300 acres of wheat. He had two mechanical cotton pickers, and they each picked two rows at a time. He first applied chemicals to make all the leaves fall off and to cause all the cotton bolls to open. I believe he leased most of that land, and I don't know how much he owned, if any.

He let cattle graze on his wheat crop when the plants were young. When a cow bites off a wheat plant, two new shoots usually grow out instead of one, producing additional stalks and additional wheat grains. Fattening the cattle is a bonus, just as honey is a bonus when hives of bees help pollinate an orange grove.

Noah had suffered a back injury from a bomb blast in 1943 when he was serving as a member of a gun crew on a transport ship. His physical condition grew worse until he had to retire from farming after the 1973 season. He moved back to Tennessee and lived in a big mobile home near Rossboro Creek, a couple of miles from his old home place. He had pain in his back for fifty years, and after numerous consultations he finally had an operation that eased his back pain.

Noah smoked most of his life and had an operation at the VA hospital in Murfreesboro, Tennessee, to remove part of his lung. The doctors thought they got all the malignancy, but apparently did not. He told me in 1995 that he stopped smoking for a long time but didn't feel any better, so he started again. He died in 1996.

Eugene Robinson, the oldest child, told me he moved first to Missouri and farmed there for a time. When his boys grew up, they wanted farms of their own, but nobody wanted to sell them enough land. Then he heard about 400 acres for sale near Wisner, Louisiana. It was covered with trees that had been growing there since the civil war, so he bought it and then cut and sold enough timber from it to pay for the entire purchase. Now he and his two older sons are doing business as Robinson Enterprises and own more than two thousand acres of the "richest farmland this side of the river Nile", to borrow a line from "Big Daddy" Burl Ives in the *movie Cat on a Hot Tin Roof.* Over one thousand acres is in the name of his oldest son, Larry, and he raises cotton and corn. It is all in a high state of cultivation, and they regularly get two bales of cotton to the acre, or more than 160 bushels of corn. Another thousand plus acres in the same area is in the name of the second son, Terry,

A third son, Jerry, has a business in New Orleans and Dallas, Texas. The youngest son, Gary, lives in the state of New York and works as a millwright.

Eugene still lives there but has had some health problems. At age 88 his activities are limited. He is another man who was "forged in a country crucible," and he has done exceedingly well for himself and his family. Uncle George died about a year after they moved to Louisiana, and Aunt Alice lived several years longer. She moved to Arkansas and lived with Evelyn for a few years. She later moved to Illinois and died in a nursing home in Bloomington in November 1979.

Lucy Jane married Charley Sides, a neighbor boy, and died August 13, 1996, two weeks after her brother Noah died. A couple of years ago Evelyn Robinson wrote an essay about life on the farm in Giles County when she was growing up. She has given me permission to use some of it.

The following is excerpted from her article that appeared in the Lawrence County Advocate on Wednesday, July 24, 2002.

The road dividing the two counties ran between their house and their barn, with the house in Lawrence County and the barn in Giles. The boys delighted in saying to those unfamiliar with the situation, "I have to go clear over to Giles County every morning to feed the horses before I can eat breakfast."

The West Side elementary school was in Giles County, and the first grade class in 1932-1933 consisted of four cousins: Auvene Robinson, Lydell Robinson, Geneva Hadder, and Evelyn Robinson. They had their seventieth anniversary reunion in 2002 to celebrate the beginning of their education. Evelyn remained to finish all eight grades at West Side. She then graduated from Bodenham High School in Giles County. She earned a BS degree from Tennessee Tech at Cookeville and a BA degree from Bryan College in Dayton, Tennessee. She taught at Summertown in Lawrence County, and later was Home Demonstration Agent in Rhea County, Tennessee. Still later she did Overseas work under World Wide Evangelization Crusade in Liberia West Africa and filled in for a year at Faith Academy in Manila Philippines, which is a school for children of missionaries who work in southeast Asia.

Evelyn writes, "One day Miss Hayes (the teacher) had a request to allow Auvene to come home after his last class. She allowed him to go at the designated time. Almost immediately after he left, a sudden wind storm appeared. Miss Hayes first thought was of Auvene. She rushed outside to get him back, but she could not see him, nor could she make him hear her calling.....The next day Auvene was asked how he could walk in that wind. 'When it would blow me down," he said, "I would just get up and keep going.' I believe Auvene's words express the spirit of West Side in those days."

* * * * *

Dad's parents, Monroe and Hester Ann White, also moved from Winston County to Tennessee when we did. They were living in Cullman, Alabama when my father was born. Grandpa was thirty years older than Dad, who was thirty years older than I was.

Dad had four brothers: Arthur, McKinley, Buren, and Thomas Carlie. He also had three sisters. Dora married Henry Wakefield, Leila married Virgil Canada, and the youngest, Annis, married Ernest Roberts. Buren had TB in the 1920's, and T. C. took him to Arizona where they lived for several years until Buren died in 1930. They couldn't do much about TB then except move the patient to a dry climate. After Buren died, T. C. worked as the purchasing agent for one of the Six Companies, Inc, the contractors that built Hoover dam across the Colorado River. He had twenty people working under his supervision, and his salary was fifty dollars a week—-a princely income at the time. The dam was once called Boulder Dam after the name of the nearby town of Boulder, Colorado.

"Hoover Dam is a huge concrete structure 726 feet high and 1,244 feet across. It was built between 1930 and 1935, and workers were paid as little as 50 cents an hour. There were as many as 5,000 workers on the payroll at a time. It is in the Mojave Desert, about 30 miles from Las Vegas. Its reservoir, Lake Mead, is the largest human-made lake in the United States. The highway on top of the dam is a connecting link between Phoenix, Arizona and Las Vegas, Nevada."

Microsoft Encarta Encyclopedia 99

Uncle T. C. White worked there as a purchasing agent from the time construction started until it was completed.

Grandpa and Grandma White lived near Haleyville, Alabama, while Dad was in France during World War I. My mother-to-be was a friend of the youngest daughter, Annis, and lived with them while teaching at a nearby elementary school. She married my father in August 1919, soon after he came home. I was born in July of the following year. I think my parents knew each other before he went overseas, and that may have helped her decide to live with his parents while he was away at war.

The White family and several of our neighbors came from the Scots-Irish group that settled in the Middle Atlantic states many years ago, and we still have some of their language habits. The Scots-Irish influence gave us the a- before-the-ing form of verbs (I'm a-going to town Saturday.)

The summer when I was fourteen I stayed with Grandpa and Grandma White a couple of weeks to help them with the chores and some of the field work. Grandma usually made two big, country-sized biscuits in the morning, one for herself and one for Grandpa, so the first morning she made one extra biscuit for me. Since I still looked hungry, she made me two biscuits the next morning, three the following morning, and four the next. Finally she asked me how many biscuits I usually ate for breakfast. I told her I could make out very well with five or six, so after that she always made me six.

Once when I was about ten I was riding with Grandpa in the wagon and he let me drive the mules. I was feeling really grown up, especially when he said I was a good driver. He paused a few seconds, and then smiled and said it took a good driver to hit ALL the bumps.

Grandma was a rocking-chair invalid for years, but before that she made dried fruit tarts in the summer. She peeled and cut up apples and peaches and put them in the sun to dry. She rolled out the dough for the crust with a rolling pin, and made it round. Then she put the cooked dried fruit on one half of the crust, folded the other half over the fruit, and pressed down all around the half moon with the tines of a fork to seal it and to make it look more artistic. After she baked it to a light brown color, it was soul food .

Sometimes she fried them in butter, and that made them even better. She made at least a half dozen at a time, and she never had to worry about any of them going to waste. She kept them in the warming closet of her stove, and that little storage area pulled me like a magnet any time I was in her house.

Grandpa White never used tobacco, but grandma dipped Bruton's snuff. She used little brushes that she had the kids make for her by chewing the ends of small green sweet gum twigs. She called them breshes, and she used them to dip snuff out of the box and put it behind her lower lip.

Dad was addicted to tobacco. He quit cigarettes and took up chewing tobacco. Then he quit chewing and started to dip snuff. Eventually he quit snuff and went back to cigarettes, and that started the cycle again. He said it was easy to stop smoking. He had done it 100 times.

Grandma White had a spinning wheel, a pair of cards, and some knitting needles. She put a handful of cotton lint between the two cards— she called them cyards—and rolled the cotton back and forth until she formed the cotton into a long roll. The cards looked something like ping pong paddles, except they were rectangular. They were about a foot wide and perhaps six inches long. The inside surfaces consisted of short, small wires placed close together. When she got a big stack of these rolls of cotton, she started the spinning wheel.

There were usually some scattered cotton bolls left in the field after we had ginned all the bales we could get, and we went into the field in the late fall and gathered them. The gin took the seeds out but didn't compress the cotton into a bale. The women used this for spinning string for knitting and as batting for quilts and mattresses.

The spinning wheel sat on three legs, two long ones on one end and one short one on the other. One end had a big wheel, perhaps four feet in diameter. The spokes were far enough apart so Grandma could get her fingers between them to spin the wheel clockwise. A belt went around the perimeter of the wheel and then around a small pulley on the other end of the machine. The pulley drove a small spindle that turned at a high speed.

She laid out a stack of these cotton rolls and started the wheel to turning. When the spindle was spinning fast she touched the end of a roll to it and it grabbed the cotton and twisted it. Grandma gradually pulled the roll away from the spindle as it twisted, and it formed a long cotton string. Before the roll of cotton became all string, she twisted another roll of cotton into the first roll. This made a long continuous string that she rolled into a big ball. Later, she knitted this string into something the family could use, such as mittens or socks.

Aunt Annis was the last of Grandpa White's family to go. She died in 2002 at the age of approximately 102. She spent her last few years in a nursing home in Nashville, Tennessee, near where my sister lived at the time. Her daughter Elrose lived nearby and visited her regularly. Elrose was married to Pete Harper, and they have six grown children. She died in February, 2003.

Annis had four daughters with Ernest Roberts: Genevieve, Bernice, Elrose, and Maylene, who died of Leukemia a few years ago. Genevieve is also deceased, and Berniece is the only one left alive. Ernest died from an accident in his forties, and a few years later Annis married a Mr. Ward and moved to a little farm on the Fall River Road a couple of miles from Lawrenceburg. There were two houses on the place, and Grandpa and Grandma White moved into the smaller one when they sold their farm in 1941.

After grandpa died in 1948, Aunt Annis and her husband moved to Winter Garden, Florida. She took Grandma with them, but she feared she would die and they would not bring her back to Gum Springs to be buried with grandpa. Finally, they brought her back to Tennessee to live at Dad's house. That didn't work out either, because he had married Willie Mason two years after mama died, the two women in the same house was not a happy arrangement.

Grandma finally went into a nursing home in Columbia, Tennessee, a few miles north of Lawrenceburg. She was not happy there either, and kept talking about going on to be with grandpa. In 1954 she fell and broke her hip, and she died soon thereafter at the age of ninety.

Arthur White was the oldest child. He moved to Bay City Texas in the late 20's, and worked in the oil fields. He raised his family there and stayed until he died. He lived too far away to help his parents personally, so he sent Grandpa a few dollars each month for many years.

During the first few years on the farm we had no car. When I was young my father came home from town one day with a new two-horse wagon. It had a full-sized wagon bed, complete with a spring-supported wooden seat wide enough to seat three adults side by side. When taking it to church or to town, we folded a quilt several times and put it on the seat for extra comfort. As I recall, it cost thirty-five dollars; and it was totally on credit, to be paid for when and as we could. Dad paid for it, because he always paid his debts, but I don't know how long it took him to do it.

Later we had an old Model T Ford. I recall making trips in it to Double Springs to see our grandparents, and spending most of the day to get there. Halfway there we stopped at Happy Hollow for a rest and a picnic lunch. There was a good spring for drinking water and benches for resting. It was only 100 miles to Grandma's house, but we usually had one or two flat tires on the way.

The tires required inner tubes, and everybody carried a small repair kit, plus a couple of boots to put inside a tire when it was necessary to reinforce a weak spot. We never had to balance the tires, because we didn't drive fast enough to make them vibrate. The repair kit was in a small round can with a metal lid. One half of the outside top of the lid had many little sharp metal projections, to be used to rough up a spot on the tube. The kit contained a tube of glue to spread on the spot, different sized rubber patches with peel-off cloth coverings, and a larger sheet of patching material that could be cut to make larger patches.

The directions said to clean and rough up the area around the hole in the tube and then smear it with glue. Next, select the right-sized patch and peel off the cover, thereby uncovering the sticky side, and stick it over the hole in the inner tube. Finally, put the inner tube back into the tire and inflate it with a hand pump, which was a necessary tool for every car. The tires were rubber and the inner tubes were rubber. In hot weather the patches had a tendency to slip off and let the air out.

The gasoline tank of the Model T was in the back. It had no fuel pump and depended on gravity to take gas from the tank to the engine. That normally worked, because the tank was mounted higher than the engine. But when the gas tank was almost empty and the car was going up a steep hill, the engine was above the level of the gas in the tank. The car then sputtered and died, even though there was still gas in the tank. The solution was to turn the car around and back it up the hill so the gas in the tank would be higher and gravity would take it to the engine.

* * * * *

When we were kids, we always went to church on Sunday. We didn't work, and we didn't hunt or fish, but none of our relatives seemed as seriously religious as Grandpa and Mama. My sister became so in later years, and it helped her through some rough times. If she ever had any doubts about her religious convictions she never let them show.

Her first husband, Alvin Powell, was handsome and charming and gave her two beautiful daughters. But he was a construction foreman and went away on long work assignments. She usually went with him until after the babies were born, but sometimes there were no facilities for them near the job site and they weren't allowed to go. Then he sometimes stayed away for weeks at a time and didn't write or call or send money for living expenses. Finally, when she had no money for food or rent she had to go to Iron City to live with Dad. Some time later he walked into the living room unannounced, as if he had left for work just that morning. "Hello, honey," he said, with a big smile on his face, and Dad hit him on the jaw with his fist and knocked him cold. She finally left him and he later died.

After that she was alone with her daughters for a few years until she met Forrest Thompson, whose first wife had died. She was working for the Tennessee Valley Authority, where he was a supervisor over a crew erecting towers for power lines. During their courtship he often invited the children to go along when they went on dates. After they were married he adopted her two daughters, Judy and Janice, and gave them his name. He always was a kind and loving father to them "The most fun we ever had," the girls said later, "was when we were dating Daddy."

After living in Florence, Alabama a few years, they sold their house, and in 1962 bought a new brick home in Donalson, Tennessee, a suburb of Nashville. Forrest died of a sudden heart attack at age sixty-two. Some years later she met Jack Curtis at a church-sponsored event and eventually married him. He had two sons from a previous marriage, but his wife had died. They had a few years together, and when he died of Emphysema she continued to live in the house. Eunice had no children from her marriages to Forrest Thompson or to Jack Curtis.

A few years later, after our brother Billie died, she sold the house and bought a new mobile home. She has it on land alongside the home of Jerry and Judy Baggett, her son in law and daughter. They live near the Tennessee state line in Green Hill, Alabama.

When his parents died, Jerry inherited the house where he grew up, together with several acres of land. They have made extensive renovations to the house and it is like new. Judy has a masters degree and teaches at New Prospect School, not far from Lawrenceburg. Jerry is also a well-qualified teacher, but he prefers to manage his used-car business, which is located near their home.

* * * * *

After Mama died in 1938, Dad had more than he could handle with the handicapped twins, and Eunice stayed out of high school two years to help. Then in 1940, after Bobbie died, he married Willie Mason from Iron City, a small town near the Alabama state line. A childhood illness had hindered the growth of her right leg, and it was underdeveloped and about four inches shorter than the other. She had a higher heel on that shoe, but she still bobbed up and down when she walked.

Her father was Bill Mason, a Constable in Iron City, and Dad met her through him. He was so fat and his belly so big he had trouble getting into and out of his car. I saw him only two or three times, and I never met his wife.

* * * * *

My brother Quinton was in the CCC two years, and when World War II started he got out and joined the Navy. We were both discharged in late 1945, and the government paid us $100 a month each for the first year to help us adjust to civilian life. We talked it over with Dad and agreed to stay and work the farm in 1946. Old man Crum had a five-acre tract next to our land, and we rented it to add to what we had already.

Dad had bought a few gallons of Davis Everbright paint several years earlier, but it sat in storage and we had never used it. One person could run the turning plow, so in the Spring I did the plowing and Quinton painted the house. The house was twenty years old and had never been painted, but he did the best he could with the old stale paint.

We worked hard that year and made twelve bales of cotton, the most the farm had ever produced. Since we had more money we applied more fertilizer than ever before, and we got forty cents a pound for most of our cotton, or about two hundred dollars a bale. We repaid all our expenses and then divided the rest of the proceeds into three equal parts, between the two of us and Dad. That was the most money he had ever made in one year on that farm.

In 1947, after Quinton and I had assured them we were through with farming, they sold the farm and all the equipment and bought a little house with a few acres near Willie's old home in Iron City. Eunice was married, Bobbie was dead, Bruce was in Idaho with his Uncle T. C., I was in Florida, and Quinton was in Detroit. Edgar and Billie moved to Iron City with the family. Dad had a small pension from his war service, and he raised watermelons and other produce and kept a few hives of bees.

After I joined the border patrol, I visited him when he was 64 and learned he had never paid social security taxes, although the law had been changed to allow farmers to participate. We learned he needed only six quarters of coverage to retire with the minimum benefit after age sixty-five, and he needed to earn only fifty dollars in each three-month period to qualify for coverage. So he started a simple bookkeeping system and documented that he was doing business raising chickens, garden produce, honey, and watermelons. He didn't net much, but it was enough.

He made the reports and paid the taxes each quarter for a year and a half and then applied for retirement. The law prescribed a minimum benefit for anyone who was eligible to retire, and that's all he got because he had paid very little into the fund. It took three months for the application to be processed, but the first check included the back payments. Each monthly check was for more than all the money he had paid into the system during the qualifying period.

He died two years later; but his widow, who was disabled because of her short leg, drew benefits for many years until she also died. Billie was always disabled and collected Social Security benefits for forty years and medicare benefits for thirty years. Edgar was totally disabled from epilepsy and collected Social Security benefits for several years.

"Social Security ain't fair," my step-mother often complained, because she knew some other widow whose survivor's benefit was more than hers. The other woman's husband had worked for many years under Social Security and had paid several hundred dollars into the system, but nobody could explain that to Willie because she refused to listen. "My husband paid that inshorance just like everybody else," she insisted, "and I ort t'git the same money."

Yet Dad, his widow, his son Billie, and his son Edgar each collected either social security or medicare benefits or both, all based on Dad's contributions in social security taxes of less than thirty dollars. The benefits started when Dad started collecting in 1956 and ended when Billie died in 1997. It totaled many thousands of dollars. If Social Security is unfair, it is only to the other workers who provided all that money by paying social security taxes. Dad would never accept charity when he was alive— said he never needed it—but this could be called charity after his death. Nevertheless, nobody took anything more than what the law provided.

When Social Security first started in 1935 someone recorded a song titled The 65 Blues. All I remember is, "With a frock-tailed coat on Saturday night, I'm a bear-cat papa and I'm ready to fight. I've got more money than I can use, and I've got them mean old 65 blues."

* * * * *

My brother Bruce had a disagreement with Dad while I was in the service; and he went to Jasper, Alabama, and lived at least a year with his aunt Eunice Bailey and her family. He had no contact with his father during all that time, but the Baileys wrote Dad and told him he was there and was all right. I don't know the details and didn't ask, but apparently he and Dad were on good terms later. He subsequently went into the Air Force and never went to high school.

After the war he went to visit his Uncle T. C. White in Moscow, Idaho. His uncle had married for a fourth time, and was living on a 500-acre wheat farm near the Canadian border. His new wife had influence with the officials at the nearby University of Idaho; and she got Bruce admitted as a special student, even though he had never gone to high school. He took several make-up classes as he waited to enter, and still more as he went along. These were in addition to his regular courses. He worked on the wheat farm during summer vacations and on weekends, and worked as a bartender in his spare time during the winter. It was a long struggle, but he finally got a college degree in finance, at age 30, without having gone to high school.

He met his wife, Kristin, in college. She was from that area, and he went to work for the Idaho State Department of Highways. They had a house on twenty acres in Meridian, a suburb of Boise, where they raised cattle and Alfalfa hay to feed them. He was head of the Right-of-Way Division for many years and stayed in Idaho when he retired.

Uncle Tom's wife died, and sometime thereafter he met and married the widow of one of the founders of Safeway Supermarkets. She lived in Texas, and they drove from there to his wheat farm near Moscow, Idaho. The old farmhouse had been vacant for some time, and the living conditions there were priitave. She stayed one night and then packed up and returned to Texas.

Uncle Tom had a Volkswagen Microbus at that time, and he spent much of his time for many months on the road between the wheat farm and her home in Texas. He would drive from Moscow to Meridian, spend a couple of nights with Bruce and Kristin, and take off for the long drive to Texas, sleeping in the bus at night. He would stay a few days there and then return the same way, stopping with Bruce and Kris for a couple of days on the way home. He seemed to enjoy traveling like that. Eventually they either divorced or got an annulment, and he then married another widow who also had a wheat farm near Moscow. He lived there with her until he died at age 96.

Bruce had smoked for many years. He had a coronary bypass operation when in his forties and another one a few years later. He quit smoking, but he had problems with his lungs later in life. He also developed prostate cancer in his late 60's, and underwent several months of chemotherapy. He eventually died at age 71.

He and Kristin had three children, Allison, Steven, and Eric. All of them are married with families of their own. Bruce always liked to hunt and fish, and kept his freezer well stocked with venison, salmon, pheasant, and grouse.

* * * * *

My brother Quinton married his wife, Beverly, and worked for Great Lakes Steel as an electrician for more than thirty years. Any time he completed an electrical installation he sprayed it with asbestos from an aerosol can, and his lungs were in bad condition by the time he retired. Company doctors insisted, however, that his problems were not work related. Beverly had three children by a former marriage, and they had three of their own. When they met, Quinton was playing guitar in a string band managed by Beverly's mother.

After he retired, they bought a few acres with a mobile home about twenty-five miles from Nashville. Beverly had a long illness and died in the early nineties, and Quinton took her to Michigan for burial as she had asked. He bought a big tombstone with her name on one side and his on the other. He died in 1996 and is now at rest with her in Michigan.

CHAPTER TWENTY-ONE

At first the CCC would take nobody unless the family was on relief. We never accepted relief, so I didn't apply. They later removed that requirement, and I enlisted. The pay was thirty dollars a month and all expenses. They gave me eight dollars and sent the rest to my family.

In April, 1938, Dad took me to Pulaski to board the train for Chicago. I had to change there to another train that took me to California A railroad went through Lawrenceburg, but it didn't go to Chicago. I should have graduated from high school in June of that year, but I had already skipped one semester to work on the farm and I lost another semester when I left for the CCC. That left me one year behind the rest of the class that started in 1934. I didn't have the option of waiting until the end of the school year to go to the CCC. It was go then or wait for the next call, and that might have been a year later.

Pulaski is eighteen miles east of Lawrenceburg on route 64. They named the town for Count Pulaski of Poland, who helped us in the Revolutionary War. Some claim the Ku Klux Klan originated there, but we never had any KKK activity where we lived.

I sat up on the train four days and nights, and there was no air conditioning in the railroad cars. We could open the windows, but that let in the smoke, soot, and cinders from the coal-fired steam locomotive. Now and then they stopped and let us get out to stretch our legs. One place was at Tennessee Pass in the Rocky Mountains, where the altitude was 10,000 feet above sea level. It was snowing in early April. The engine had been laboring long before we reached the top, because it had been going uphill for many miles.

We also stopped in Colorado at the Royal Gorge, a long, narrow canyon formed by the Arkansas River, with near-vertical walls more than 1,000 feet high. The railroad tracks followed the river, as they often do crossing mountains. A bridge across the gorge was so high above us it looked like a toy bridge from where we were.

I worked hard in the CCC, and spent about half my time during the summer in a gravel pit shoveling gravel into a dump truck. Part of the time I dug post holes and built fences. At other times I built watering places for livestock and wild animals.

First I located a damp place on a hillside and dug down until I found the source of water. Then I arranged big rocks to prevent dirt from filling in and choking off the water supply. Afterwards I installed an iron pipe to carry the spring water downhill. Finally, I built a wooden trough below the spring to catch the water from the pipe and hold it for animals to drink. We built these watering places primarily for cattle, but wild animals also used them.

I was at the main camp at Susanville, California, for two months. We lived in barracks buildings and ate in a big mess hall, military style. I had kitchen duty one month, and that included working late at night making lunches for the work crews to take out the next day. Several big trucks took the workers to their assigned jobs, and they were too far away to come back to camp for lunch. We had garbage cans on a back porch, and had to make the lids secure because coyotes knocked the cans over looking for scraps of food.

We got our electricity from a gasoline-powered generator located a hundred yards from the barracks. It ran at full speed 24 hours a day. When we left camp for a work detail, it felt strange not having that constant drone in our ears.

One day I was playing catch with another kid who aspired to be a pitcher in the big leagues. The sun was hot, and we were standing very close to the barracks building in order to be in a narrow strip of shade. He threw me a fast ball, and it bounced off the barracks wall and hit me on the side of my nose. Some time later I noticed that my nose was crooked. The camp doctor said he could straighten it but he would have to break it again to do it. I declined the offer, but many years later I finally had the operation, primarily to help me breathe easier.

Reno, Nevada, was a couple of hours away, and they sent an excursion truck there once a month, the first weekend after payday. The main attractions were brothels and casinos and I had no interest in either, so I never went. At the processing center of the CCC we had taken eleven shots and vaccinations in two days and had sat through a movie showing the horrible things that can result from promiscuous sexual activity. That got my full attention, and I stayed away from Reno. Of all the vaccinations and shots I had to take, the aftereffect from the shot for Rocky Mountain spotted fever was by far the worst. A big lump appeared where the shot went into my arm, and it didn't disappear for two or three days.

Ray Baxter had bought a Recording King guitar from Montgomery Ward. He paid $17. 50 for it, a huge price at the time. It had a hand carved spruce top and a rosewood fingerboard that was comfortable to use. Its tone was as good as any I had ever heard. Ray wanted to sell it and buy something fancier, but I didn't have any money,

When I left for the CCC, Dad bought it for me for eight dollars and 1 took it with me. I sent him two dollars a month and paid for it in four months. When my brother Quinton went into the Navy, I let him take it with him. It held up well aboard his ship, and he played it for many years.

When Mama died they finally got word to me the day of the funeral, my eighteenth birthday. I was working at a camp far up in the woods, and there was no telephone. There was no possible way I could have come home in time, because it had taken me four days to get out there on the train. I had a six-month contract that I could renew for additional six-month periods. I had planned to stay at least a year and maybe longer, but since I couldn't make a temporary visit home, I left after six months.

After the war the high-school authorities accepted my certificates from military courses I had taken and counted that as sufficient for graduation. They gave me a diploma in 1946. One was a six-month aircraft Mechanic's course, and another was a flying training course. That lasted eight months and got me Airplane Pilot's wings and a commission as a Second Lieutenant in the Army Air Corps.

* * * * *

After I left the CCC Dad got a job for me on the Lawrence County bridge crew, and I worked there for more than a year. He had some influence because he was a Justice of the Peace, and as such he was a member of the County Court. I commuted to work with Red Powell, who also worked at Lawrenceburg, and I walked to and from our meeting place on Fall River

Road. My pay was twenty-five cents an hour, which came to ten dollars a week.

Joe Graves was the crew Foreman, a man named Carden was the truck driver, and Troy McAfee was one of the crew members. Troy was about my age, and he and Carden had a long-lasting disagreement about using brakes when going down a steep hill. Carden said he put the truck in a lower gear to hold it back from speeding and save the brakes, and Troy argued it was better to wear out the brakes than the engine. Neither of them mentioned the most important reason, which I learned much later is to give the driver better control for the sake of safety. Brakes sometimes fail when a loaded truck goes down a hill, and by the time the driver discovers he is in trouble it is too late to do much about it.

The crew left for work from the office located next to the hitch yard. We rode on a flat-bed truck with four-foot-high railings around the sides and across the back. The truck then took us to some wooden bridge in the county that had fallen in or broken through, and we repaired it. Sometimes it involved only replacing a few two-by-eight planks and nailing them to the sills with twenty-penny nails hammered in with eight-pound sledge hammers.

Sometimes we cut a nearby tree from the road right of way to get two logs for new sills in order to replace the bridge entirely. We carried the two-by-eight planks with us, but not the sills. We placed the logs one on each side, parallel to the sides of the road; and placed the 2-by-8 planks crosswise and nailed them to the logs to hold them in place. We dug into the dirt and made beds for the ends of the logs, so they would be low enough for the 2 by 8's to lie even with the surface of the road.

For the biggest jobs we built forms and poured concrete for the foundations, the supports, and even the floor of the bridge. We had carpenters on the crew to build the forms. The Works Projects Administration had assigned them to work with our crew. They made 27.5 cents an hour, slightly more than I did. One of them told me he paid twenty-five dollars a month to rent his house, and that was about half of his total income.

For our concrete work we used a mixer powered by a small gasoline engine. We put in the sand, gravel, cement, and water; and when the mixture was ready we poured it into a wheelbarrow and pushed it up a ramp made of two-by-eight boards. Since the forms were sometimes fifteen or twenty feet above the ground, we had two or three landings on the way up where we changed directions. This made the slope more gradual so it was possible to push the loaded wheelbarrow. Since I was younger, bigger, and stronger than many of the other crew members; I spent most of my time pushing that wheelbarrow up and down the ramp. After the concrete set, we removed the forms and rubbed the raw concrete with a wet stone to make it smoother. That was child's play compared to some of the previous work.

Sometimes we had a bigger job where we had to use timbers treated with creosote, a black preservative used to treat crossties for railroads. It is derived from tar, and in hot weather it gives off invisible fumes that burn the skin. They treat the timbers with it because it prevents the wood from rotting and from being eaten by termites.

* * * * *

In 1940, I got a better job with the shirt factory in Lawrenceburg, which was owned and operated by Salant & Salant. It closed many years ago, but the old buildings are still there. I operated a big press that would do six shirts at once, two rows of three shirts each. The shirts came to me already folded, and I had to line them up on the press and pull the top part down on the shirts with pressure. Then I depressed a treadle with my foot to give them a shot of steam. Next I raised the top part of the press, turned the six shirts over, and went through the same process again. I earned 32.5 cents an hour for that work. There were a couple of other pressers working in the section, but they used older presses that did only two shirts at a time.

The foreman of our wing of the building was Thomas J. Davidson, a first lieutenant in our national guard company and an older brother of my high school classmate, the algebra whiz kid. He supervised about thirty people and earned twenty- five dollars a week. That was enough to support a wife and drive a new Plymouth car. After I worked there three or four months, they had a cutback and closed the entire wing where I was working. That worked out OK, because very soon thereafter they federalized the national guard and I was in the army.

* * * * *

When I came back from the CCC, I was eighteen, so I joined the Tennessee National Guard. We went to Lawrenceburg on Thursday night of each week for two hours of drill. The salary was thirty dollars a month, or one dollar for a night's drill. They paid us four times a year, and I usually got thirteen dollars. The company kept a fund from which they would lend you the one dollar for that night's pay, but you had to pay back $1.25 on payday. If you borrowed the dollar four weeks in a row, then you couldn't borrow a dollar on the fifth night. You had to use that dollar to pay the four twenty-five-cent charges you owed from the previous four weeks. I never did know what they did with the interest they collected.

I was in Company G, 117th Infantry, 30th Division. Each drill night I walked about a mile to Fall River Road where I got a ride to Lawrenceburg and back with Wesley and Everett Hayes, who were also in the National Guard. I paid them ten cents for each round trip.

One night in 1939 the temperature was below zero, ice covered the road, and we had to get out and push the car to get it up a long hill. Both of my ears were frostbitten, and they swelled up and turned black for a few days. My left ear still has a hard rim around the top edge, and my doctor says it is the result of that frostbite.

Sometimes after drill we stayed to see the late movie at the Princess Theater in Lawrenceburg. The usual admission price was twenty-five cents, but for the last showing on Thursday night we got in for a dime.

The National High-power rifle championships were held in September, 1940, and the Tennessee National Guard sent a team. They had the tryouts at Tullahoma, Tennessee, in August. I had never shot a high-power rifle, but I had done well with the 22 caliber qualifying and they let me go to the tryouts. I made the team and went to Camp Perry, Ohio and stayed several days on official-duty status. We were still there on September 16, when the National Guard became the Army of the United States. When we returned home, we went to Fort Jackson, South Carolina.

After we had been there a few months we had rifle qualification shooting with the then-new M-1 Rifle. Colonel Bond was the regimental Commander, and he announced that the soldier with the highest qualifying score in the Regiment (of about 2,000 soldiers) would get a seven-day pass and be allowed to go home for a week.

The qualification course was the thousand-inch range—about 28 yards—and the three positions were standing, sitting, and prone. We shot one magazine (eight shots) standing. A hit in the bullseye counted five points, and hits in he larger scoring rings counted lesser points. We then shot ten shots each at sitting and prone, with a little more than a minute time limit for each. We loaded two magazines, one with two cartridges and one with eight. That required us to change magazines once during the allotted time. I got four fives and four fours standing for a score of 36 out of 40 points, and all bullseyes at sitting and prone for scores of 50 on each. That gave me 136 out of a possible 140, and that was enough to win. I traveled the better part of a day each way on the bus, but I had five days at home. I served in the military five years, but that is another story.

After I got out of the military service, the Republican party in Lawrence County asked me to run for sheriff, probably because my father had been successful in other elections. I was flattered, but I declined, because the democrat nominee was Claude McAfee, the older brother of Troy and a well known and immensely popular figure in the county. I didn't want to be humiliated by a lop-sided loss, and I had no burning desire to be sheriff. They got the son of a prominent Republican lawyer in Lawrenceburg to run instead, and he lost by a wide margin.

* * * * *

In December 1946, I drove to Florida with Ezra Voss, and we got jobs with a field crew foreman who worked for the Florida Gold Company. We picked fruit a few days and made fifteen or eighteen dollars a day. We got fifteen cents a box and could average a little over a hundred boxes of oranges a day. Some of the fast pickers could get more. The foreman gave each of us a supply of little cardboard tickets each morning, each with our own identification number on it. When we filled a box, we stuck one of our tickets on it. The boxes all had thin metal strips nailed around the tops, and the ends of the tickets slid easily under them.

When the loaders came by to load the boxes on the truck, they pulled the tickets off the boxes and gave them to the foreman at the end of the day. The foreman separated the tickets by the identification numbers and counted them to find out how many boxes each worker had filled. A box held one and four-fifths bushels. It was made of wood and was eighteen inches wide, a little more than a foot deep, and about three feet long. It had a divider in the middle, and a hand hold was cut into the center of each end of the box, near the top, to make it easier to handle.

A crew consisted of a foreman, a truck driver, three loaders, and several pickers, usually twenty or more. The pickers used wooden ladders made with lightweight cypress poles to get to the oranges they couldn't reach from the ground. Most of the trees were less than fifteen feet tall, but some trees grown from seed were much taller.

The bud or the cutting grafted to the tree controlled the variety. Nurseries grew little trees from Rough Lemon or Sour Orange seeds, because they had the strongest root systems. They then grafted buds or cuttings to the seedling trees when they were very small to control the variety of oranges the trees would bear. The shoots then became the main trunks of the trees and the trees bore only fruit relating to the grafted buds or cuttings. Nothing was left of the original trees except the root systems and part of the trunks below the branches.

When a grower placed an order with a nursery for trees, he designated the number of trees and the variety. The nursery then grafted the baby trees according to the buyer's wishes. Three of the more popular varieties of oranges were Temple, Pineapple, and Valencia. Duncan, Marsh Seedless, and Texas Ruby were the more popular varieties of grapefruit.

Temples were easy to eat from the hand, because they had thin rinds that came off easily and the flesh of the orange came apart in sections, almost like Tangerines. The flavor was slightly tart, however, and Temples were not as durable as some others for shipping and storage.

Pineapple oranges ripened earlier than some, usually in November or December. They were sweet, had plenty of juice, and stored and shipped well.

Valencias were the best from the standpoint of the grower, because they were especially durable for shipping and storing and were sweet and packed with juice. They matured late and could stay on the tree for several weeks after they were ripe without suffering any damage. The trees were often in full bloom in the spring with a crop of ripe oranges still on the trees. They commanded a higher price than most of the others, and the growers called them the old mortgage lifters. My personal favorites were Navel oranges because they were seedless and I liked their flavor, but we saw very few of them.

Duncan Grapefruit had many seeds and were used extensively for canned grapefruit sections because the individual sections separated easily. Sectionizers, mostly women, sat in the canning plant all day flicking out the seeds and dividing the fruit into sections. Marsh seedless Grapefruit were usually sold as fresh fruit, because the sections didn't divide easily. Texas Ruby Grapefruit were excellent for fresh fruit because the flesh was red and sweet.

When our picking crew started in a grove, someone from the fruit company parked a big semi-trailer near the grove and left it there. The crew's truck driver drove a goat, a small dump truck with a body only five feet wide. It had to be narrow so it could go between the rows of trees. It had sideboards that reached about six and a half feet above the ground, and it held fifty boxes of fruit.

The driver brought the goat down the middles and stopped where the full boxes were lined up. Two of the loaders then picked up a box, one loader on each end of the box, and emptied it into the goat. The boxes were sturdy, weighed fifteen pounds empty, and held 100 pounds of oranges. A box of grapefruit weighed ten or fifteen pounds less than a box of oranges.

Each loader used the hand nearer to the truck so he didn't have to cross his hand across his body to dump the box into the truck. Since both loaders needed to face the box, one had to use the left hand and the other had to use the right hand. After loading one truck, they usually changed hands for the next load.

The pickers put all the filled boxes on the same side of the row of trees, so the loaders didn't have to waste time going to the other side of the truck. They had to lift the box over their heads so it would clear the sides when they dumped the fruit into the truck bed.

When they shipped the oranges as fresh fruit they left them in the boxes. In that case we used a flat-bed truck and stacked the boxes on the truck bed. One of the loaders picked up the boxes and set them on the truck bed, and the other loader stacked the boxes in two rows, four high. This was harder work than dumping the boxes of juice oranges into the goat.

After the goat was full of juice oranges or grapefruit, the driver dumped the load on an escalator that took it up and into the semi-trailer. Then he came back for another load. Sometimes he and one of the loaders had to move the empty boxes to another part of the grove.

Three loaders were in the crew, and they rotated assignments each day. Two of the loaders threw the boxes up and emptied them into the goat, and the third loader moved the emptied boxes over to the next two rows for the convenience of the pickers. Sometimes he had to carry them down the rows to trees out ahead. He usually carried four boxes at a time, two in each hand placed end-to-end. That was not an easy job, but it was easier than loading fruit and much easier than picking cotton.

The loaders got three cents for each box loaded, and the three loaders shared the money equally. After I had been picking a couple of weeks one of the loaders quit, and I asked for the job and got it. We had a big crew and were picking about three thousand boxes a day at that time, so suddenly I was making thirty dollars a day. Two or three weeks later another loader quit and Ezra Voss got the job. The third loader was Villard Taylor, Dave Webb's nephew. The three of us then did all the loading until the end of the season.

The first week that I worked as a loader my arms and shoulders ached so I could hardly sleep. Finally my muscles became accustomed to the strain, and I had no further problem. I calculated one day that 115 pounds a box times 3,000 boxes came to more than 170 tons we loaded in a day. And each box had to be lifted from the ground to a point over our heads and dumped into the goat.

Ezra and I roomed and boarded with another worker named Foot Smith. They called him Foot because he wore a size thirteen shoe. We paid the Smiths ten dollars a week, and we ate so much I don't think they made a profit. Foot and his wife went to the store one evening and were not there when Ezra and I ate supper. As they were coming back Mrs. Smith wondered aloud what we had left for them. "I know what they left us," Foot replied, "A bunch of empty bowls."

Finally Ezra brought his wife and kids to Florida. He bought a big canvas tent and set it up on a vacant lot that belonged to Shirley Taylor, Villard's sister. After that, I moved in with the Taylor family and paid them the same ten dollars a week. They had beds dormitory style in the attic, and all the boys slept there.

The managers of the groves arranged for beekeepers to bring hives on trucks and install them in or near the groves when the trees were in bloom. They took the hives away after the blossoms were gone and before they sprayed the trees. The bees went around gathering nectar and pollen, and in the process they moved pollen to all the blossoms. The production of honey was a by-product of that more important function. The flavor of honey depends on the kind of flowers the bees visit, and orange blossom honey had a delightful taste.

* * * * *

The crew didn't work one day because of rain, and I went by the office of the Citrus Worker's Union because some of my friends had been urging me to join. The secretary in the office was Agnes Colvin, a married woman who had a young son. When she learned I was single and unattached, she invited me to her house for dinner to meet her younger sister, Annie. I don't remember much about the dinner, but later the grandmother asked the sister what she thought of me. She said I was O. K., but I was too big and too old. I was 26 and she was 18 at the time. Also, her father had done hard manual labor all of his life, and she couldn't be expected to get too excited about someone who worked in the groves for a living. I think she was hoping for someone like a dentist. Nevertheless, we were married several months later.

* * * * *

Finally a hurricane came through Florida and shook the trees so hard most of the fruit fell off. We had several days of frantic work to get the oranges picked up and to the juice plant while they were still good. After that there was so little fruit left on the trees we could barely make a living.

My foreman had applied for a job with the Hercules Powder Company as a foreman trainee, but they told him they wanted someone younger. He told me how to apply, and I got the job. I lived in their company housing in Zephyr Hills, Florida, about forty miles Northwest of Auburndale.

Some lumber company had cut hundreds of acres of old-growth pine trees and left the stumps in the ground. The Zephyr Hills project was to harvest the stumps. They were taking them out of the ground and hauling them to their processing plant in Waycross, Georgia, to extract certain valuable properties from them. I never knew exactly what they got, but the stumps had a great deal of resin in them. Caterpillar tractor drivers pushed the stumps out of the ground and into piles. A man with a little dragline picked them up and loaded them into semi-trailers, and drivers hauled the big loads to the railroad siding where they were loaded onto boxcars for delivery to the processing plant. I was to work at different jobs until I was familiar with them all, and would eventually become a foreman. This also did not last, because they phased out the foreman trainee program. They offered to keep me permanently as a truck driver, but I declined.

About that time my sister and her husband moved to Tampa, Florida. He was a millwright foreman on a big job building a cement plant near Tampa. He got me a job there making $83.00 for a five day week. We were installing machinery for the plant, and they managed to find something for me to do that I could handle. That was better than picking fruit, so we decided to go ahead and get married. About a month later, that phase of the construction was finished and there was to be no more work for a few months.

Annie got a job in Tampa with the telephone company as a long-distance operator. That was before direct dialing was available, and the operator placed all long distance calls. I went back to picking fruit for a few weeks, commuting 40 miles each way daily to Auburndale. One night I saw an ad by Kistner Realty for a real estate salesman and went for an interview. He hired me, and I started as soon as I got a license.

Spear Realty conducted a twenty-hour course at night in the office to prepare applicants for the state examination—-two hours a night for ten nights for twenty-five dollars. Mr. Spear was about sixty and portly, and had a red, bulbous nose. His voice came from deep down in his throat and sounded as if he were gargling gravel. "During this course," he told us the first night, "We will teach you everything there is to know about the real estate business." That was the overstatement of the year.

The two Spears, father and son, had collected a large number of questions and answers from previous examinations for both real estate salesman and broker. They talked to us about how to write a listing and a few other things, but they didn't seem to know much. After the first five nights I took the examination and passed it and didn't go back.

Time was passing. I was 27 years old and newly married. "To load fruit in the groves," a foreman once told me, "you need a strong back and a weak mind." It was time to move on to another line of work, and real estate looked promising. That will be the basis for another story.

ABOUT THE AUTHOR

The oldest of seven children, the author grew up on a hardscrabble farm in Tennessee during the worst part of the great depression of the 1930s. They had no electricity, no gas, and no indoor plumbing. The WPA built them a privy in 1933, and before that they went either behind the barn or across the road and into the woods. The family got electricity while the author was serving as an army air corps pilot during World War II.

After the war he became a real estate salesman, broker, and investor. In 1953 he joined the US Border Patrol as a GS-6 trainee, and he retired twenty-one years later in GS-15. He gained national recognition as a competitive pistol shooter, and after retirement was national senior pistol champion six times (age 60 or older). He also worked in the executive suite of the national rifle association for three and a half years, the last two years as deputy to Harlon Carter, the CEO. He has written two other memoirs and is working on a novel about romance in the mountains of East Tennessee.

He lives with his wife, Linda, in South Carolina. He has three adult children and his wife has two, in each case by former marriages. His E-mail address is josephcwhite@comporium.net, and he would welcome comments or questions from readers.

www.ingramcontent.com/pod-product-compliance
Lightning Source LLC
Chambersburg PA
CBHW061348280526
45784CB00001B/184